DEATH IN CHILE

TONY GOULD

Death in Chile

A MEMOIR AND A JOURNEY

PICADOR
PUBLISHED BY PAN BOOKS

First published in 1992 by
PAN BOOKS LIMITED
a division of Pan Macmillan Publishers Limited
Cavaye Place London SW10 9PG

1 3 5 7 9 8 6 4 2

ISBN 0 330 32271 0

Phototypeset by Intype, London
Printed and bound by Billing and Sons Limited, Worcester

To Jen

'. . . But why, my friend persisted in her question, this interest of mine over so many years in Spain and Latin America? Perhaps the answer lies in this: in those countries politics have seldom meant a mere alternation between rival electoral parties but have been a matter of life and death.'

Graham Greene
Getting to Know the General

ACKNOWLEDGEMENTS

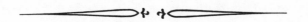

Many people in England and in Chile have contributed to the writing of this book. Grateful thanks are due to the Leverhulme Trustees, whose generous grant enabled me to go to Chile in the first place; to the *New Statesman and Society* and its then editor, Stuart Weir, for giving me six months' leave of absence; to the many Chileans named in the text who allowed themselves to be interviewed by a foreigner and did not complain when he asked them impertinent questions; to my attentive agent, Gill Coleridge, and encouraging editor, Martin Fletcher, whose role as midwife has been crucial; and to my old friends Michael Wood, for much useful advice, and Simon Gray, whose critical comments on a draft of a very different book prevented me from attempting to publish a work which I would have come to regret.

If I select some out of the many people who helped me in Chile for special mention, it is because their contribution was way beyond anything I had a right to expect. Paz Errázuriz not only provided me with a home from home throughout my stay, but also put herself out in countless other ways to further a project about which she had every justification in feeling ambivalent, to say the least. Adriana Valdés was also unbelievably generous with her time and hospitality and acted, as I say in the book, as my guide and mentor to the Chilean intellectual scene. The *Guardian* correspondent Malcolm Coad and his wife 'Coca' Rudolphy looked after me when I was ill; and Malcolm, like Paz and Adriana, read the book in draft form, correcting many errors (those that may remain are my responsibility) and making perceptive comments. Soledad Marchant generously entertained both me and my wife at the beautifully appointed avocado farm in Cabildo. Mario Valenzuela, now happily restored to diplomatic eminence under the democratic regime, and his wife Milka showed Jenny and me more of their country than we would otherwise have seen. And finally Marcos García de la Huerta took an infinity of trouble to get me – with my inadequate grasp of *castellano* – to understand the intricate politics of the University of Chile.

Further thanks are due to Francis Greene and the Bodley Head for permission to quote from Graham Greene's *Getting to Know the General*; to the estate of Dylan Thomas and Dent for permission to quote from *Under Milk Wood*; to the estate of W. H. Auden and Faber & Faber for permission to quote from *Collected Shorter Poems*; to Ray Gosling and Faber & Faber for permission to quote from *Sum Total*; to Brian Loveman and Oxford University Press for permission to quote from *Chile: The Legacy of Hispanic Capitalism*; to the estate of Vladimir Nabokov and Weidenfeld & Nicholson for permission to quote from *The Real Life of Sebastian Knight*; to Heberto Padilla and Faber & Faber for permission to quote from *Self-Portrait of the Other*; to Jorge Edwards and the Bodley Head for permission to quote from *Persona Non Grata*; to the estate of Cristián Huneeus and to Pehuén Editores ltda, for permission to quote from *Autobiografía por encargo*; and to the estate of Cristián Huneeus for permission to quote from Cristián's letters to me and from earlier books of his, the publishers of which are no longer in existence.

PART I

Parallel Lives

1

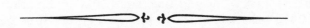

In the stillness of a bitterly cold February weekend the phone rang sharply.

'Tony?' The disembodied voice was female, foreign and, at first, a little tentative; but on receiving confirmation it became bright and teasing: 'Guess who?'

I had to admit defeat. In my befuddlement I only knew that the voice did not belong to that time or place. I connected it with summer, but still couldn't place it.

Even when she identified herself, I remained confused.

'But Soledad, where are you?'

'In London,' she replied, as though it were the most natural thing in the world for her to have popped over from Chile.

She told me she had come on a flying visit to Europe with her daughter, and it took me a further moment or two to realize what this signified.

'Cristián . . . ?' I was unable to formulate the question except by inflecting his name.

'He died – in November,' she said, all the brightness draining from her voice. 'Soon after we returned.'

Five months after this conversation I was walking – not without difficulty: I walk with sticks as a consequence of polio – along the cliff path at Gara Rock on the most southerly coast of Devon. Almost exactly a year before, I had brought Cristián and Soledad to this spot. Soledad had taken photos of Cristián and me, and I had photographed the two of them with her camera. As they put their arms around each other's shoulders and smiled at the camera I watched Soledad.

For she knew he was dying. Soon after they had arrived in London, the three of us had dinner together in a restaurant; and while Cristián was out of the room I took the opportunity to ask Soledad if all was really as well with him as he had indicated in the last letter he had written me. She shook her head and said that, according to the experts – and what she had been told in England only confirmed what she already knew – he had three months to live. Cristián himself, she added quickly before he rejoined us, did not know this; as far as he knew, the operation he had undergone to remove a tumour from his brain had been a complete success.

Did not know, or did not want to know? It was impossible to say. I listened to him and watched him closely whenever we were together and nothing he said indicated anything other than a normal expectation of life. He had plans for writing, for his university teaching and for his avocado farm. He arranged to have books sent to him in Santiago from London, and he was reading old Chilean volumes as part of his research for a novel which was gestating in his mind. Even the tender way he treated Soledad, his consideration of her, his sweetness and affection towards her, might have been no more than a grateful response to her solicitude for him.

I rounded a corner on the cliff path and looked across the mouth of the estuary to Bolt Head where, twenty-one years earlier, I had stood beside Paz, Cristián's first wife, while he had photographed the two of us from above and slightly to one side. I still have that black-and-white photo. They were staying in Kingsbridge with my friends, the Sharpes. Cristián and Paz . . . Paz so beautiful, Cristián so clever. Beauty and the brain. I was proud of my exotic Chilean friends: I liked to be seen with Paz, to talk with Cristián.

Cristián was not the closest friend I have ever had; I saw him too rarely for that. But our friendship began at a crucial time for us both, and was maintained, if not developed, over two decades when we were living through very different, yet in certain respects complementary, experiences at opposite ends of the earth.

During that period, Chile was – unusually for such a remote country – often headline news: first, through Salvador Allende's 'peaceful road to socialism' when, after several attempts, he finally won the presidential election of 1970 and his left-wing coalition known as the *Unidad Popular* came to power; then again, three years later, when the military coup put an abrupt end to Chile's socialist experiment and introduced a Communist witch-hunt and reign of terror seemingly out of all proportion to the offences of the previous regime. Allende himself preferred to commit suicide (as nearly everyone now agrees, though isolated voices on the extreme left still maintain he was murdered) in the presidential palace of the Moneda rather than fall into the hands of the military, thus transforming himself from a vacillating (or Machiavellian) politician into a heroic martyr, whose legend has been the stuff of countless songs, films and books.

Cristián was a writer, not a politician; but one of the things that had brought us together in the first place had been a mutual interest in politics. To be a writer – and not just a novelist, but a journalist and broadcaster as well – in a country where politics had become, quite literally, a matter of life and death, was to take risks. For most of my life I had been cocooned in the comfortable greyness of post-imperial Britain, and the question of how I might have behaved in similar circumstances preoccupied me when I met him again after all those years. Would politics have become more, or less, important to me had I lived under a regime which tortured and killed people for their ideological beliefs?

From a distance, of course, political reality is reassuringly black and white: the military junta against the Communists, torturers and victims, the powerful and the powerless. How could anyone with a heart and conscience put up with, let alone support, General Pinochet, the army commander turned dictator? Yet many in Chile, who were neither torturers nor tortured, did. Most had no choice, they were intent upon survival; and among those who did have a choice, it did not always appear so obvious as it did to us, living thousands of miles away and enlightened by articulate exiles, who were inevitably *parti pris*.

Political changes in Britain may not have been as dramatic as those in Chile, but in the Sixties I could have as little predicted the dismantling of the welfare state and the return of beggars to the streets of London in the Thatcher era as Cristián could have foreseen that he would live his last years under a military dictator.

In the Sixties everything seemed possible, not just politically, but individually as well. Naturally, both Cristián and I would become important writers in our respective countries; and I suppose I saw his career blossoming along the lines of, say, his Peruvian neighbour, Mario Vargas Llosa, whose early novels were just beginning to make an impact then, and who would go on to make a bid for the presidency of his country in 1990. In South America, a diplomatic career seemed part and parcel of a writer's life: think of Octavio Paz, Pablo Neruda, Rubén Darío, Alejo Carpentier, Carlos Fuentes and countless others. Cristián had the intellect and, I had no reason to doubt, the artistic ability. He looked the part; why should he not play it as well? With Paz beside him to complete the picture, there seemed no limit to what might be achieved by this talented Chilean.

I wanted Cristián and Paz to come to Kingsbridge because it was my home. I had grown up on a farm four miles from the town, and I returned there when I was invalided out of the army in the spring of 1960, after nearly two years in the Far East and another year in various hospitals and rehabilitation centres. And I wanted them to meet the Sharpes because it was with them – with Bill in particular – that my political education began.

My upbringing had not prepared me for life with a severe disability: it had been, in a word, physical. From just after the war, when I was seven and we moved to the remote and broken-down farm that a schoolfriend later dubbed 'Wuthering Heights' at the end of a mile-long, muddy lane, I was required to do physical work, alternating with my elder brother as 'outdoor' and 'indoor staff' – in other words, helping either my father or my mother. It was a tough regime with little respite and I was often relieved to get back to boarding school, once I had got over the initial spasm of homesickness.

At school, too, I sought to shine at games rather than intellectually, though I did manage to get an exhibition to public school. This reduced the fees a little, but not enough for my father's liking. When I was sixteen, and had just taken my GCE 'O' levels, he asked me whether I wanted to stay on or leave school. The question took me by surprise – just as, five years later, I would be surprised when the Medical Officer at the rehabilitation centre I was attending suggested that the time had come for me to leave the protected environment of hospitals and other institutions and go out into the big, wide world again. But in contrast to the latter occasion, when I felt let down by the very person who had buoyed me up during my fight for fitness – this doctor who was now calmly telling me that I must become reconciled to lifelong disability – I welcomed the opportunity of escape provided by my father.

My headmaster was opposed to this move: he had visions of my taking a classical scholarship to Cambridge – visions, it has to be said, that seemed a little over-optimistic when I failed Greek at 'O' level. But he did his utmost to persuade my father to let me stay, offering to negotiate reduced fees with the school governors and even to make me a house prefect – a generous gesture that was not endorsed by my housemaster, who said it would be 'over his dead body'. But I had grown to loathe school and for our different reasons my father and I were in rare accord over the question of my leaving.

Faced with the prospect of National Service – and no possibility of deferring it, now that I had stepped off the academic ladder – I had to plan my future around it. There seemed to be only two possible 'careers' that could be started before call-up and resumed on demob: banking and insurance. Neither held the slightest appeal for me, but I went for insurance, landing a job, which I stuck for four months, in an office overlooking Piccadilly Circus. It was not quite the blacking factory, but it did make farming seem an attractive option. When I handed in my notice, the manager cheerfully told me that had I not got in first, he would have been obliged to give me my cards. So we parted amicably, and I returned to the farm to work for my father for the few remaining months before the army claimed me.

My public school education, however inadequate in

other respects, ensured that I was hived off from the majority of my fellow recruits into a platoon of similarly privileged 'Potential Officers'. If we successfully negotiated the various hoops – basic training, 'Wosby' (as the War Office Selection Board was familiarly known) and Eaton Hall, where National Service infantry officers were trained for four months – we ended up with a single pip on each shoulder, blushing when a grizzled sergeant twice our age addressed us as 'Sir'. In my case, at least, there was the additional embarrassment of not yet needing to shave. But since I was commissioned into the Gurkhas, whose faces, by and large, are hairless, this mattered less than I had anticipated.

So, for the next eighteen months I was a 'Sahib', which seemed even grander than a 'Sir', and I am afraid it went to my head. I sometimes forgot that I was only playing at soldiers and confused it with real life. I even thought of making a career of it: after all, it had considerably more *cachet* than banking or insurance, and it was less mucky than farming. And it was physical: when we weren't tramping through the Malayan jungle, or marching up and down for the Queen's Birthday parade in Hong Kong, we put on our sports gear and played football or basketball.

According to the doctors, that made polio, when it struck, the more severe: if I had not been playing football the night before, I might have got off more lightly. As it was, first I lost the use of my limbs; then my breathing went and they shoved me into the iron lung. Thus incarcerated for several weeks, I had fantasies of climbing the Himalayas, where, just a few months earlier, I had walked in the foothills and caught occasional glimpses of the eternal snows.

Slowly, but slowly, I returned to earth and the deeply unglamorous business of rebuilding a shattered body. In this I succeeded – up to a point at least, the point at which the RAF Medical Officer told me there was nothing more he could do for me. I was not to despair, however: for up to two years I might make further progress, and I would certainly become more adept at doing things, but I should not expect a miracle and the hundred per cent fitness which had been my target was now out of the question.

you could think of, including a battalion of very dis-
gruntled Indians, whose attitude suggested they might
actually have preferred to be at the front getting blown to
bits. I don't know what they had done to deserve their fate
– perhaps they were tinged with the dreaded nationalism
and the brass-hats feared another mutiny. But they were
just one element of that forgotten army, likely to remain
there along with the rest of us until someone woke up to
the fact that there were thousands of perfectly able-bodied
men   doing   absolutely   bugger-all,   miles   from
anywhere . . .'

He looked at Delia, who had started to nod off on the
sofa.

'She's got the right attitude: go to sleep. Anyway she's
heard it all before,' he said with a cheerful grin, lunging at
her ankle. 'Hey, wake up, woman. I'll shut up if you'll
make the coffee.'

Delia stretched and yawned. 'That'd be nice,' she said
sweetly, as she got to her feet.

A product of grammar school and provincial university,
Bill might have stepped out of the pages of *Lucky Jim* or
Hurry on Down; he was part of the movement that swept
Attlee to power after the war. For my father's generation
and class this had been the ultimate betrayal, a slap in
the face for Churchill, the 'architect of victory', 'man of
destiny', and so forth. Bill and his contemporaries were
sceptical about great men and cynical about Great Britain
and its pretensions, in particular the double standard of
democracy at home and empire overseas, and regarded
Suez as a kind of nemesis.

My father, though by no means a lifelong Tory, was a
Conservative-voting *Daily Telegraph* reader throughout the
years when I was growing up. I remember him sporting a
little blue badge depicting a rodent in a top hat; when I
asked him what it signified, he told me it was his member-
ship of the Vermin Club, which was a jokey right-wing
response to a remark of Nye Bevan's to the effect that Tory
voters were 'lower than vermin'. So it was not altogether
surprising that Bill and my father didn't see eye-to-eye.
Bill found my father buttoned-up, ungiving of himself;

and my father dismissed Bill as a garrulous schoolmaster, 'too fond of the sound of his own voice'.

But I was young and malleable, and my experience in hospital made me receptive to Bill's egalitarianism. Much to my father's irritation, I took to calling myself a socialist, and one day, when I was inveighing against the inequities of private education, he responded bitterly, 'If I'd known how you'd feel, I wouldn't have wasted all that money sending you to public school.' I was shocked that he should take it so personally: didn't he understand that I was not attacking him, just arguing the – as I saw it – irrefutable case for social justice? But my father and I never argued without acrimony; as a consequence we seldom argued at all, and the silences between us grew longer.

He was less critical of my other unofficial and unpaid tutor, however. For Robert Pim was an Oxford man, a university extra-mural lecturer whose literary enthusiasms did not spill over into politics in the way Bill's did. But it was Robert who started me reading poetry again after a long lapse. At the age of sixteen, I had discovered Dylan Thomas; I either read or heard *Under Milk Wood* on the radio, and its sonorous rhythms and lively reJoycings (though I did not yet recognize them as such) enchanted me: 'It is spring, moonless night in the small town, starless and bible-black, the cobblestreets silent and the hunched, courters'-and-rabbits' wood limping invisible down to the sloeblack, slow, black, crowblack, fishingboat-bobbing sea', and so on. This then seemed to me the very essence of poetry, and I bought everything Thomas ever wrote, committing whole poems to memory. When I had to think of a topic for a five-minute lecturette that I, along with every other Potential Officer, had to give at my War Office Selection Board, I chose the poetry of Dylan Thomas and timed my talk so badly that I had barely begun when the five minutes were up. After that I forgot about poetry for two or three years.

Now, under Robert's tuition, I began to read the poetry of the Thirties, and Auden, Day Lewis and MacNeice replaced Dylan Thomas in my literary pantheon. Along with chunks of *Hamlet* and William Cowper, demanded by the 'A' level syllabus, I memorized such lines as 'Lay your sleeping head, my love,/Human on my faithless arm' and 'Lady, weeping at the crossroads/Would you meet your love/In the twilight with his greyhounds,/And the hawk on his glove?' They became, in my view, the epitome of sophistication.

My reawakened enthusiasm for poetry was also the result of being in love. But it outlived my affair with Ruth, which ended when my over-earnest pursuit of her frightened her – not to mention her parents – off.

In the spring of 1962, when I was two-thirds of the way through my first – and last – year at the School of Oriental and African Studies in London, reading Hindi (which was a throwback to my old life, rather than the new direction I was seeking), I read an article in *Encounter* by the playwright Arnold Wesker. In it, he described the organization, Centre 42, which he and a number of other writers and artists had set up to combat elitism in the arts and make the best available to ordinary citizens, courtesy of the trade union movement. I was fired with missionary zeal and wrote to Wesker, offering my services. I received a reply, not from Wesker himself, but from one of his henchmen, a theatre director called Clive Barker, who invited me to come and see him.

Clive proclaimed himself a Marxist; it was the first thing I learned about him. He came from Middlesbrough and, after his National Service, had studied acting at the Bristol Old Vic, where he was made doubly welcome since he was not only working-class but heterosexual as well. His formative theatrical experience, however, had been working with Joan Littlewood's Theatre Workshop in the East End of London. Clive was an enthusiast, and I liked him immediately. For his part, he professed himself happy to take me on as a volunteer, since I had a car and was prepared to drive people around. Centre 42 was mounting six week-long arts festivals in the early autumn, in places as diverse as Wellingborough, Hayes and Southall, Birmingham and Bristol, and Clive needed all the help he could get in organizing such an ambitious programme.

Centre 42 had an office in Fitzroy Square, and perhaps there was a connection, through the Euston Road School of Painting and Drawing, with the old Fitzrovia. The art school of the Thirties, which involved itself in such initiatives as the documentary film movement and Mass Observation and produced posters in support of the Republican side in the Spanish Civil War, demonstrated the same sort of political commitment on the part of artists as was evident in Wesker's latter-day crusade. Both might be praised for their generous idealism or condemned as patronizing and simple-minded. Centre 42 evoked the sneer of 'Art for the masses'; but I had no doubt that it was a worthy cause, one which gave the lie to the ranting of characters such as Osborne's Jimmy Porter about there being 'no brave good causes left'.

Yet, despite the egalitarian thrust of the enterprise, Centre 42's offices, which consisted of three or four rooms on the ground floor and a basement beneath, had a distinctly hierarchical atmosphere. Wesker himself, short of stature but not of presence, strutted around like a pocket Napoleon, usually accompanied by his *éminence grise*, Beba Lavrin. Beba was generally dressed in purple and wore dark glasses; her office was large and tastefully decorated and her leather-topped desk, it was muttered in the basement, had cost Centre 42 money it could ill-afford to squander. But Beba was keen on appearances and wanted the best not just for the masses, but also for herself; and she argued that trade unionists, whose Resolution 42 – a gesture towards supporting the arts – was behind the creation of Centre 42, would be unimpressed if they were ushered into dingy offices when they came to see her and 'Wizzy'.

When she emerged from her office and came to the tiny communal area where the tea was made and the post sorted, Beba would say, in her heavily accented English, 'Darling, I have ze headache. Could you get me aspirin?' Or it would be something else she wanted; and someone, usually Nancy, an American volunteer, would trot off to do her shopping for her.

Apart from Arnold and Beba, and Clive Barker, there was Michael Kustow, newly arrived from Oxford and already embarked on a brilliant career in the field (yet to be named) of radical chic, which would take him to the Royal

Shakespeare Company, the Institute of Contemporary Arts, the National Theatre and Channel 4, and the accountant, Michael Henshaw, who in his self-confident, authoritative way patronized even the artists he professed to serve. Then there was the girl Nancy, with whom I fell hopelessly in love – hopelessly, because although she was happy to have me as a *friend*, she did not want me as a *boy*friend. Our friendship, as is the way with some American girls, could even be *intense*; what it could not be was *sexual*.

Soon after I joined Centre 42 I made the shocking discovery that not everyone involved was a true believer. For example, Arnold's fellow East Ender, Bernard Kops, whose play *Enter Solly Gold* was to be premiered in the festivals, enjoyed playing the role of sceptic on his frequent visits to the office. I was still at that stage of innocence and conviction when I thought that every artist and intellectual *must* be a committed socialist, especially if, like Bernie, he had a working-class background. If ever I showed signs of wavering, Clive was there to bolster my faith; he was the person I respected most at Centre 42, the one who made least fuss and did most work. His commitment was total, he was prodigiously active and he seemed inexhaustible. Unlike the others, he was quite unconcerned about status; he did not have a fancy office; if something needed to be done and no one else showed any sign of doing it, then Clive got on with it. He was the one genuine egalitarian in an office overstaffed with prima donnas.

Through Centre 42 I discovered an England I had previously only read about. For the first time in my life I visited towns such as Wellingborough, Leicester and Nottingham, where many of our contacts were trade unionists. In Nottingham, I made friends with the Trades Council Secretary, Jack Charlesworth, who was also General Secretary of the Nottingham and District Hosiery Finishers' Association. Jack was in his early sixties, a little man with a fine sense of humour. He was so small he almost disappeared behind the wheel of his union's Humber saloon. Once, when we were driving through the Park, the smart residential district below Nottingham

Castle, I asked him what sort of people lived there. He said, 'Oh, you know, wealthy people like lawyers, doctors, professors, trade union leaders . . .' In fact, he himself lived on a council estate in Basford, within walking distance of his union office. On another occasion he said to me, 'I was born in Buckingham Terrace: if it had been Buckingham Palace instead of Terrace . . . well, there's very little in it really.' He had changed jobs twice in his life, each time taking less money.

Jack had joined the Independent Labour Party in the Twenties and the Communist Party in the Thirties, but his approach to industrial politics was undogmatic and humane: he always put his members' interests first and his attitude towards employers was amused and sceptical. He once told me: 'An old member of mine said to me many years ago, "You catch more flies with treacle than with vinegar", and that's perfectly true. They don't all try to buy you with money, though quite honestly I've been offered money as a gift. A roll of notes, as a Christmas box. I wouldn't accept it of course, and the employer said, "Oh, I'm not trying to buy you". He must have said that because, you know, I blushed: I was really embarrassed – embarrassed that he should think I was a person who might accept it.'

Jack had been in the army in Egypt for three years immediately after the First World War. He had taken the opportunity to improve his education (he had left school at thirteen) and might have stayed on and become an army teacher if it had not been for the fact that his parents were on their own and he felt he should come home for their sake.

'When I was in the army,' he told me, 'I probably imagined myself a Conservative if I thought about politics at all. But coming out of the army I worked up against a lad who was certainly a socialist and for whom I've always had the greatest respect. I remember once we were on a bus and we was passing the cinema where there was a lot of unemployed all waiting outside to get in for a penny – a penny was the price then. And he said, "There they go: two hours of living in fantasy, then back to the bread and lard." That stood in my memory.'

Jack and his wife Ada had two sons, Ken and Roy. Roy was living at home when I first knew them, while Ken lived elsewhere in Nottingham with his wife and son, but they all went on holidays together. Jack's union owned a holiday bungalow at Mablethorpe, where I once went with them for a weekend. Other weekends I stayed with them in Nottingham and on Saturday afternoons Jack would take me to watch Notts County play. His football loyalty was as absolute as his political loyalty: he preferred to stand in his regular spot on the thinly populated terraces of Third Division Notts County and hurl good-natured abuse at the ref rather than follow fashion and join the larger queues outside First Division Forest's ground up the road.

Jack was for me – to quote what another friend I made at this time wrote about another working-class hero, a railwayman called Wispy – 'the first contact of any depth I had with the old-world divisions, the solidarity of the working classes, rich and poor, workers and bosses, and the greatness of the Labour movement'. These lines appear in Ray Gosling's autobiography, *Sum Total*, which was published that same year, when Ray was a mere twenty-two years of age. Even before I met him, I had stayed in his flat in Nottingham, opposite the Players factory, and wondered about this fellow who had pictures of himself pinned up on the wall, alongside those of James Dean and other cult heroes of the time.

Ray was interested in the activities of Centre 42 but was critical both of its generally *de haut en bas* approach to the provinces and of its conservative choice of events to represent the best, for example, in music: Stravinsky's *The Soldier's Tale*, a sixteen-piece jazz band, and warbling folk singers. Didn't Wesker & Co understand what was going on under their very noses? Or if they did, why did they shun it, other than out of an elitism quite as pernicious as the one they set out to oppose?

It's strange [Ray wrote in his book], that for all the efforts of the Elders of our tribes to provide the younger generation with fitting and suitable heroes, we've got heroes in a set of unzipping the banana young men, and women of maturity to cuddle and comfort the poor banana once it's bin unzipped, and young girls who look like boys. But let's be honest, all the Soviet achievements, they're a little unsatisfying, emotionally. The moralists have tried to provide the world with honest, happily married two kids, secondary modern to tec at night and skilled technocrat to Party member and Government commission sitter; provincial ordinary suburban ever so nice and normal, fit and healthy and the heroes are still a long list of Ishmaels. The figure is on the stage, the banana, the Boy-god, the Ishmael. The backing starts up. He moves into a solitary blue spot. He cannot sing, talk, express; but the youth and the beauty he has are worth more than all the other qualities he does not have. The other cerebral and emotional qualities we can have all through life, but the youth and the beauty are over before you have the chance to put them across. He moves alone across the desert of the stage. It is the face, the look, the loneliness, the uncommunicable, unclubbable – the figure we would all like to be or be in physical contact with – tall, dark, slim. Letting in a little light, bringing in a little life. With our 7/6's we must buy him and kill him and then love the image and read the magazines and start all over again . . .

This homo-erotic picture of the pop star as sacrificial victim was something new in my experience. On its own it would have had little appeal, though by now the rock music which had delighted the newly emancipated teen-agers and appalled their parents in the late Fifties was becoming generally acceptable; but what was special about Ray was not his modish worship of the Boy-god but his attempt to ally it with a traditional, caring, radical, if not socialistic, concern with the poor.

Ray was an early, pre-Sixties 'drop-out' from Leicester University, where he had gone from grammar school in his native Northampton. After an attempt to promote a local pop group, he went on to set up a club for young people in Leicester to be run by its members. The idea, as he explained in his Fabian pamphlet, *Lady Albermarle's Boys* (the title refers to the fund which provided the money), was to bypass the Youth Service, with its bureaucratic and patronizing approach to the young, and give young people themselves the opportunity to make decisions and be responsible for their activities. Because Ray was attracted to the rough, Teddy-Boy-into-Rocker, motor-mechanic young, he went out of his way to recruit these 'unclubbable' elements into the club; and it was his very success that brought about its downfall. Drink flowed, fights broke out and the police were called in. Ray himself became suspect for what he had written in his pamphlet and had to leave town after he had been subjected to an almost ritualistic beating-up.

Ray was essentially a grass-roots politician, more concerned with people than policies, with action than protest. He had a kind of love-hate relationship with the then fashionable New Left, and with Stuart Hall in particular, whose move in the Sixties from the *New Left Review* into academic life puzzled and disappointed him.

Later, Ray spearheaded a campaign to ensure that the rebuilding of the St Ann's district of Nottingham was done for the benefit – rather than at the expense – of the residents, who included some of the poorest people in the city. SATRA (the St Ann's Tenants and Residents Association) was the kind of organization he had tried to bring into being among the Leicester young and 'unclubbable'; only this was the grown-up version and it achieved what it set out to do.

Centre 42, by contrast, failed because it lacked a proper constituency. The TUC's Resolution 42 was no more than window-dressing; it did not reflect a heartfelt desire on the part of the unions for artistic experience or involvement; it was the brainchild of a group of artists who, either because they had lost touch with their own roots or because they wanted to reach a wider audience, or both, badgered the unions into accepting a small measure of responsibility for patronage of the arts. The 1962 festivals cost a great deal of money and Centre 42 never recovered from the losses it incurred then. It became associated with the Roundhouse in Chalk Farm, a disused railway engine-shed which – again at vast expense – was turned into an arts centre and then taken over by other organizations for trendy, Sixties-ish events, while Centre 42 itself faded and died, a relic of an earlier, less materialistic era.

I had to leave Centre 42 after only two of the six festivals to go up to Cambridge, where I had succeeded in gaining a

place to read English. I went straight from Jack Charlesworth's council house in Basford to Trinity College's New
Court. I looked forward to discussing my recent experiences with like-minded fellow students, who I imagined
would flock to join me in setting up a Cambridge branch
of Centre 42. Workers and students together, we would
change the world. In a very short time I learned the error
of my ways. Politically-minded dons, such as Raymond
Williams and Bill (later Lord) Wedderburn, supported my
efforts, but the mass of undergraduates were as indifferent to the idea as the mass of working people had been.
Enthusiasm, I soon discovered, was frowned upon in
Cambridge.

A month or so later, still suffering from culture shock, I
found myself sitting down at midnight in a friend's
exquisitely furnished rooms in Great Court, a glass of malt
whisky at my elbow, to play a game of piquet, and I
thought: was it for *this* I came to Cambridge?

My supervisor, who was an elderly gentleman from one
of the villages outside Cambridge, had once edited an
anthology of mystical verse; he was a kindly, twinkling-
eyed fellow much given to hushed recitals of Keats's 'Ode
to a Nightingale'. I only once saw him display irritation:
that was when, in the middle of one of these readings, a
military jet screeched overhead and drowned his reverent
tones. He took it as a personal affront. He looked up
almost angrily. 'I do wish they'd stop flying over Cambridge,' he said. 'Now Lord Tedder, he's the Chancellor of
this university and Marshal of the Royal Air Force, isn't
he? Why doesn't *he* stop the aeroplanes flying over Cambridge?' I had to keep reminding myself that this was also
the university of Dr F. R. Leavis, who was reputed to have
carried his copy of Milton into the trenches during the
First World War.

Gradually, I came to understand that Cambridge – literary Cambridge at least – was all about Personal Relations.
There was political activity and debate, of course, but
superior minds tended to regard all that as rather vulgar,
better suited to Oxford, perhaps. In Cambridge it was
fineness of sensibility that counted. I was still trying to
find a niche for myself there when I met Cristián and Paz.

Our friendship began in an unlikely way: I was attempting
to chat up Paz at a party when she stopped me by saying,
'You must meet my husband.' I hadn't realized she had
one. But they became very much a couple in my eyes and I
grew equally fond of them both. Paz, though not so dark
as to be a conventional Latin beauty, was both Latin and
beautiful; Cristián, though striking, was neither. Paz was
small, exquisitely formed, and had light brown hair; Cristián was tall, thin and blond, with a northern coldness in
his blue eyes, magnified by his glasses. He looked more
German or Scandinavian than Spanish. There was about
him an aristocratic *hauteur* which assorted oddly with the
Marxism he professed at the time.

Neither Cristián nor I had ever expected to go to Cambridge. We were both rather amazed to be there – he
because it was, after all, a long way from Chile; I because I
had left school so young and imagined that was the end of
my education. There was a further bond between us: I had
been in the army, and he had been at the Military School
in Santiago before going to the University of Chile. We
both were, or felt ourselves to be, outsiders, studying at
Cambridge by happy chance rather than design. Just as I
had come there via the London School of Oriental and
African Studies, so Cristián had arrived by way of Hull
and then London, where he and Paz had spent several
months before he succeeded in getting into Cambridge.

They lived in a small, first-floor flat in Fitzwilliam Street,
handy for both the Fitzwilliam Museum and Corpus
Christi, Cristián's college. I took to dropping in on them
on my way to and from Trinity. I learned that they had
been married shortly before they left Chile and had
decided (but who had decided what precisely?) that since
they wanted to travel in Europe – it might be their only
opportunity to do so – they would defer having children.
There would be time enough to think about a family when
they returned to Chile; for the moment, like young eight-
eenth-century aristocrats, they were doing the Grand
Tour.

Perhaps this is why my most vivid memories of them
are of the times when we travelled together. One day we
drove from Cambridge to Aldeburgh. I have a photo that

Cristián must have taken of Paz and me on the beach; it could almost be a still from an Antonioni film. Paz has her back to the camera; she is wearing a short suede overcoat and a headscarf which the wind has blown off her head but which still clings to her neck. I am standing two yards away from her, dressed all in black, wearing dark glasses – an affectation – and leaning on my stick, my head thrown back and laughing. What was the joke? Probably that we were there at all, shivering on a deserted beach beside a leaden sea, under a leaden sky.

On another occasion – a beautiful spring day this time – I drove Paz to a village church not far from Cambridge which was famous for its brasses (Paz was decorating their flat with brass rubbings). We had a picnic lunch in the churchyard and afterwards, stretched out on a rug, smoking and talking together, we must have come as near as we ever did to admitting to an attraction which friendship made taboo.

Then there was the time they came with me to Devon and stayed with the Sharpes in Kingsbridge, when we walked to Bolt Head and Cristián took the photo I was remembering as I observed the headland across the mouth of the estuary – and across the chasm of years.

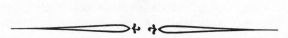

2

Cristián was that rarity among Cambridge under- or, in his case, post-graduate students: a published writer. A volume of short stories and a novel had already come out in Chile. I couldn't read them, though, as I was not then conversant with Spanish. But Cristián was the first person to whom I showed my own early efforts at writing, and he encouraged me. Mostly we talked about books and writers, which in Cambridge at that time meant F. R. Leavis, D. H. Lawrence, and Joseph Conrad, whom we both admired.

To Cristián, *Nostromo* was a revelation. 'Good God,' he exclaimed. 'I mean, the man hardly touched land there and yet he has written *the* Latin American novel.' How could an anglicized Polish sea captain like Conrad have understood so clearly the turbulence of South American politics? Cristián found it little short of miraculous. Not all South American states were dictatorships, of course, and despite his Marxist leanings Cristián was proud of his own country's democratic tradition and told me that Chile was known as 'the England of South America'.

Towards the end of my second year at Cambridge, I became one of three editors of what was then the undergraduate literary magazine, *Granta*; the other two were Jim Philip, a poet, and Reg Gadney, an enthusiast for kinetic art at that time but subsequently a writer of thrillers and television scripts. We were an unlikely trio, with very different interests. We did not choose one another, though Jim, in particular, was a friend of mine; we were selected by the previous three editors, who probably wanted to ensure a continuing eclecticism. My aim was to bring in outside contributors, such as Ray Gosling, who wrote a piece for us about hitch-hiking, called 'Code of Hitch', and the BBC radio producer Charles Parker, who wrote about

the radio ballads he created along with the folksingers
Ewan MacColl and Peggy Seeger. These were products of
my Centre 42 experience and indicated a continuing desire
on my part to attack the provincialism of Cambridge and
open the eyes of my fellow students to a wider culture, if
no longer to convert them politically. I was learning the
value of an oblique approach.

Another of my initiatives turned out badly. I persuaded
my fellow editors that we should invite the pop artist
Antony Donaldson, who was also a friend, to design the
cover for us, not for a single issue but for a whole year's
worth of magazines – twelve in all. Tony came up with the
very Sixties idea of cutting up a black and white photograph of a nude into twelve squares, which would be collected by avid readers and stuck together at the end of the
year. It was a sort of jigsaw, and you would not be quite
sure which bit went where until you had acquired the
lot. It seemed like a clever wheeze, guaranteeing faithful
readership throughout the year; and we even inserted a
copy of what was on the cover inside every issue so that
readers would not have to destroy the magazine in order
to compose their pin-up. The trouble was, the reality did
not match the idea and the bits of very grainy, black and
white thigh or armpit that adorned the first two or three
covers were mystifying rather than mysterious and
encouraged no one to buy the magazine; and the whole
idea was quietly dropped when I resigned as editor (in
order to concentrate on academic work during my last
year) after three issues. At least there were no complaints
of sexism, as there certainly would have been a decade or
so later when Cambridge colleges became mixed and there
were far more women students; in some ways, the early
Sixties was still a time of innocence.

Before I left *Granta*, I invited Cristián to be guest editor
of a special issue devoted to Chilean short story writing,
and he and I translated one of his own stories from the
original Spanish. He did the actual translation; I tried to
render his English more idiomatic – a task in which, I have
to confess on re-reading the translation, I was none too
successful.

The story is called 'Don Patricio' and it has pride of place in Cristián's collection, *La Casa en Algarrobo* ('The House in Algarrobo'), which was published in Buenos Aires in 1968 and dedicated *'a Tony y Lesley'* – to me and my first wife – though I didn't see a copy of the book for many years, indeed not until I was married a second time (and Cristián a third).

It is the story of a young man with a political conscience. Patricio rejects his social role as the son of a wealthy land-owner and professes Marxist ideas. His parents do not take these ideas seriously, though his sisters are irritated by them and by Patricio's contempt for their own Catholic beliefs, as well as by his position as their mother's favour-ite. The workers on his father's farm remain resolutely deferential despite his egalitarian overtures.

No such deference, however, is shown him by one of the workers on a neighbouring rented farm, and the story hinges on a tussle of wills between this rather shadowy figure and the young Patricio, culminating in a murder for which Patricio is indirectly responsible. His solution to his personal predicament is to run away: 'That day he would leave the farm'. But he may not even be up to that; easier to stay in his room, get drunk and spew it all up . . .

Patricio, like his creator, is a privileged being; he can indulge in radical fantasies without being called to account; he is not a bad man, merely ineffectual. He is a divided being: his instinctive loyalties are at odds with his perception of the world about him. He would change the world but cannot change himself. Was Cristián testing the strength of his own Marxism? And if so, did he find it wanting? At all events, after reading 'Don Patricio' it would be difficult, even without benefit of hindsight, to see Chile as 'the England of South America'.

I spent the long summer vacation of 1964 in Spain, reading Thomas Mann and trying to be a writer, though it was more than a little daunting – even for a Cambridge under-graduate – to essay a novel about illness in the shadow of *The Magic Mountain*. I stayed at Peñíscola, a village on the Costa Blanca between Barcelona and Valencia. Even then it was a tourist resort, though not to the extent it has become since, with closely packed high-rise hotels and blocks of holiday flats disfiguring the magnificent sweep of coast which was the dramatic setting for the finale of the epic film *El Cid*. Peñíscola's chief claim to fame, prior to the filming of *El Cid* at least, was as the domicile of Papa Luna, one of no less than *three* Popes who disputed the papal supremacy in the early fifteenth century – the other two being at Rome and Avignon. Papa Luna lost out, but his castle still dominates the rock on which it sits.

On the rock itself the houses are old, the streets narrow and stepped, mercifully impenetrable to motor vehicles. I set up my typewriter in a room close to the Bar Altamira, where I ate my meals. There I met an American couple, Jake and Judy, with a flaxen-haired four-year-old called Lorne, whom the Spaniards idolized. Jake was a research student, in Spain on a Fulbright scholarship. Spain and most things Spanish (though not bullfights, over which we had several arguments) enchanted Jake; he was an enthusiast and a romantic. Loud, slovenly, lantern-jawed and bristly-jowled, Jake preferred life on the rock to the sybaritic pleasures of the beach below. He was never happier than when he was pottering, or passing the time of day with fishermen in bars. He spoke fluent Spanish. But even Fulbrights don't last for ever and, though Jake would have preferred to remain indefinitely in Spain, Judy was homesick for America and anxious about Lorne's education.

Boisterously American though he was, Jake dreaded going home. At the end of the summer he practically had to be dragged on to the ship that was to ferry them across the Atlantic. Judy and Lorne enjoyed the crossing, he wrote to me later, but he had hated every moment. He summed up the awfulness of it by telling me how, when the band struck up the tune of 'Over the Rainbow' for the hundredth time, he found himself offering them money if only they would desist, or at least play something else.

Jake tried to teach me Spanish. And he accompanied me south when I drove down to Nerja on the Costa del Sol, where Cristián and Paz had rented a villa. Soon after our arrival, the four of us set off in my car for a few days in Seville. I have a colour photo of Cristián and Paz sitting side by side, his arms encircling her and his hands resting lightly on hers, taken in a park in Seville. I was just thinking that I must have been the photographer when, looking at it again, I spotted myself in the bottom left-hand corner of the picture, practically hidden not only behind dark glasses (which Paz, too, wore) but also in a black T-shirt, which perfectly blends with the background foliage; only half my face is visible, smiling up at my friends, who in turn smile at the camera. The photo seems to symbolize our relationship at the time: they were the glamorous foreign couple for whom I acted almost as a kind of impresario, introducing them to other friends, such as Jake, who in this instance must have been the one holding the camera.

So I was disappointed when I sensed that Cristián, though impeccably courteous, did not altogether take to Jake, or vice versa. The South American *hidalgo* and the brash North American might have come from different planets. Jake was in love with Spain, Cristián was simply at home there; there was no mistaking who was the more European. But while Cristián might look irritated and challenge some of Jake's wilder assertions, Paz seemed to be amused by him and they got on well. When Jake and I drove off after dropping the others at Nerja, I attributed any lack of warmth towards me on Cristián's part to Jake's rumbustious and rather alien presence. Once we were back in Cambridge, I felt sure, we would quickly re-establish our former intimacy.

But Cristián and Paz did not return to Cambridge at the beginning of the academic year and I acquired a new set of friends with whom I often played poker in the evenings. Like Cristián, they were mostly my age or slightly older and included Simon Gray, who was beginning to make a name for himself as a novelist while still a post-graduate student, and who supervised me for the Tragedy paper in Part II of the English tripos; Roger Gard, who commuted to London, where he was a lecturer in English at Queen Mary College, and his wife Liz, née Kenrick, who had been in the glamorous world of television between graduation and marriage (and whose brother David was the person I had found myself playing piquet with soon after my arrival at Trinity); Michael Tanner, a philosophy don at

Corpus Christi with a passion for Wagner and Nietszche, and a student of his, Malcolm Budd, who would later marry Liz, after she and Roger split up. It was a diverse group, but the men at least were all more or less apolitical, sharing a Leavisite view of the world and regarding Liz's – and no doubt my – leftish political enthusiasms with a measure of scorn. Under these influences, I was tempted to equate political commitment with simple-mindedness, but I drew strength from the example of another of my supervisors, Raymond Williams, whose radical socialism somehow did not detract from his donnish *gravitas*.

In addition to these new friends, I had met an English girl in Spain who became my main preoccupation at weekends, when either I went to London to see her or she came to Cambridge to stay with me. So I missed Cristián and Paz less than I might have expected.

I had rented a flat in Panton Street; it was more of a room, with a minute kitchen and bathroom attached, over a garage at the bottom of a garden. My landlady, who taught French to students of English literature, was a stocky woman with close-cropped hair and half-frame spectacles perched on the end of her nose. Her favourite reading was the memoirs of Second World War generals, and she considered herself something of an expert on military strategy.

One wet evening, when I was settling down to study, I heard a heavy tread on the wrought-iron spiral staircase leading up to the flat, followed by a knock on the door. I was not expecting anyone but in Cambridge people often dropped in unannounced, so I did not give much thought as to who it might be. But I was very surprised to see Cristián. He had come all the way from Heathrow airport in a taxi. He was alone. Paz, it transpired, was still at Nerja.

I poured him a glass of whisky and before long he was reminding me that when I had last seen them together on the beach, holding hands, I had commented, 'Still the honeymoon couple, I see'. It had been a painfully inapposite remark. Paz had now left him to go and live with a Frenchman. Cristián had had an affair, too; indeed, he had been the first to do so. They had been quarrelling, apparently, even when I was at Nerja. I began to understand that the atmosphere of tension, which I had ascribed to Jake's unsympathetic presence, had had little, if anything, to do with that. My friends' marriage had been collapsing and I had had no inkling of the fact.

Cristián's affair had soon come to an end, but Paz's had continued. Cristián was contemptuous of her Frenchman and did not take him seriously as a rival; he felt that he himself had driven her into the affair. Now he agonized over what to do next: should he go straight back to Spain to try and persuade her to return with him to Cambridge? It could well be a wasted journey; she might not want to come and, even if she did, what kind of reconciliation was possible once they were back in Cambridge? Wouldn't Paz resent being slotted back into the role she was rejecting – camp-follower in Cristián's Cambridge career? Furthermore, did Cristián really want her back rightaway? Didn't they both need a little time away from one another to work out how they felt? And even if he was certain he did want her back, wouldn't he do better to leave her where she was and trust in time and her good sense to bring about a reconciliation?

I suspect that Cristián came to me not because I was his closest friend in England but because I was a friend of them both. He knew that I was as close to Paz as I was to him. So I might go along with his quixotic scheme of rescuing her from the clutches of the feckless Frenchman regardless of its merits. For me, it was true, Cristián was a diminished being without Paz, and the sooner he got her back the better.

The rescue bid was a failure, of course. Cristián's swift return, far from delighting Paz, infuriated her and ruled out any possibility of an early reconciliation. If there was one thing she needed to establish, it was that she could manage without him. So Cristián had to acknowledge defeat and, for the third time in less than forty-eight hours, clamber aboard an aeroplane . . .

When Cristián was back in Cambridge he and I rather avoided one another, as if we shared a guilty secret. Paz's absence came between us. The flat in Fitzwilliam Street had lost its welcoming homeliness; it became like countless other rooms in Cambridge, the temporary lodgings of single people who would soon move out and on. And now that he was living alone, Cristián was seldom in when I did call.

Meanwhile my own romance, which in the pitiless light of Cambridge came to seem increasingly misconceived, had ended. I resigned myself to weeks or months, if not years, of celibacy. So I was surprised when Marta, a Hungarian domiciled in Paris who was a lodger in my landlady's house, manoeuvred me into bed in the middle of what I had taken to be an intellectual conversation. I was grateful to her for that, but I was not in love with her; she was older than me, rather mannish in her forcefulness and intelligence, and our relationship was altogether too matter-of-fact. I needed a tortuous and complicated situation in order to pull out all the emotional stops; and given life's propensity for providing what we imagine we desire, I did not have to wait long.

Jane lived opposite. She had been married for only a short time; her husband was a decent and dependable sort who gave her the security she needed, though not perhaps the adventure she craved. To go from school to Cambridge was fine; but then to marry and settle there, possibly for life, was to limit one's options. There was a restlessness, not to say recklessness, in Jane that found a ready echo in me. Our affair seemed to develop without our active volition, from the day when we suddenly found ourselves holding hands without either of us being aware of precisely how we had arrived at this degree of intimacy.

Paz returned to Cambridge in due course, the Frenchman having proved, as Cristián had predicted, unsatisfactory in the long run. By that time, however, Cristián had got used to being on his own and their reunion was a muted one. I was pleased to see them together again but saddened by their mutual wariness. Paz, too, knowing that Cristián had confided in me, was now inclined to regard me as Cristián's friend rather than hers – the two no longer being quite synonymous.

The honeymoon was over, for them and for me. We all

had a more critical awareness of one another; if Cambridge fosters nothing else, it fosters that. What they thought of me, I am in no position to say, but I began to ask myself questions about them: wasn't there something just a little bit inhuman about Cristián's detachment? It might serve for artistic purposes – though how good a writer was he *really*? – but didn't he perhaps lack a basic emotional warmth? Paz could never be accused of that, but did her physical attractiveness incline one to overlook a certain shallowness, a lack of direction in her life . . . ? It was probably because I had been so close to them that I had always, if unconsciously, seen them as they saw each other; and now that the scales had fallen from their eyes, they were bound to fall from mine, too.

We remained friends, but were no longer the threesome we had been for the previous eighteen months. While my new friendships and new love took up all the time I had left over from working for my finals, they turned inwards on themselves in an attempt to renew their commitment to marriage and each other. There was one obvious way of doing that and, in the spring of 1965, Cristián announced that Paz was pregnant. Though they were not yet ready to go back to Chile, the prospect of a family turned their thoughts homewards. In a year's time, perhaps, they might think of returning, but for the moment there were plenty of things they wanted to do, plenty of places still to visit. When they did go back to Chile, of course, I must come and visit them there.

As soon as my finals were over I ran away to Spain. An Australian family I had met the year before at Peñíscola had taken a house a few kilometres up the coast at a village called Casas de Alcanar and they urged me to come and stay. I was glad of an opportunity to escape from Cambridge and to have time – and space – in which to test my resolve to pursue a relationship with a married woman. Jane was not going to give me the satisfaction of following me to Spain, in spite of the fact that distance inflamed rather than doused our desire and we wrote each other passionate letters. Instead, she went to Paris, away from both her husband and me, and had a brief fling with a visiting American beat poet before I flew in to reclaim her. We had a few intense days in Paris, but she still refused to come with me when I returned to Spain.

Cristián and Paz went to Italy for the summer. Early in July Cristián wrote to me from Rome; he was full of the beauties of Italian cities: 'No wonder the education of wealthy eighteenth- and nineteenth-century Germans included a *Wanderjahre* – a whole year travelling and studying in Italy. One wishes one's sensibility were finer and one's memory better.' They were seeing Chilean friends in Rome, 'which received us literally covered in Chilean flags – Chilean flags absolutely everywhere. [President] Frei was visiting and the ruling C[hristian] D[emocrat] Party went out of its way to salute him. It was very moving.'

Eduardo Frei had won the 1964 presidential election for the Christian Democrats in Chile, much to Cristián's disgust. Cristián had supported Allende, and wrote to me at the time:

> Our candidate lost, as you may have learnt in one of your few moments of un-provincialness. Bad anti-climax it was. Everyone expecting the bloody country to occupy the news for ages as the one, first, eccentric, remarkable, funny, out of the way little place that votes in a Marxist government, and we turn up an undistinguished form of lawful socialism. That's okay for you settled imperialist industrial moveless mammoth societies, but not for feudal geographical areas in bad need of a good shake-up. I am terribly sad but I must acknowledge the existence in my fathomless ambiguity of that little devil that feels rather relieved in the hope that things might now move without having to face the alternative of running into a totalitarian regime . . . If they do move, I'll begin to think that we are, after all, somewhat civilized.

For the moment, though, Cristián welcomed the distraction from politics that Italy provided, despite Frei's visit. He and Paz were getting on well. He described how, when they were staying in Florence, they had walked up the hill to the Belvedere fort overlooking the city and stretched out on the grass, reading and talking companionably. In Rome their walks took them to the floodlit fountains; there were fountains everywhere, he wrote.

He was eager for news of my love affair; Jane, he informed me, had 'dropped in briefly' on the day they had left Cambridge. He wanted to know whether I had got the travel studentship I had applied for (it was administered by St John's College and called the Harper-Wood, and that year it was awarded jointly: to Roger Scruton and to me). And he asked after the progress of the novel I was writing: 'You must write soon so [that I can] make up my mind whether to envy you or not.'

By October he and Paz were back in Cambridge and I had finally persuaded Jane to come and live with me in Madrid. We found a room in the bohemian quarter of the city, an area full of bars with *tapas* on offer. We went to the Prado and admired Goya's black paintings and Bosch's *The Garden of Delights*. We made a trip to Toledo and gawped at the attenuated figures of El Greco. Jane got a part-time job teaching English, and we settled into a kind of domestic routine, though ours was a tempestuous affair, physically exciting but mentally wearing as we argued back and forth over what right we had to be together in the first place. Half the time we were not even sure we liked each other: Jane would close up against me whenever she thought affectionately of her husband, or got a letter from him reaffirming his love for her despite everything; and I would try to wear her down, accusing her of vacillating, of denying the evidence of her senses. It was easy for me, she said, I didn't have a choice to make; and the more I tried to persuade her to leave her husband, the more obstinately she refused to make the definitive break.

Cristián wrote that I sounded 'quite tortured'; he asked if there were reasons 'beyond the wholly inevitable ones' and admonished me thus: 'I ask because it may be that you are not altogether exempt from a certain tendency to make things harder than they need be.' He and Paz, he said, had laughed over my description of the room (of which I have only the haziest of memories) Jane and I rented in Madrid: 'Your establishment does sound to me like a *casa de cita* or, in Chilean slang, *culeadero*.' He did not share my enthusiasm for Madrid. 'I find it rather appalling as a city,' he wrote, adding sniffily, 'but then, I'm not an English tourist.'

The bulk of his letter was taken up with his anxieties over the possibility that they might have to return to Chile sooner than they had planned. In August he had written: 'Our everyday life has slowly begun to adjust itself to the idea that we are leaving. It seems to be an irrevocable decision. Deep down in our hearts we are, even if slightly scared, full of excitement and great expectations about the return.' But since then his mother had been taken into hospital for a breast cancer operation and Cristián had written to the doctor to find out how serious it was. He couldn't face the thought of returning to Chile empty-handed, so he put aside his thesis – possibly on Henry James at this point; the subject changed more than once – in favour of a novel he was determined to finish. So far, he reported, he had completed forty pages of typescript, but he was still being cautious: 'So many things I've begun with enthusiasm and . . . abandoned for some reason or other halfway (and scarcely that) through! Still, this one must come out, if only because the fact of returning presses me to do it.'

There was a postscript in Paz's handwriting. 'I'm looking so funny now,' she told me, 'the baby moves so much and it's big. I wish I could have it soon; we are so happy and I feel marvellous and great!'

I was feeling anything but 'marvellous and great'. I had lost my battle with Jane, who insisted on returning to England to her husband, and I could not bear the thought of staying in Madrid without her. It was now nearly December and I had been in Spain since mid-June; I had fulfilled the conditions of the Harper-Wood, which stipulated that the recipient must spend a minimum of three months abroad. But in contrast to Cristián, I felt no excitement when I looked at the thickening pile of typescript on my table, only distaste. The novel I was writing was like my affair with Jane, a lost cause; but abandoning it, like ending the affair, would leave me with nothing. The affair, however, did end without much further ado; the novel lingered on.

*

Cristián's mother's condition was not so serious that they were obliged to make a hasty return. Paz, in particular, was relieved as she wanted to have her baby in England, away from family pressures. I was at my parents' home in Devon when I received a letter dated December 12th, 1965. Cristián wrote ecstatically: 'Daniela was born on Thursday at 6.40 p.m. We are absolutely delighted that she should have been a girl. She is very tiny, very silent and very pretty though she tends to take up funny crumpled positions when you hold her in your arms, as if she were still inside the womb, and she looks a bit like a monkey . . .'

There followed a breathless description of the build-up to the birth: the anxious nights in which, despite taking sleeping pills, neither Cristián nor Paz could sleep; the morning when it all started and the prompt arrival of the ambulance; the ward where Paz went swiftly into labour and practised, with Cristián's help, the breathing exercises recommended in 'the admirable Mrs Wright's book on natural childbirth'; Cristián's forays into the outside world, his calls on mutual friends of ours with children of their own who were prepared to put up with his 'attack of loquacity' and let him 'vent it all out'; his reappearance at the hospital in order to reassure himself and give more help and encouragement to Paz; the doctor's warning that nothing would happen for the next two or three hours; Cristián's need to go out and get something to eat before he fainted from hunger; and his return, only to find an empty bed and a nurse calmly changing the sheets.

'Your wife was taken into the delivery ward fifteen minutes ago,' she said. 'Did you want to be in?' We both rushed up to the sister's room to ask the number of the ward. The sister smilingly said, 'Oh, it was a girl.' I went in and there was Paz, very tired, very dazed, a bit weepy, half seated on the bed, with the little noiseless Daniela with her face all wrinkled, as if menaced by a hive of bees, wrapped up inside a cot by Paz's side. She had literally been born a few minutes ago.

The doctor responsible for my absence saw me afterwards in a corridor and came along . . . to say how sorry he was.

Cristián blamed himself for having gone off when he did; he wrote that he felt like 'a very guilty fool'. Afterwards he went round to a friend's and got drunk, though this friend had been 'mean enough not to get drunk as well'. He wished I had been there to celebrate with him. Now he was looking forward impatiently to Paz's return from hospital.

The spring of 1966 – that *annus mirabilis* in which England staged and won the World Cup, in which the Beatles were at the peak of their amazing career and union jacks blossomed on every shopping bag in an extraordinary marriage of pop art and patriotism – found me still languishing in Devon, grinding out the last chapters of 'the novel', which was in reality nothing more than thinly disguised autobiography, aimless as life itself in its casual meanderings. Cristián chided me in a letter for telling him in one and the same breath that I had finished the novel and that 'there is really very little news'. It would have been better if I had written 'finished *off*', in the sense of delivering the *coup de grâce*, then he might have understood that I had no sense of triumph, only a conviction of failure.

Instead, he looked for other reasons for my depressed state of mind, and concluded: 'Probably you are too sociable an animal to survive in wild deserted Devon.' He had met Jane at a dinner party and found that he liked her less than before. 'Don't get me wrong,' he wrote. 'She is very attractive, very charming and also very bright. But something absolutely awful, something painful to watch, happens to her . . . It is as if she had completely lost her innocence without having lost her naïveté, which allows her to be shockingly smart and equally shockingly wrong.' Perhaps he was just seeking to reassure me, for he added, 'Ultimately, it is better for you that you didn't marry.'

But by now I was intent upon marrying, though as yet I had no idea whom. At twenty-seven years of age, I was growing tired of playing at life, of making false starts, whether personal or professional; I was ready to commit myself to someone, if only I could find someone prepared to accept my commitment. I told the friends I was staying with in London, when I finally escaped from Devon that summer, that I wanted three things in life: to get married, to find a job and to have somewhere to live, though not necessarily in that order. As it happened, in less than three months I was married and living in a flat in Notting Hill; finding a job took a little longer.

I was standing outside a butcher's shop and thinking, 'There's an attractive girl,' when I realized she was coming towards me and smiling. I knew her, but for a moment I had her muddled with someone else and couldn't place her. She said hello and, sensing my confusion, went on: 'In Cambridge, you remember? I was with Simon at the time. We had dinner at Roger's.'

Of course. Lesley was her name: she was then a leggy art student, wearing shocking pink tights. I remembered the dinner well. I had felt an instant rapport with Lesley; she seemed out of place in Cambridge and would surely have been more at home in, say, Centre 42. At any rate, she and I had found ourselves on the same side of a political argument and, when she had left the table and gone up to the sitting-room, Simon had remained behind. As we followed the others up the stairs, he had muttered, 'Seems like you're the coming man', and I hadn't been sure how to take it. They seemed an incongruous couple but he was my friend, and when the affair ended I made no effort to see her. Apart from any other consideration, I was then involved with Jane.

Several months later, when Simon and I were sharing a taxi in Holborn, I asked him what had become of Lesley. He said he'd heard that a mutual friend of ours was taking her out, but he didn't know for sure – 'I couldn't do that, could you? I mean, take up with a friend's ex-girlfriend . . .' No doubt I agreed at the time; but now her appearance seemed providential.

We went into a pub. She was wearing a kind of loose-weave T-shirt, with white and lime-green hoops, and Levis. Her hair was cut short, very short, like a boy's. I remembered that she had drunk whisky and ginger and asked her if she still liked it, and that was what we had. She was impressed that I should remember. How delightful it was that we should remember so much, yet still have so much to discover. She had heard that Simon was married and asked me if I was. We quickly established that neither of us was engaged, and she told me she was still living at home with her parents.

I had nowhere to say in London that weekend, and I said to her that if only it had been Paris it would have been different: I had friends there who would put me up. From there it was but a step to suggesting that we went to Paris for a few days. Lesley was game: it was only our second day together, but she had no ties to keep her. She was already playing truant from her job as deckchair attendant in Hyde Park; her parents wouldn't mind and her friends would be pleased for her; as for lovers, it was all over with Dudley – she said it was impossible to have a decent relationship with an alcoholic; she was fed up with being knocked about when he was pissed.

Those days in Paris were a kind of honeymoon, the only one we had. A walk to the local launderette was as enchanting, as novel, as a trip on the Seine or a visit to the Louvre. And the races: we went to Longchamp, where they wouldn't let us into the enclosure because Lesley was improperly dressed – wearing trousers, or not wearing stockings, I forget which. Not that it mattered. We didn't win any money, but the heat and the wine and our determination to enjoy ourselves with our friends more than made up for that. In the warm-up to one of the races, Lester Piggott came trotting by and we yelled out in concert, 'Go back to Lower Lambourne', and he fell off his horse, we were convinced, out of surprise that we should know where he came from. And then he disappointed us by coming nowhere in the race.

By the time we got back to London we had decided to get married. Neither of us had a job but it was, after all, the Sixties and no one worried too much about that sort of thing. Besides, I'd had a promising interview with the BBC and, while they couldn't offer anything immediately, there was this radio producer's job coming up, for which I might like to apply . . .

Cristián, meanwhile, was vacillating between going home to Chile and staying on, if not in England, at least in Europe. One minute he could write:

I spend hours swamped in sticky descriptions of the ways of peasants and the forms of nature in the South or in the North or the mountains of Chile. I cannot say that it doesn't in some pretty obvious way touch me deeply, however offended my aesthetic and my moral sense can be by the clumsiness of our local worthies' attempts at studying the human heart . . . Neruda has said that he likes poetry so much that he can even enjoy the work of bad poets. I can say the same – but only insofar as Chilean literature is concerned. It always has a documentary value.

The next minute he was telling me excitedly that he'd had a story accepted by *Mundo Nuevo*, the Latin American equivalent of *Encounter*, and that he'd been so impressed by the editor, a Uruguayan and a former student of Leavis's at Downing, that he was going to write to him, as he'd heard that he was looking for an editorial assistant in the office in Paris. 'Can you imagine,' he added enthusiastically, 'a few more years in this part of the world? Paz couldn't be happier with the dreams we've built on this possibility.'

But dreams they were. Reality was pulling in the opposite direction.

I'm trying very hard to get a [teaching] job in Santiago [Cristián wrote to me in May], and there is a big chance that I shall, in spite of petty intrigues which are already reaching my oversensitive ears. Chile is hell. I don't think we'll be able to stand it for long. We came back from London, that microcosmos of Chilean life, only yesterday . . . A most depressing pit of jealousy, competitiveness and envy. We Chileans are petty and provincial and savage. One sees a bit of them, just a bit, and leaves them exhausted by the amount of emotional energy spent in coping with them. We both, Paz and myself, have an increasing fear about the return. As if we were throwing ourselves bang into the middle of the lion's den, just for the sake of doing it. And this kind of thing brings out the worst in oneself and one becomes another of them. The trouble is that one *is* one of them. By this I mean that I am by no means free of our kind of animosity and aggressiveness. It is easier to live in the ivory tower of Cambridge, where one chooses one's friends. To think that we know that it won't do – that we *wish* to go back for the sake of our personal growth. Anyway, enough. The problems are not new. They have become acute due to the proximity of the return and to my frustration with my work (works) which also affects Paz and puts us both in a position we may call anything but strong –

The letter breaks off at this point. Cristián was interrupted by the arrival of visitors, and when he resumed he didn't return to the theme. This was the last letter, as it turned out, that he wrote to me in England.

We met in London once or twice before he and Paz finally left for Chile. When they took the train to Liverpool to embark on their transatlantic voyage, they entrusted to my care an avocado plant which Paz had grown from the stone of an avocado. I remembered it from its earliest days in their flat in Cambridge. First, it had been suspended over a jar of water, held in position by three pins resting on the lip of the jar; then, when it sprouted at both ends, it had been transplanted into a pot, in which it grew to a fair size and, until it came into my hands, flourished. But it did not long survive its removal from Cambridge; bereft of its nurturing mistress and rather neglected by its new owner, it shed its leaves and finally gave up the ghost. Its demise touched my conscience and I was reluctant to throw it out; it was, after all, my last tangible link with my departed friends.

3

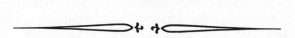

'The keynote of our recent exiles-feeling towards Chile was our fear,' Christián wrote from Santiago at the tail end of 1966. He and Paz had experienced violent culture shock when they boarded the Chilean boat, the *Andalien*, at Liverpool docks: 'There we were, already back in our homeland, at a couple of yards' distance from English soil.' They anticipated clashes everywhere, quarrels with everyone; they were ready to take offence at the slightest provocation. But the long voyage south, into a warmer clime, soothed their jagged feelings and gave them time to adjust to the reality of homecoming.

Cristián's parents had travelled north to the Peruvian port of Callao to greet them.

'Paz had been frightfully nervous the night before,' Cristián reported. 'I was, I suppose, as usual; quite calm and waiting to feel whatever I might come to feel once the actual event was over. I wasn't moved to tears then, but I am moved to tears every time I recall it.'

He gave me a graphic account of this meeting, their first for five years: how his father and mother approached the *Andalien* in a motor boat and had to wait while the port authorities came on board; how they waved from the gently rocking boat, which emitted puffs of exhaust like smoke signals; how a woman came and stood beside them at the rails of the ship, saying, 'I can't miss this moving meeting, I can't'; how the two Indians aboard the motor boat looked from the younger to the older couple, wide-eyed and expectant; how he himself, holding Daniela aloft, called out, 'You look just the same, you haven't changed a bit!' and his father tried to take photos but was too nervous to hold the camera steady; how his mother pointed at Daniela and said, 'Look at her! ¡Qué amor más grande! But look at her!' and his father echoed, '¡Mírala, *pero por Dios Mírala como hace con la manito!'*; how his mother, whose hair was whiter than he remembered, clung to his father, who had grown balder but was otherwise unchanged, while they waited in silence for the port authorities' boat to move away and let them come on board.

'My mother is, thanks God,' Cristián wrote (that misplaced 's' so characteristic of his fluent but idiosyncratic English), 'in perfect health.' She was inclined to be depressed and was unenthusiastic about doing things, but then she had always been like that. His father, he found, had 'developed certain obsessions and has a tendency to over-exert himself in anti-government tirades. Taxation, agrarian reform, bureaucracy, irresponsibility, madness have taken over the country. No respect for private life any more, etc.' Cristián was amazed how much easier it was to be conciliatory in person than by letter, where he often found he was being assertive, if not downright aggressive. He succeeded in the double task of reassuring his father about his rectitude and, at the same time, standing up for reform.

Still on board the *Andalien*, Cristián was stirred by the first sight of his homeland: 'Then came the long series of Chilean ports and the long bleak dry roasted Chilean northern coast. The landscape is one of the most impressive in the world. It is pre-human and anti-human. The light has a golden transparent shine; it is fresh and pure and impeccable.'

Eventually they reached Valparaíso and the end of their voyage. They arrived late at night and, as they sailed slowly into the horseshoe of the bay, the lights on the surrounding hills were twinkling and they could see lines of cars racing along the avenues: 'It was like finding a jewel after a long, long search. It seemed unbelievable to be in such a beautiful place so far away from the world' (Valparaíso, of course, is no longer the port-of-call it once was, before the Panama Canal was opened). Paz's parents, who were waiting at the docks – 'the old docks with their hundreds of beautiful cranes' – came on board to complete the family circle.

They disembarked in the morning and after lunch at Viña del Mar, Cristián's birthplace, they drove to Santiago, a journey of nearly two hours. The countryside was 'full of wild bushes and flowers', but Santiago was 'huge and horrid, dirty, untrammelled, unchanged, flat, noisy, hot'. That night Paz's parents gave a party for them and the next day they visited Cristián's father's *hacienda*, Santo Tomás. Despite himself, Cristián was impressed by what he saw, the new crops, the improvements in the peasants' houses and, above all, his father's enthusiasm: 'I liked him more than ever. His farm is his life. I should (rather) say his feudal property is his life. But it's a beauty. And it always improves.' He admired what his mother had done in the garden and then went to say hello to the peasants: 'They were a bit older, had more children, their wives looked very spent. They found me much the same but taller.'

According to the historian Brian Loveman, the large rural estates in Chile's central valley

> constituted the single most important political and social institution in Chile. Their owners belonged to a small social elite that has controlled most of Chile's best agricultural land as well as its political institutions . . . The tremendous power exercised by landowners or proprietors over the rural labour force made each rural estate a quasi-political unit. The landowner controlled access to land, housing, and employment. The resident rural labourer who disobeyed the landlord's orders risked being fined, whipped, dispossessed, or otherwise punished.

As a result, *campesinos* were cringingly subservient and listened to their orders with 'bowed head, eyes toward the ground, hat held over genital area'. Between 1964 and 1973 however, 'the *hacienda* system seemed destined for the scrapheap of Chilean history, and the future of Chilean agriculture appeared tied to thousands of newly formed peasant organizations'. Cristián approved of this agrarian reform; his father did not. But in the euphoria of their reunion they easily overlooked their political differences.

*

Cristián's top priority was to get a job. He hoped to find something at the University of Chile in Santiago and went first to the Faculty of Philosophy and Letters, the Instituto Pedagógico, where he had been a student. There he came up against the system, which rewarded political loyalty rather than merit. He was offered a little teaching, for very little money, and told that he should hang on and apply for a job which would soon become vacant, as the man who currently held it was dying. Even then, he would have to work like a politician for the votes of other faculty members and student representatives, competing with the favourite for the job, a woman, who had been waiting years for someone to die . . . Chileans, Cristián informed me, 'never say no directly'. He was on the point of resigning himself 'to the tedium of provincial life' in Concepción (where he had been offered work) when he had a stroke of luck.

A friend advised him to try to get a job in the Centro de Estudios Humanísticos in the Engineering Faculty. A priest of his acquaintance, in whose library he was working ('he's got the best library in the country, it's his private library'), asked him what he planned to do, and he told him he would like to get into the Centro, little knowing that the padre was a close friend of the *decano*, the dean of the faculty. Two days later, Cristián was summoned for an interview and, shortly after that, offered a job. Best of all, the *decano* encouraged him to continue working for his Cambridge degree *as part of the job*.

Two months later, Cristián wrote that the honeymoon with his family was over. The *casus belli* was a house – or rather, two houses. The one they already had was 'new, cramped and miles away from everything, in one of those housing developments, uncomfortable and ugly, where young couples are supposed to start life'. The one they wanted was a big old Chilean house, 'ruinous and enormous: eleven rooms, with a huge back garden, a U-shape and a glassed [-in] gallery going round the interior. All on one floor. And cheap . . . It's also ideal for the nursery school which Paz has often thought of having.' The trouble was that his parents claimed to have bought the new house for them and regarded it as their property, whereas in actual fact it 'was bought with money *we* had left behind plus something like £300 which my father put from his pocket, not as a present – as he's insistently pointed out – but as a loan. We were much too far from this business in England to trouble over what was what and we accepted a rosy version whose origin, now lost in the past, is untraceable: that they had given us the house as a superb wedding present.'

Now, ungratefully, Cristián and Paz planned to sell this love-nest and buy a monster of a house that no one in his senses could possibly want. Worse still, Cristián had the gall to ask for a loan to make up the shortfall on the exchange – this on top of the allowance his father was already paying him until he started his job at the university. It was too much for the old man: he refused the loan and tried to prevent the sale of the bijou residence, telling the estate agent to await his instructions and plaguing Cristián, who was staying at Paz's parents' farm at Los Andes, with long-distance late-night calls.

> 'You are irresponsible, you are mad, you're a crank.' I forced myself to listen patiently, never raised my voice a bit, waited for him to finish. He could only finish with a question: 'What are you going to do with the house?' 'Well, father, sell it, of course.' Bang. Hung up. Silence. Operator's voice: 'Are you through with your call, have you finished, sir?' Next day *I* had to ring up, to ask whether he had any of the documents I needed to formalize the sale. His voice had gone ages away, it sounded weak, terribly weak: he was a man defeated. Poor foolish man, he was so hurt. But he had given way. So the house is sold.

One house might be sold, but the other still had to be bought: 'This is the present state of the house saga. You'll find its dramatic end in the next chapter: "The young writer-critic-traveller-bum C. Huneeus life-sentenced for murdering his father".'

Eventually, they got the old house, on terms they could just about afford; Cristián's parents were obliged to accept the *fait accompli* and gave them, by way of a peace offering, some lovely old furniture they had stored in a barn on their estate. The balance of power had shifted decisively in favour of the younger generation.

Cristián and Paz were soon sucked into the whirlpool of social life in Santiago. As they were not yet in their own house, they could not invite people round; but they often dined out or went to the cinema. When they saw Antonioni's portrayal of 'swinging London' in *Blow-Up*, they could scarcely believe that they themselves had so recently been living in England, it all seemed so remote from their present lives – or at least from Cristián's; he admitted that Paz felt differently: 'not having a social activity, she lives more in the glorious memories of our European past'. Cristián was both more involved in Chilean life and, through his Cambridge thesis, which was now on D. H. Lawrence, more in touch with their recent English past.

While Paz earned some money doing translations, Cristián started work at the Engineering Faculty. His office was on the top floor of a nine-storey building; he could look out over the whole of Santiago when the smog permitted. There was a chain of hills to the north and, further east, the snowy peaks of the Andes. After rain when the atmosphere cleared he would open a window to let out the smoke from his cigarettes and breathe in the cold, fresh air; sometimes he amused himself by scrunching up a piece of paper and dropping it out of the window to see how long it took to reach the ground. Then he would return to his thesis and engross himself in 'the wild rose-bush scene or Gerald's death or Tom and Lydia or even poor Rico [who] become much more real to me than anything else in life'.

But there was another reality competing for his attention, the reality of Latin America in general and of his own country in particular:

Chile is hopeless, yes, but in doing or trying to do things, in endlessly grumbling, in bitterly crying out one's despair, in quarrelling and shocking people, one feels, as it were, part of a secret society of conspirators, who don't really ever do anything but dream and dream and dream and always feel on the verge of a cataclysmic change. That's the ethos in a new

pre-revolutionary country. Not that anyone in his senses actually expects a revolution to take place in Chile, but, again, no
one in his senses rules out the possibility.

The Cuban strategy, according to Cristián, was to 'Viet-
namize' South America, to bypass the traditional left-wing
parties, both socialist and Communist, and instigate guer-
illa warfare all the way down the Pacific coast, in Venezuela, Colombia (though apparently not Ecuador), Peru
and Bolivia (also in Guatemala), but not yet in Chile.
There, the revolutionaries contented themselves with
milder forms of insurrection:

> Slum dwellers have lately invaded several farms near and
> around Santiago, and the government obviously can't take
> them out after they've got in, since it would be too unpopular
> a measure. Slum dwellers in England are princes in compari-
> son to slum dwellers in Chile, and even if the most conserva-
> tive people in the country would go to any length to protect
> their own property, they would not do much to uphold, as
> such, the principle of private property, since it would have no
> effect whatsoever on anything or anybody. Mind you, they do
> protest in Parliament, but it is one thing to protest in Parlia-
> ment when you are in the opposition and quite another to
> take measures when you are in government. Before Frei,
> Allessandri, as you know, a Conservative, legally ratified one
> or two of these invasions once they had taken place.

Cristián was still on the side of revolution, but he was
far from sanguine about its success. The problem for all
Latin American countries was that the rapid growth of
social discontent outstripped their potential for development. There were two possible future scenarios: either
'give and take reform' which might be successful in terms
of survival but could never eradicate misery or alleviate
frustration, 'which, in other words, will maintain us as
purposeless poisoned miserable countries'; or revolution,
which – no matter how glorious the prospect – was
doomed to failure because 'the Americans won't allow
it . . . they won't allow another Cuba'. It was as simple as
that: there was no way to solve the problems of Latin
America short of revolution, yet equally there was no way
the Americans would stand for that, so 'one ought to

preach it through loudspeakers: no revolutions ahead, blocked road, branch off right . . . For us, American imperialism is like the law of gravity. That the poor will have to remain poor, that despair will continue to be the key feeling in South America would also seem to be something like the law of gravity.'

The impact of American imperialism touched Cristián more nearly, too, through his Uruguayan friend, the editor of *Mundo Nuevo*, Rodríguez Monegal, who was trying to weather the storm caused by the revelation that the Congress for Cultural Freedom (which sponsored *Mundo Nuevo*) was funded, or had been until very recently, by the CIA. Cristián wrote, 'I myself am, as usual, torn between two things: my personal loyalty to him, he's a good friend and even if I've been a very minor contributor to the magazine, I wouldn't like to leave him in the lurch; and some ethical principles which I'm supposed to uphold, one of them being that in the situation much good may come from collaborating with the Americans but within decency, and that collaborating with the CIA lies entirely outside decency.' He wished he were capable of 'a passion for ideas', so that he might divest himself of his painful ambivalence and throw in his lot with the Communists. But then, 'even Communists have their little moral problems, don't they?'

In England, too, in the spring of 1967, there had been a row when Stephen Spender and Frank Kermode resigned as consultant editor and co-editor, respectively, of *Encounter*, following Conor Cruise O'Brien's revelation of the CIA financing of that journal through the same channel. But it is a measure of the difference between the two places that what Cristián described as 'a thunderstorm' in Latin America was no more than a storm in a teacup on this side of the Atlantic, though intellectuals opposed to United States foreign policy in Vietnam and Latin America, such as the philosopher Richard Wollheim, were much exercised by this discovery and ceased writing for *Encounter* forthwith.

The Wilson era in Britain, despite its energetic 'white heat of technology' phrase-making, was not remarkable for political passion; the later Sixties were the years of the counter-culture, when politics turned personal, and drugs and the anti-psychiatry of R. D. Laing and other gurus (a late Sixties keyword) were dominant. But, just as sexual intercourse, which in Philip Larkin's words 'began/In nineteen sixty-three' and was 'rather late' for him, so drugs and hippy behaviour in general passed me by, though Lesley, who was a crucial few years younger, was not immune to their appeal.

I had joined the ranks of the nine-to-fivers, queueing for the No. 52 bus morning and evening, pushing my way in and out of the massive portals of Broadcasting House, where I had an office, and a half-share of a secretary, on the seventh floor (if there was no view of the Andes from my window, at least I was spared the smog of Santiago). My work as a General Talks Producer was as interesting and varied as I cared to make it: it was up to me to come up with ideas for talks and documentaries to be broadcast on either Radio 3 or Radio 4; and then, provided they were acceptable to the network Controllers, to go away and make the programmes. I enjoyed the hours spent in studios and editing channels, polishing someone's performance or cutting and shaping a tape to fit the time allocated for the broadcast; but I was a reluctant Organisation Man and found the internal politics of the BBC and the interminable weekly meetings unutterably boring.

Then there was the delicate question of 'balance', the apparent neutrality of the BBC on political issues, its Olympian detachment, which I tried to subvert in whatever small ways I could. Not that my work as a producer was ever censored; the more insidious danger was self-censorship, the lure of the bland. Invariably, the programmes with – in the jargon – the highest RI (Reaction Index), or greatest appeal to that cross-section of the audience which constituted the Listening Panel at any given time, were the ones which gave least offence to any particular section of the community. Anything remotely controversial and the figure dropped, because, while a few listeners might respond very positively, others would be outraged and mark it right down. Under another system of reckoning, I maintained, programmes which

challenged the audience, instead of pandering to its com-
placency, would be regarded as successes, not failures.
Despite its monopoly of national sound broadcasting, the
BBC was as obsessed with figures and market research as
the manufacturers of breakfast cereals. It was as though it
had to compete with imaginary rivals in preparation for
the day when real ones would come along.

At home, in our poky little flat in Notting Hill, I could
forget about the BBC. Lesley, who wanted more than anything to have a baby, was pregnant and happy. Our min-
uscule bathroom, tucked away under the stairs to the flat
above, was the topographical and emotional centre of the
flat, cosy, warm in winter and cool in summer, and a little
claustrophobic. It had no windows, and the noise of traffic
in the street was blotted out by the ventilator which came
on with the light. There we read to one another in the bath
or simply talked.

Marriage had an almost supernatural significance for
Lesley; it had to work. Her anxiety was that I would cease
to love her when she grew older. One day she gave me a
Donald McGill-type postcard, with a sentimental tag. It
depicted a large woman, all bottom and bust, and a little
man with a red nose and a bowler hat; and the caption
ran, 'Will you still love me when I'm old and grey?'

All the time she was growing larger. Pregnancy suited
her. She suffered little sickness, had all the usual cravings
for strange foods and acquired a distaste for cigarettes.
She got so fat all over that I began to wonder if she'd ever
again be the beautiful, slender creature I had married. It
worried her, too, but not much. She was too proud of
what was going on inside her. She wanted people to
notice, so she stuck out her belly when she walked along
the street.

The last month was the worst: waiting for it to happen.
It was mid-summer and unusually hot, and when I came
home from work I would find her sprawled heavily on a
bench in the communal garden at the back of the flat. The
sun and the weight she was carrying made her drowsy,
and it was too much of an effort even to read or knit.
Mostly she talked with the young mothers, whose ranks

she could hardly wait to join, and watched their children playing. Soon . . . ah, make it soon.

The night before, she was fretful. It seemed it would never happen. Then in the early hours she woke me and said she thought it was starting. I phoned for an ambulance and we dressed and waited in the thin light of dawn, not saying much. I knew how she was feeling: she had waited so long for this moment, but now that it had arrived she was totally unprepared for it. I went with her in the ambulance, but when we reached the hospital I could see that she wanted me to go. She wanted to face the ordeal alone, though afterwards she said she wished I had been there at the end to share her joy.

I phoned at midday and they told me to phone back in an hour. At one o'clock they told me, 'It's a boy. Mother and baby doing fine.' You've done it, I thought, you've really done it, and I wanted to cry. But I had to go to lunch with a politician, who kindly bought a bottle of wine to celebrate.

Because Lesley had a cold they had put her in an isolation ward. When I visited her that evening, the sun was still streaming in over the prison walls of neighbouring Wormwood Scrubs. It was the hottest day of the summer and her upper lip was flecked with perspiration. She was radiant, speechless with happiness, and there, in a crib at the end of the bed, was the tiny creature she had just brought into the world, his eyes tight shut against the light.

At that moment, she wasn't Lesley; she was something archetypal, more animal than human. I half expected her to break into little whimpering sounds of pleasure. It was weird and awe-inspiring and I ached with love for her. For the child, the product of our love, I felt nothing except a sort of bemused curiosity, tinged with apprehension. He was a fact, but as yet it seemed ludicrous that he should have a name – especially such an adult name as Conrad.

Late that night, after I had gone home, Lesley wrote me a letter, euphorically describing the sun setting over the Scrubs – until she realized it was no longer sunlight but the prison searchlight that was illuminating the ward while Conrad noisily sucked his thumb and she herself drifted into a drug-induced sleep . . .

Our choice of name for our firstborn delighted Cristián, who felt himself haunted by 'the ghost of the sombre wise sage' and planned to hold a seminar for members of the Engineering Faculty on *Nostromo*. Meanwhile, he wrote, 'Your letter actually performed the miracle of breaking through one of the worst postal strikes we've had in Costaguana since the dark times of Guzmán Bento.' He and Paz, he told me, were thinking of having a second child. Whenever they watched Daniela playing with other infants they felt they should provide her with a sibling. But Daniela herself had recently caused them some anxiety: she had woken up one morning looking 'strangely cross-eyed'. They discovered she was suffering from a condition known as strabismus, inherited through Paz's family, and she was obliged to wear a white patch over one eye to correct it.

Because they were still waiting to move into their 'grand old house' Cristián turned his office into a study and worked on his thesis till seven or eight in the evening. This was his 'main activity', though he made his mark in other ways, too. Soon after his arrival he had organized a series of debates on *Problemas de Chile en 1967*; these covered such topics as the press and the State, the agricultural situation, and the educational crisis and aroused considerable interest as Cristián succeeded in getting VIPs – such as Allende and the Minister of Education, a number of senators and the editors of the three most important newspapers – to participate: 'Nothing of this sort had ever been done in the faculty before, so you can imagine how well it went down.'

In his teaching, too, he tried out new ideas. Not content merely to lecture his students on D. H. Lawrence, he set up a *Taller Literario*, or writers' workshop. This was not so successful since his students were engineers, not writers, and the stuff they produced was 'simply horrid'. They met once a fortnight and Cristián began to suffer excruciating headaches before each session; soon the numbers fell off and, though the students begged him to continue, he used this as an excuse to drop the project:

I must admit that I felt sad, because I had managed to attract to the blessed *Taller* the handful of desperadoes in the faculty, those who dislike engineering, who run the Student Centre, work on the abominable magazine, take part in play productions, write revolutionary tirades and love Che Guevara . . . And their avidity, their thirst, their desperate need to have their spiritual emptiness – the emptiness of a young boy who spends twenty-four hours a day trying to become an engineer – filled by a 'teacher' (in the real sense of the word) were as large as the mouth of a whale and I knew that if I was incautious the whale would swallow me up. My headaches were telling me so.

More rewarding were the postgraduate seminars – on Lawrence, inevitably – which he held with a group of English teachers, mainly older women, and a mini-series of lectures on the poetry of Neruda that he gave to two lots of American students. These, he added cryptically, were 'probably spies'.

I heard nothing from Cristián between July 1967 and January 1970, during which time I was absorbed in the vicissitudes of my own life: the birth of a second child, a failing marriage and a stalled career.

I cannot say I was sacked by the BBC, that's not the way a liberally-minded organization likes to go about things. But, whereas a producer was normally taken on to the permanent staff at the end of an initial two-year probationary period, in my case this did not happen. I was at liberty – nay, I was encouraged – to apply for jobs within the Corporation, and I did apply for one for which I was well qualified. But though I was short-listed and interviewed, I was not offered the job.

What had I done to deserve the bum's rush? Had I been idle, incompetent, or unprofessional? Apparently not, since within three months of my 'dismissal', if that word can be applied to the non-renewal of my contract, I was invited back, on a short-term basis, to produce a series of documentaries. No, my crime was to have taken BBC professions of liberalism at their face value and not to have understood that, though we were all on Christian-name terms, there was a rigid hierarchy in which I was – to use the appropriate analogy – a very junior subaltern. So when I refused to do an attachment to a folksy magazine programme called *Home This Afternoon* – aimed at the old and, it sometimes seemed, senile; and quietly dropped soon after this – on the grounds that I had nothing useful to contribute to it, this brought out all the latent authoritarianism within the liberal psyche and was seen by my superiors as insubordination.

What they wanted to say was 'How dare you?' but that would have exposed the iron fist. What the benevolent-looking man with the flowing white locks – like Selah Tarrant in *The Bostonians*, as Leavis once said with deadly venom about his one-time associate, I. A. Richards – actually said was: 'I would remind you that you have a wife and two young children.' I had my revenge when I was invited to comment on his report of the dispute – BBC liberalism once again. I underlined all the words such as 'discipline' and 'training', of which there were several, and wrote: 'I have come across this sort of language before. I, too, was in the army.'

'Selah Tarrant' was outraged. Instead of summoning me to his office, as he would normally have done, he stepped down to mine to tell me what a 'dirty trick' he thought I'd pulled. But it was on the record and there was nothing he could do about it. The upshot was, to pursue the military metaphor, that I won the battle – I was not made to do the attachment – but lost the war. As one of my bosses, a fat and florid woman who spent her lunch hours in the bar, a lipstick-stained cigarette between her fingers, remarked to a third party: 'Tony Gould? So obstinate, dear, and' – referring to my prominent canines – 'those dreadful fangs . . .'

Lesley's second pregnancy had not been as happy as her first; she had wanted another baby but she was now familiar with the constraints of motherhood and knew that two children would be twice as demanding as one. She didn't put on weight or grow lethargic; only her stomach swelled and that seemed more of a burden than a blessing. She was more worried about losing her looks than proud of the child inside her. She had also, for whatever reason, fallen out of love with me. At one time she could not sleep if there was the merest hint of a disagreement between us. Now it had ceased to matter. And she began to look at other men.

I date the decline of our relationship from the moment we moved into her parents' flat in Holland Park which they vacated for our sake. We rationalized the move, saying we needed the extra space to accommodate the baby – and that was certainly true. But it was not *our* place. For Lesley, the flat was, quite literally, home: she had left it in order to marry me, and now she was back in the cage, so to speak, only I was her keeper instead of her parents; she had needed to escape from them, did she now need to run away from me as well? Whereas we had both been involved in Conrad's birth and shared the pleasure, if not the pain, of it, our daughter Frankie's birth was very much a private affair, her affair, from which I felt that not only I, but Conrad too, was excluded.

She had wanted to have the baby at home, but for medical reasons, she had to go into hospital. She was very upset at parting with Conrad – for the first time ever. I thought her grief was out of all proportion and found it irritating, but she explained it later. It was, she said, like cutting the umbilical cord. The first day in hospital she could think of nothing but Conrad. It upset her so much that she censored her thoughts and, by an effort of will, made her mind go blank in that direction. And it worked. After two or three days she ceased to think of him *in that way*; and when Frankie was born, the girl she had always wanted (she was so convinced it would be another boy that the midwife had to say to her, 'Well, aren't you going to look and see what sex it is?'), she was ready to commit herself exclusively to her.

A few days after she came out of hospital, she was nursing Frankie in the sitting-room when she noticed Conrad cowering in the corner and called him over. But even that gesture misfired when Conrad burned himself on the cigarette she had carelessly left on the side of the ashtray.

Despite our differences, I could not imagine that we would not come through. Ours was a good marriage, wasn't it? We never had rows, were considerate with one another and had the sort of jokey relationship that outsiders found attractively intimate (though perhaps it needed a third party to define it in this way; when there were no witnesses, wasn't there a hollowness at the core, a frightening vacuum where true intimacy should have been?). Then there was Conrad, the son we both adored; and now Frankie. As Cristián, in describing his own experience, put it in his long-awaited letter: 'It's hard, hard to end a marriage.'

Yet that was what he had done. Instead of having a second child, he and Paz had separated at the beginning of 1968. He had run off with a Frenchwoman (shades of Paz's affair in Nerja). She was married to a wealthy industrialist who kept their house and children, just as Paz kept Daniela and the 'grand old house' that she and Cristián were still struggling to pay for. Eventually he'd settled with Marie Claire in a dilapidated studio on the slopes of the San Cristóbal hill in Santiago, lent to them by an architect friend. Paz, meanwhile, had started a relationship with a neighbour, a North American painter long resident in Chile, whose own marriage had recently broken down.

Six months later, Cristián's father fell ill with lung cancer; and in August he died. His death had practical and emotional consequences. Cristián took over the management of the *hacienda* and began to study agriculture and fruit-growing, in addition to spending two days a week on the farm. He managed to stay on at the university, as 'the near-total abandonment of my students it entailed wasn't really noticed'. The university was anyway undergoing a crisis (it was 1968) and during the last three months of his father's life Cristián had devoted himself entirely to university politics, becoming at one point a member of a twenty-man junta which ran the faculty.

His father's death also brought him closer to Paz, who had got on well with the old man, and put his affair with the Frenchwoman into perspective. There was even talk of a reconciliation, but since both Cristián and Paz were physically in love with other people, this was no more than wishful thinking; yet 'if pressed to commit myself, I would still have said that Paz was my woman and not Marie Claire'.

In November Cristián moved to the farm for the cherry

harvest, leaving Marie Claire in Santiago, 'and it was a strange thing to be living again, completely alone, where I spent my childhood and adolescence'; his book of stories, *La Casa en Algarrobo*, came out and proved 'a disgusting flop'; and he took up again with 'an old flame' called Catalina, another married woman, who had four children. All these things, coming so soon after his father's death, precipitated a crisis.

> . . . I once held a loaded gun in my hand [he wrote], and walked into the farm after dinner, and [put] the gun to my temple and thought out very carefully what I was: a frustrated writer, with a bad book brought out by a good publisher through the influence of friends; I had tortured Paz day in and day out for years and years; I was a fake as a lecturer; I had lost my daughter; I still owed large sums of money for Paz's house; I was betraying Marie Claire's faith in me; I was ruining Catalina's married life, which, however awful it might have been, had never had anything to do with me; I could not write a single word worth the paper's value; I had trailed for years and years that unfinished – unstarted – thesis which I had committed myself to doing, for which I had got money, on which I had justified my loafing at Cambridge for a century, oh my lord; I was trying to run a farm and I was doing it successfully – that was the one thing that gave me a horrid scare and I fired the gun's-load at a tree trunk, and walked back to the house. A labourer came out of the dark, 'Anything wrong, *patrón*?' 'No, nothing, just a number of bloody fools coming to steal the cherries.'

That was the nadir of his fortunes. After that, things began to look up. He broke with Marie Claire, who had reached a settlement with her husband and was now living with her daughter in a decent house in Santiago. Catalina took him in hand and 'started to deal with poor Cristián's chronic trouble: the thesis'; she kept him at it, every afternoon and evening for five months, until it was finished; then he worked with a translator and finally posted it off to Cambridge in November 1969. This freed him to start, or re-start, the novel which he had tried to write both in England and in Spain: 'This time it will come [out]. I am working steadily and, for the first time in my life, with no impatience or anxiety, enjoying it tremendously, because it is funny, loose, insolent, show-offy and moving. It seems to be telling itself: no need to invent situations – I've been through so many . . .'

In addition to all this – the farming, the university teaching, the writing – Cristián had joined the advertising agency in which his father had been a partner to try to sort out the mess it had got into due to the other partner's drinking habits. Yet he was happy: 'Life with Paz seemed to be a sealed tunnel. With Catalina it's an endless adventure.' They had quarrels of 'truly Lawrentian' proportions: 'But I am proud of her, I am proud of myself, and of my success on the farm, which to everybody's amazement, including my own, is beginning to shine, and in the firm, and in the faculty, where, considering the little time I devote to it, I ought to be buried in chaos. Most of all, I am proud of the fact that I am writing my novel. Yes, we are happy.'

Cristián's letter reached me at a bad moment: I was just entering the tunnel from which he was claiming to have emerged triumphant. I did not like the tone of it, the self-centredness of someone in love. Even in his account of his suffering there seemed to be an element of boasting, an unseemly sense of the melodramatic. Or was I being too stiff, too English in my disapproval?

It was, as I say, a bad time. I was out of work; I worried about money and what I would do next. I didn't enjoy being on the dole: it only confirmed my growing sense of failure. I suppose I began to blame Lesley. Her faults, real or imagined, which I had glossed over for so long, now seemed glaring. The flat was a mess, she only cared for the children, she was thoughtless with money . . . But none of these things would have mattered if I'd felt that she loved me.

Then I got a lecturing job at a polytechnic in the Midlands. We thought we'd buy a house, yes, we'd buy a house. But where? In the town or the country? In the country, Lesley said; she didn't want to live in the town, of that she was certain. When I pointed out that we were likely to make more friends in the town, she said, 'Yes, but they'd be your friends. I'd be dependent on your friends.'

The way she talked about living in the country reminded me of those characters in Chekhov plays who are always on the point of leaving for Moscow, but never will. The difference was that whereas they want to get away from the boring provinces to the big city, Lesley wanted to make the journey in reverse – back to the simple life. But the impetus was the same; to go to the promised land where a new life would begin.

She wrote off to estate agents, explaining what we wanted, but the response was depressing. In nearly every case the ingenuity of the blurb-writer counted for nothing against the evidence of the photographer: all those featureless modern houses that carry the greyness of suburbia deep into the countryside. But we were easily put off. I don't think Lesley believed in her dream any more than I did; it was just that she needed it more.

Then, for a day or two, we thought we'd found it, our house in the country. Even allowing for estate agents' hyperbole, it sounded ideal. Cheap, too. It was to be auctioned, but it was not expected to fetch more than £2000 to £3000. There were major repairs needed, but that was to be expected . . . We decided to look at it.

We dumped the kids for the day and set off in high spirits. Our friend Neil accompanied us because he knew about houses and could assess what needed to be done. Everything conspired to make us optimistic. The spring sunshine and the open, rolling country seduced us, and as we neared the village a bird I didn't recognize came out of the hedge in front of the car and ran ahead of us for a while, clucking all the way. It seemed a good omen; but then we were always looking for signs.

The village had some fine houses, only 'ours' wasn't one of them. The rooms were dark and mean and there were relics of the previous inhabitants: an open packet of cornflakes on the kitchen table and a pair of worn-out boots by the cold stove. They were lonely old folks, kicked out when the owners decided to sell. The woman said as much. They must have been poor, too, living in that damp and dismal place. It was eerie, and we were glad to get away.

We had lunch in nearby Market Harborough and visited

a couple of estate agents. We thought we should look at more houses but decided against it. Lesley said she could never live there: it was neither one thing nor the other. So we went on to Leicester itself. Lesley had never been there before, but she had set her heart against living in the town and nothing would alter her resolution. I resented her attitude. After all, I was going to have to work in the place. But she couldn't get out of it fast enough.

After this daytrip we tacitly dropped the idea of moving, though the issue wasn't finally resolved until I started work and discovered that I need only spend three days a week there in any case. So we stayed in London and I commuted.

One night Lesley surprised me by saying casually that she wouldn't mind if I had an affair – this after the many promises of eternal fidelity she had extracted from me. Then she told me about an affair she nearly had a year and a half before with a television designer she had met at a party in the flat next door. I remembered that party; I had seen her flirting with the man but, rather than create a scene, I left early and went to bed. I had no idea that she had subsequently gone to see him and was only prevented from going to bed with him by his religious scruples. Now we discussed the possibility of one or other of us having an affair and she said she was sure she would be the one. I never got used to the detached way in which she talked about herself as if of another person whose actions were not her responsibility, and I found it disturbing.

We tried to analyze what had gone wrong: of course it had to do with sex. She accused me of 'cold sensuality' and I retorted that that was the role she forced on me by her lack of response. We saw a production of *The Merchant of Venice* in which Jessica, the Jew, is made to feel like a whore by her gentile lover, and Lesley identified with her and said that was how I made her feel. I protested my innocence of any such intention and argued that she never showed me any tenderness . . . And so it went on through the early months of the summer: accusations and counter-accusations, punctuated by uneasy truces and protestations of love (she once sent me a flower, pressed between a folded sheet of notepaper on which she had written, 'I love you'). Neither of us was ready for the showdown, though it was only a matter of time.

I noticed that she was withdrawing from those of our friends whom she considered *my* friends, particularly the married ones. Except where the children were concerned it was as if she stood apart from our joint life. But then her manner was ever thus: she herself told me that once, when she was in a pub with her boyfriend Dudley, a friend of his had said to her, 'Why is it that you never look at Dudley? You are with him, aren't you?'

Ah, the boredom and loneliness of all those afternoons in the park with the baby in the pushchair, among the nannies and those of the mothers who deigned to look after their own children, with their loud voices and upper-class opinions, so different from the homeliness of the communal garden outside our first flat. And there was Vincent, sitting apart and leaning against the fence of the big lawn, an obvious outcast. It wasn't so much that he was a hippy, there were plenty of them – they settled in droves all over the lawn with their beads, guitars and flutes – no, it was because he was alone and seemed a little lost that he attracted her, that and her nostalgia for the freer life. Lesley took him up, mothered him a bit and he became her friend. I wasn't jealous of Vincent, there was so obviously nothing sexual in the relationship. If I resented her friendship with him, it was because I took it as a veiled criticism of my 'straight' way of life.

The point of it was, I suppose, that she was giving and getting in friendship what marriage should have provided, but didn't – not sex, but companionship. As long as the friend was Vincent, I wasn't particularly alarmed. But after the conversation in which she told me how nearly she had taken a lover, I wondered uneasily who her next friend might be.

We'd looked forward to our summer holiday; a change was what we needed, a different atmosphere. We spent a week in Devon and it rained. It was no fun for the children: nothing to do in the house and too wet and cold for the beach. We did spend one afternoon at the seaside, but it wasn't a success. The kids soon tired of the sand and didn't like the look of the waves, while I sat huddled in a deckchair making facetious comments about the weather which failed to amuse Lesley. She went riding a couple of times, and in the evenings we played Scrabble with my parents. We slept in separate rooms that week, Lesley with the children and me on my own. I appreciated the uninterrupted nights and she didn't seem to mind our apartness.

Then we went to a friend's farm in Dorset where Neil was also staying. The weather improved and with it Lesley's mood, though the kids still whined and Conrad kept asking what he could do. Lesley went for walks along the lane; she cut down nettles in a field; she was happy. And I was desolate, because her happiness excluded me. I might as well not have been there. Indeed, when I suggested that I return to London early and come back later to collect her and the children, she was perfectly ready to fall in with the plan.

I didn't go; I was too miserable even to leave. In the face of Lesley's growing indifference, I had wild daydreams: I would give up my work and start again, become a doctor (in my mind I skipped over the years of training) and get a country practice. Then we could have a house in the country and some land, and she could have the horse she'd always wanted. The children would grow up healthy and strong, with plenty to do, and she would love me again . . .

It was laughable, of course, but I hung on to this vision. Yet, at the same time, as each bright morning beckoned us out to enjoy it while it lasted, I could only think of getting away and going back to London where the bleakness of my mood would be less apparent. But when Lesley came to me one afternoon and said, 'Let's go back to London', I was so surprised that I could only ask, 'What, now, this afternoon?' And she said, yes, she felt we were unwanted, a nuisance, we were getting in the way of the necessary work, the children . . . and so forth. This conversation brought us together again, if only momentarily, and I at once became reasonable and pointed out why it would be better if we stayed a few more days as we'd originally planned.

We were leaving on the Thursday and we'd promised to give Neil a lift to London. The night before he and I had an argument about films and novels and the differences between them, and I noticed two things: one was that, silly as the argument was, he was unusually persistent; and the other was that Lesley joined in on *my* side and took a much greater interest than I had come to expect from her in such an argument. Normally she would have been bored and indifferent and, if anything, hostile to me for going on about it.

Oh yes, the signs were there, if I had been alert enough to read them.

She came into the sitting-room and sat on the bed and her face went hard and she said, 'I'm bored, I'm so bored.'

That was how it began. She went on to say that she didn't love me, couldn't love me, had never loved me. I said to her, 'You once told me you could never leave a man unless you had someone else to go to', and she replied, 'I've never been married for four years before.' That was what I couldn't understand, how you could cease to love someone, just like that. I heard myself asking her if she wanted a separation and she said yes.

I went outside. The summer night was clear and warm, and I remembered the occasion when, after three months, Jane had told me it was no good, she had to go back to her husband, and I'd walked the streets of Madrid in the night and said to myself she was right and I must let her go. But that was different – upsetting, certainly but that affair was the stuff of romance; this was my life. Lesley was a part of me; she had borne my children, our children, beautiful children, who were even now asleep in our home. Wife, children, home, all gone. I sat on a bench in the park. I said, 'But you leave me with nothing!' and surprised myself by saying it aloud. Only there was no one around to hear me.

All the time I was wandering about, Lesley lay curled up on the sitting-room bed (she told me later), sucking her thumb and calling alternately on me and her mother. But when I reappeared she seemed utterly self-possessed. We went to bed in separate rooms and when I burst in on her in the middle of the night she thought I was going to kill her. If I had known there was someone else I might have felt like it, but I believed her when she told me she had just stopped loving me and could no longer live with me. In my abject state I was ready to shoulder all the blame for the failure of our relationship. I thought of various things I had done or left undone and they amounted to a massive indictment. All those Saturday afternoons at Stamford Bridge, watching Chelsea with the lads instead of being at home with her and the children. It wasn't that I had been, in a literal sense, unfaithful, but there were countless occasions when I might have been more sympathetic, more loving . . . If only she would give me another chance.

She agreed with some reluctance, said she didn't think it would do any good but we could try, only she must be allowed to go out in the evenings to see her friends. Of course, I said, of course, I don't want our home to be your prison. I cursed myself for not having encouraged her to go out on her own more often, until I remembered she hadn't wanted to before. A year, two years earlier, we had been having dinner at the house of friends and Harriet (who'd been married before) was saying how, in the early days of her first marriage, she used to look forward to the moment when her husband came home from work, and rely on him to entertain her; in the event, she said, she was often disappointed because he was tired and preoccupied. She said that a woman must have a life of her own apart from her husband, otherwise the dependence became mutually irksome. I saw that Lesley was listening intently; she was a little in awe of Harriet, who seemed to be so much more in control of her life than she was.

What I could not admit, even to myself, was that our disenchantment had been mutual. While Lesley had looked to procreation to give her life a purpose and had found more drudgery than fulfilment in it, I had expected marriage and children to intensify our love instead of undermining it. The difference was that she was not prepared to compromise because – it must have seemed to her – the whole of her life was involved, whereas for me there was always an escape in work or with friends. In that sense our marriage foundered on the rock of tradition: I was the husband who went out to work, she the wife who stayed at home, earning pin money by writing scripts for BBC schools broadcasts. That was no life for a child of the Sixties.

Now that I thought I was losing her I couldn't leave Lesley alone. I reasoned and pleaded and wept, but to no avail; the more I argued, the more she resisted. At lunch the next day we were still at it. I felt I was wearing her down without making any real progress. She was squatting on the floor, feeding Frankie, when she said with an angry disdain which contradicted her words, 'I want my freedom, but I can't bear your suffering.'

What puzzled me was how she could be so cheerful so much of the time. When I went to look for her at a lunchtime party where I could barely manage the common civilities, I found her chattering gaily to a young doctor. Instead of suspecting her, however, I despised myself for my boorishness.

It wasn't until she chose to go out one evening when it seemed important that we should be together that the truth began to percolate through the fog of my misery. She had gone to see a friend called Frank, whom she knew I didn't like: it seemed an odd thing to do at a moment when we'd achieved a small measure of harmony. I sat down to read Joseph Conrad's *Victory*, but my mind refused to focus on the print. Suddenly I started laughing: of course – how could I have been so blind? – she was having an affair, and not with any of a number of people I had suspected, but with Neil, whom I had never regarded as a rival.

This explained everything: her moment of panic at the farm, when she had wanted us to leave immediately; the argument with Neil which she had so unaccountably found interesting; her stipulation that she be allowed to go out and see her friends in the evenings if we stayed together; and her need to go out on this night of all nights. It was so obvious that I marvelled at my obtuseness. But Neil was such an unlikely suspect: he seemed disqualified by his virtues, his seriousness and sense of responsibility. Lesley's dreams, it had always seemed to me, were pure Hollywood and I automatically assumed that any lover she took would conform to that image – the poet B, for example, on whom I had expended a fair amount of vitriol before I had to admit that my suspicions were baseless. But Neil?

I was filled with relief. I was no longer dealing with an unknown quantity, but with something tangible. There were precedents – my God, were there not? This was the very stuff of fiction.

So that's it, I said to myself with a glow of self-righteousness, my wife is having an affair. I looked at my watch: it was nearly half-past eleven. She'd promised to be home shortly after midnight and I knew she would keep her promise.

I hadn't thought out what I would say to her when she came in, so I began by behaving as though everything were perfectly normal. I asked her how Frank was, and marvelled at the subtlety of her reply: 'Oh he's fine. But a ten-year-old kid was drowned in the canal near him yesterday – don't you think that's terrible?' Could she have invented such a story on the spur of the moment? She stuck to her story as it was, in part, true. She had been to Frank's, but had only stayed there long enough to acquire an alibi. Then she'd had dinner with Neil.

She was agreeably surprised at how coolly I took the news; she had expected an explosion. What she didn't realize was that the affair gave me new hope; I now knew what I was up against. There were no secrets between us any more. We talked through the night and if, practically speaking, we got nowhere we did achieve a new intimacy. She conceded that she had loved me in the beginning and said that now we were like 'old comrades'. I didn't much like that, but I let it pass. She spoke wistfully of the past, of the days when Conrad was a baby. Neil had first seen her at that time and he'd told her that she'd looked 'blooming' then, so she had forgotten the sleepless nights and recalled only the sense of achievement.

In the morning I did a foolish thing: I got her to phone Neil. He came over and we all sat down and tried to be reasonable, but Lesley understandably took offence at the way the two rivals for her favours were calmly discussing her future as if she wasn't there. She knew it was up to her and she had already decided she couldn't live with me. Besides, the affair with Neil had hardly begun and she wasn't sure of him yet.

I went to the country for a few days. It was a kind of convalescence; I began to eat and sleep again. When I returned to London Lesley greeted me cheerily, a little too cheerily I thought. Nothing had changed; while I was away she had been inundated with visitors and people coming to stay. She had no time to herself, no time to think.

But then Neil got cold feet. It was one thing to have an affair with a married woman, but quite another to feel (in part, at least) responsible for the break-up of a marriage. He decided to end the affair.

When she told me about it on the phone she didn't attempt to hide her sadness. I was touched; I felt sorry for her and wanted to help. With Neil out of the way I could afford to be generous; I was ready to forget what had happened and make a new start. She wasn't so sure; she wished it hadn't happened but couldn't forget why it had happened, and all the time she was thinking of Neil. But she let me comfort her and we even made love on a couple of nights, though I didn't stay; she didn't want me to stay. She couldn't be sure . . .

Those were mellow days and we took the children to the park. In a way it was as if nothing had happened. In time, I thought, she would forget Neil and then she would be glad our marriage had survived. But we were both anxious and little things took on a disproportionate significance. When Conrad lost the medallion that hung on a chain round his neck, we searched and searched for it in and around the sandpit. She said it was hopeless but I wouldn't give up. Our future seemed to depend on my finding that St Christopher. And I did; I found it in the grass and held it up in triumph. It was another omen.

Term started and I had to go away to work. I promised to phone as soon as I got back to London. When I did, I knew from the tone of her voice that things had changed.

Neil had been in touch again; he found it impossible to stay away . . .

Increasingly, the children became my major concern. Frankie was too young to know what was going on, but Conrad worried me. The birth of a sister had been traumatic enough for him and, at three, he was vulnerable and oddly mature for his age; there was something quaintly adult about the way he spoke. He was never a boisterous child. He had just started at nursery school and I was relieved to learn that he was enjoying his afternoons there. I arranged that once a week I would collect him from school, take him out to friends and bring him back at bedtime; then I would stay with him and read to him in bed, so that I was still in the house when he went to sleep.

I dreaded the moment of meeting him in the lobby of the school; the headmistress would call downstairs for him and I would wait nervously, thinking he must feel that I had deserted him. How was he to know any different? But he would come upstairs and solemnly take my hand and ask where we were going. In the car he'd be silent and I'd watch his pale face anxiously, thinking he was going to be sick – which he was once. Sometimes he fell asleep before the end of the journey and I'd wake him gently. In the strange house he would cling to me; I was the only one he would allow to do anything for him. If he played at all, he played on his own; and when others spoke to him, he buried his head in my trousers.

He was like that for the first hour; then suddenly he would begin to enjoy himself. On the journey home he would chatter gaily without cease; we invented games with the street lamps and traffic lights, and when there was a moon we played hide and seek with it and sang songs like 'I see the moon'. He generally went to bed happily and sucked his thumb while I read to him. But it made me sad that one so young should have to suffer so.

At the beginning of December I went to Devon for a fortnight; and while I was there I visited my sister Jeannie in hospital, where she had just given birth to her son Matthew. Inevitably, it reminded me of when Conrad was born and how Lesley and I were then. I couldn't believe our marriage was really over; we had shared so much; we understood each other so well; we laughed at the same things . . .

When I got back to London I saw a mutual friend who told me that Lesley had surprised her by saying that though she didn't know what would happen she 'supposed we'd get together in the end'. It was a week before Christmas.

I phoned Lesley. I shouldn't have done so, but there was a valid pretext and anyway I was too dejected to care. Her voice was bright and friendly until she heard the despair in mine; then she became concerned: she would bring Conrad round to see me the next day, or would I like her to come round right away? I hesitated, she hesitated; we both knew that it was decision time again. She said she would come.

She came. Impossible to say whether it was out of hope or despair, or as a result of a sudden generous impulse. She comforted me and the words tumbled out, the debris of love, hope, tenderness. She promised to phone in the morning. Neil, who was baby-sitting, would have to be told . . .

I waited till midday and still she hadn't phoned, so I called her. She sounded weary but said, yes, come. I packed my bag and went. The first night, I remember, we made love; it was the big test, which we were bound to fail. Absurdly, we had hoped for a miracle; we needed one for sure. Instead, we were confronted with our own bleak misery. Nothing had changed; nothing could change in the circumstances.

We struggled through Christmas, the visits to family and friends, and then, a few days later, she phoned Neil. And that was that. We shared the flat for a little longer, but slept apart. One night when we were playing poker, an American friend of Lesley's called Tod came up with the offer of a room in his flat, which was no more than a few hundred yards away, on the other side of Holland Park Avenue. It seemed the ideal solution and I accepted it gratefully.

We were an odd couple, Tod and I, with nothing in common but a love of Lesley. I found him attractive but

silly, a spoilt child with more money than sense. And I
could tell that he thought I was another uptight Englishman – why couldn't I let myself go, for Chrissake? Yet
we lived together in harmony and I was touched by his
attempts at therapy. He would invite me into his room
when he got in late at night (usually as I was about to go to
bed) and get me to keep time while he played the guitar
and sang his own songs. I was not very good at this, not
being particularly musical, but this was where the therapy
came in. 'You're doing fine', he'd say. 'Just let it come, let
yourself go . . . That's it, you've got it, you've got it!' And
I'd sit there like an idiot thumping my thigh with the palm
of my hand, grateful for his interest and anxious not to
disappoint him. And so it might go on till four in the
morning with him sitting on the bed, pepped up with
Mandrax, singing and playing, and me in the chair, both
audience and accompanist, trying – as if my life depended
upon it – not to lose the time.

In the morning I would get up first, make coffee and
take him his in bed. He generally invited me to bring mine
in and sit with him while I drank it. I appreciated this as I
dreaded waking up in the morning, coming into con-
sciousness and remembering why it was I felt so desolate.
But no matter how relaxed Tod was about my being there,
I couldn't feel anything other than an interloper in that
house. As long as I remained in the flat itself, on the
ground floor, I was all right; but I tried to avoid going
upstairs to the communal bathroom, not just because it
was an icy room with a broken window, but for fear of
meeting other residents who might question my right to
be there. I remembered that a friend had once told me
how after the break-up of her first marriage she couldn't
go out of her room for days on end, not even for a pee; so
she filled up empty milk bottles with her urine and left
them standing in the bottom of her wardrobe until they
fermented and formed a green mould. If I had stayed
much longer in the flat I probably would have been doing
the same.

It is indeed 'hard, hard to end a marriage', as Cristián
had written with reference to his own. My experience
made me better able to understand how he had almost

given in to despair when he had walked out on his father's estate with a gun in his hand. Life was still precious to me, but the trauma of my separation from Lesley and the children was the emotional equivalent to the physical devastation wrought by polio.

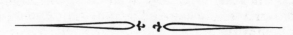

Cristián and I were separated not just by distance but by the vicissitudes of our private lives as well. When neither of us wrote to the other for several years this did not mean a failure of friendship so much as a reluctance – or a recognition of the impossibility of attempting – to describe our emotional travails while we were still caught up in them. Our intimacy dated from a time of hope for us both, and life – 'old life itself', as Simon Gray was wont to say – had played its usual tricks on us, leaving us sadder, if not wiser, people. Cristián might have temporarily dropped out of my life, but he never dropped out of my thoughts.

Sometime in the mid-Seventies I read a memoir by the Chilean writer Jorge Edwards, who had served as *chargé d'affaires* in Castro's Cuba when diplomatic relations were resumed between the two countries after Allende came to power in 1970. I was excited to see Cristián's name in print and to read of a private visit he had made to Cuba. By the time I read this, however, the military coup had taken place in Chile, Pinochet was in power and horrific stories of massacres and torture were emerging from that country. In spite of my eagerness to find out how Cristián was, I was reluctant to write to him in Chile for fear of compromising him in some way. Instead I wrote to Jorge Edwards in Barcelona, asking if he had any news of Cristián. He suggested I write direct to Cristián. But Cristián did not reply to the letter I wrote him apart from a note promising a long letter soon.

For that I had to wait many more years – until June 1984, when he wrote and announced his intention of visiting England the following summer, at the invitation of the British Council, to write a series of articles: ' "England twenty years after" sort of thing.' And he proceeded to make up for nearly fifteen years of silence with a full account of his life:

'After a number of affairs, wild and otherwise, and a second marriage in between, I've been happily married for the past eight years to my present wife, Soledad, whom you'll like, I'm sure, very much.' (He was right about that: when they came to England it was like being reunited with two old friends, not just one.) Soledad had five children from her former marriage ('imagine', Cristián wrote): four boys and a girl, all grown up or thereabouts. Daniela remained Cristián's only child, and she was now eighteen: 'She's always lived with Paz, she's been through periods of rejection of my life and ways, but on the whole we've never been far from each other for too long a time. She's always, even from the days when she was a child, spent summers and weekends with me.' Now she was at university, studying anthropology. As for Paz, she had long since married her American painter, who had been a good stepfather to Daniela.

Cristián's visit to Cuba took place during Allende's first year of office and it was this visit, he told me, that made him realize that he was no longer an *allendista* (in fact, he had almost certainly made up his mind before he went to Cuba, even before the 1970 election, in which he apparently voted, not for Allende, but for his Christian Democrat opponent, Radomiro Tomic). Whether he would have put the case quite so starkly as does Mario Vargas Llosa – who stated in an article on the Cuban Revolution '30 Years On' published in the *Daily Telegraph* on January 2nd, 1989, that 'the ideal of equality is incompatible with the ideal of freedom' – can only be a matter of conjecture; but he would certainly have agreed that the spectacle of 10,000 people milling around the Peruvian embassy in Havana, wanting asylum, in the three days following the withdrawal of its police guard in April 1980 indicated that the achievement of equality had not been without some human cost.

In addition to lecturing at the university, running the family farm and his father's advertising business, Cristián 'also got involved in a curious enterprise of my own in the early Seventies, a discotheque, which may have been a way of saying goodbye to capitalism (as many of us thought we were in those days) in the fullest possible swing'.

In 1972, he was elected Chairman of the Centro de Estudios Humanísticos – 'a quite smart department, now almost in ruins – by a strange combination of left, right and centre'. But the difficult balancing act became impossible to sustain under the Junta: 'I managed to survive up to 1975 when the military made a radical cleaning up of the remains of the opposition in the Universidad de Chile; they sacked me from the Chairmanship, and I was forced to give up the university altogether.'

He had already opted out of the advertising business, which his brother had taken over and ran with the help of two sisters, and in 1975 the family farm was sold. But Cristián, who had become addicted to the land, bought a farm of his own, some eighty acres in size, 180 kilometres north of Santiago at a place called Cabildo, 'very close to one of the most beautiful resorts on the Chilean coast, Zapallar, where we go often and, whenever money allows, rent a house during summer'.

In effect, Cristián wrote, 'I became a kind of internal exile'.

He spent a large part of 1976 in New York as Visiting Fellow in the Writing Division of the University of Columbia; otherwise for two years he concentrated on farming to the exclusion of all other activities. Then in 1977 he became a columnist on the magazine *Hoy*, 'the first opposition weekly . . . allowed to circulate' under Pinochet, and over the years built up 'quite a reputation' for his articles on art and literature. His novel *El rincón de los niños* ('The Children's Corner') was published in 1980: it was 'very successful in avant garde circles but rather rejected by ordinary mortals ("hermetic", "pretentious", "unreadable", "obscene", you know, that sort of thing)'. I have to say that when I lent my copy of the novel to a Spanish-speaking friend, his verdict placed him firmly in the ranks of 'ordinary mortals': he, too, found it pretentious and unreadable.

Another short novel, *El verano del ganadero* ('The Rancher's Summer'), followed in 1983, and a third, *Una escalera contra la pared* ('A Ladder against the Wall'), was short-listed for the prestigious prize, the *Premio Herralde*, in Barcelona. At the same time Cristián was writing an autobiography, and, after 1982, lecturing again, this time at the University of Santiago, and doing regular interviews with writers and painters on the university radio station, though 'one never knows how long such a job will last'.

People get sacked [he went on] under various stupid pretexts. And one always plays as far beyond the line as [the] situation permits. We've all been forced back into adolescence under the dictatorship. Arguments come and go as to how one ought to behave. [Though] far from being myself a Communist (how could I?), I've taken the Communist line of strategy: to act publicly as much as one can, penetrating education and the media, *using* them, to counter the ideology in power with one's views and ideas. It's a dangerous and risky attitude in all kinds of ways. But one learns, in spite of misunderstandings and misinterpretations, to stick firmly to it. I came to feel absolutely bored buried on the farm, [but] I've never, not even in the worst moments, when after the coup and for the first couple of years, many if not most of us intellectuals were closely watched by the political police, world famous then as DINA and now as CNI, interrogated by men with courteous manners (that at least and thanks God was my own experience) and sinister records, and visited in our own homes from time to time by fellows with machine guns in civilian clothes (many of my close friends have been in detention camps, sometimes because they were . . . acting in direct politics, sometimes through gruesome mistakes; many others have been tortured; quite a number have been sacked from their jobs and have had to undergo awful economic hardship), never, as I say, not even in the worst moments, have I thought of leaving the country.

What enabled Cristián to stay in Chile was the farm; although that got to be boring, it was less boring, he thought, than living in exile. But he was anxious I should not get the wrong impression: he was not bored with farming, only with his confinement to the farm. Growing things had become something of a passion with him: 'Since 1978, when I started planting, I've planted 7,000 avocados, about 12,000 papaws and numberless ornamental trees all along the lanes of the farm and in small groves here and there.' This mania for planting trees was surely less a matter of economics than a gesture of faith in the future of the country at a time when, as he felt, it was being undermined by the political extremism of both left and right.

There was no house on the farm and Cristián stayed in Cabildo; he had once owned a house in the village but had been forced to sell it at a time of rocketing inflation to pay off a bank loan. Latterly, he had been spending three or four days a week at the farm, sometimes accompanied by Soledad, sometimes by Daniela or one of Soledad's children, more often alone. He informed me that shortly 'we are going to hold in the farm buildings the first Cambridge Old Boys' *asado* [barbecue]. This is a weird group of some twelve fellows, all of them business men, some Chilean . . . and the rest all English with a very colonial background involving Africa and the Far East. This group meets once a year for the Cambridge Dinner (in black tie) in some smart restaurant, and gets awfully drunk amidst foolish dirty jokes, tall stories and some amount of commercial truck.'

Cristián's love of England and English literature tended to cut him off from his fellow countrymen. It was 'one of the problems I had to face when I returned with plans for lecturing on English Lit'. No one was interested. England, he wrote, 'is a kind of private drug, unavailable to most people in this part of the world. Many times I ask myself if it wasn't . . . a tremendous waste of time to spend so many years there rather than in France or Spain. No use asking so late, is it?'

In returning to England in his forty-ninth year Cristián wanted, as he put it, 'to recapture the past and also, somehow, to feel the pulse and attest what time has done to us all . . .' He indicated something of what time had done to him in a brief postscript: 'I've grown a little gentleman farmer's paunch and I'm going bald.'

What time had done to us all . . . I still had my hair but by 1984 I, too, had put on a little weight. Like Cristián, I had married again, but only once; unlike him, I had fathered another child, a second son, who was now eleven years old. I had been working, for almost a decade, as literary editor of the weekly *New Society*, and had written three books, the first of which was part of a *New Society* series, though it predated my employment on the journal. It was written in collaboration with the founder of the Claimants and Unemployed Workers Union, a Barnsley ex-miner called Joe Kenyon, and called, simply, *Stories from the Dole Queue*.

After the boom of the Sixties, the early Seventies – with unemployment in the United Kingdom hovering around the million mark – raised the spectre of the Depression, which was still within many people's living memory. Gone were the days of Macmillan's 'You've never had it so good' boast; gone was the optimism that greeted Wilson's first ministry; Labour now seemed bereft of ideas and powerless to prevent the slump. Claimants' unions, of which Joe Kenyon's was but one, sprang up all over England to fight for the rights of the unemployed against the bureaucratic state.

For me, paradoxically, the work I did on the *Dole Queue* book, the research and interviews with claimants and their spokesmen (and they were all men), marked a political watershed comparable, perhaps, to that reached, though not yet acknowledged, by the country as a whole. It was not a 'road to Damascus' conversion; I didn't suddenly start yelling 'Scroungers' and turn purple in the face. But I did come to realize that society's more obvious and vociferous 'victims' were not the only ones, and that the working poor, who were often the people manning the counters of Department of Health and Social Security offices and facing the abuse of the unemployed, were also victims of the system. As I noted in the book, following the introduction of Family Income Supplement (to boost the earnings of the low-paid) at the beginning of August 1971, the *Sunday Times* reported: 'Curiously, there has been a rush of applications for FIS from the Civil Service itself. To avoid embarrassment to civil servants working in Departments of Health and Social Security who wish to claim, a special branch office has been set up in Blackpool which will . . . process all civil servants' applications.'

One or two of the more perceptive reviewers of *Stories*

from the Dole Queue pointed out the discrepancy between
its overtly activist message and its cautiously ambivalent
subtext, a difference which reflected the constitutional
make-up and contrasting experiences of the two authors –
one, working-class, unemployed himself and a born politician and fighter; the other, a bourgeois lefty, perhaps
more tainted with the BBC ethos of 'fairness' and 'balance'
than he would have cared to admit. At any rate, that was
my last attempt at crusading journalism. After that, I
began to distrust political indignation in general, and the
self-righteousness of the extreme left in particular.

My father, curiously enough – and to some extent possibly under my influence, though he would never have
admitted as much – had been moving in the opposite
direction. The Vermin Club forgotten, he had long since
abandoned the *Daily Telegraph* in favour of the *Guardian*;
and he enjoyed shocking the more hidebound of his
country neighbours by proclaiming his support of the
Labour Party. Since he had retired from farming, he had
also changed in other, equally unexpected, ways.

The father I knew from my childhood would have scorned both vegetarianism and the idea of taking paying
guests, but in his old age he embraced both enthusiastically. He became a Samaritan, deriving extraordinary
pleasure from helping others and often going to considerable lengths on their behalf until a severe stroke slurred
his speech and made it impossible for him to continue. He
also developed an unlikely interest in the mystical and
rather misty end of religion and bought twee books published by obscure little presses in Cornwall. This seemed
unworthy of him; but most of the changes, probably
attributable to intimations of mortality, were for the better.
In some ways, though, I preferred the unregenerate
Adam.

He lived long enough to read – or rather, nod off over –
a typescript draft of my second book, an historical account
of the fate of five young Englishmen left behind in the
forests of the upper Congo by H. M. Stanley on his last
African expedition. My interest in this gruesome tale
of moral disintegration under pressure was one that
Cristián would have understood, since it grew out of my

researches (for a radio programme) into the Congo experiences of the novelist we both so much admired, Joseph Conrad: this Victorian scandal was – almost certainly wrongly – considered to be one of the sources of *Heart of Darkness*. I don't know what my father would have thought of the finished book, however, as he died before it came out.

The day he went into hospital, my sister Jeannie, who had earlier been summoned by my mother, called me from Devon to say that perhaps I should come too. I took a train from Paddington on a perfect summer's day in the otherwise dismally wet June of 1978. It was an old-fashioned train and, for the last stretch of the journey, the beautiful coastal run through Dawlish and Teignmouth to Newton Abbot, I went out and stood in the corridor. Outside, the air was still; it was as if the world were holding its breath. The sea's glittering immobility, the occasion for my visit and memories stretching back more than thirty years of this, the last leg of my journey home, induced in me a pleasurable melancholy.

Jeannie was waiting at the station. Her fervent embrace shook me out of my reverie.

'He's dead,' she said, and the words released the torrent of emotion she had been holding in check until that moment.

My own emotions were muted and they included, I have to admit, an element of relief: not that my father was dead – I had scarcely had time to absorb that – but that I was spared the duty of witnessing his dying; and that his death had been mercifully quick. When I had visited him in hospital two and a half years earlier, after the more severe of his two strokes, he had been uncharacteristically tearful and emotional. It was an effect of the illness, I was told, but still I didn't like to see him so nakedly vulnerable.

He did not have a last illness as such, he just grew progressively sicker and frailer. His eyes gave him trouble (it had been a great annoyance to him throughout his life that he had poor sight, which had necessitated his wearing glasses from an early age), so my mother read the *Guardian* to him in the evenings until he grew tired of newspapers and asked for poetry instead, choosing a

volume of John Donne that Jeannie had given him as a
birthday present.

The day she called me, it was obvious to Jeannie that he
had decided to die. He had had enough; all the life had
gone out of him and his eyes had clouded over. He looked
as though he were in agony and was just holding on until
the ambulance came to take him to hospital. Jeannie was
reminded of a child, who, on a long journey, keeps
saying, 'When will we be there? When will we be there?'
As long as he remained at home he obviously felt some
responsibility for himself which he couldn't wait to jetti-
son. In contrast to the day before, when he had eagerly
discussed her linguistic studies with her – she was, at
the time, doing a course in teaching English as a foreign
language – he seemed scarcely aware of Jeannie's presence; his only intimacy that day was with my mother.

When the ambulance finally arrived, his relief was pal-
pable. Jeannie found it extraordinary, almost surreal, the
way he welcomed the ambulance men as though they
were death's messengers, twin Charons who would ferry
him to the other side. My mother welcomed them, too,
but for more practical reasons: they promised to take care
of him and told him not to worry when he started to retch.
They took him away, not on a stretcher, but in a kind of
collapsible seat. Jeannie watched in horror as they folded
him into this contraption: he was like a baby, a foetus
even, there was so little of him left.

As they loaded him into the ambulance, my father
turned and looked straight at my mother. 'Goodbye, Ber',
was all he said. My mother, anxious to reassure him, told
him she would be coming to see him in the afternoon; but
it was as if he knew that would be too late – as indeed it
was: when they went into the hospital that afternoon, he
was too far gone even to recognize her, and by the time
they got home he was dead.

When Jeannie and I went to 'view' the corpse, the
undertaker greeted us in sepulchral tones, saying how
sorry he was that we should meet under such circumstances – which prompted me to ask under what other
circumstances we were likely to meet. As we entered the
viewing chamber, or whatever the cubicle in which the

corpse is displayed is called, Jeannie and I were both trying to stifle our unseemly giggles. No doubt nervousness had something to do with it too.

I don't know what I expected to feel, but I expected to feel something. My father looked so small, so *shrunken*, so familiar – and so absent. If I felt anything at all, it was simply that *he* was not there.

I never cried for my father. We were never close in the way he and Jeannie were. Yet despite the lack of intimacy in our relationship, my father was the single most important influence in my life. Other men whom I have come to love and respect, like Cristián, have all had about them certain characteristics or attitudes I associate with him; and much of what he was lives on in me.

The writer Colin MacInnes, who was the subject of my third book, *Inside Outsider* (1983), told a friend who had written to express condolence on his mother's death: 'Such events put one in the front line, don't they?' Having each lost a parent, Cristián and I were now both in the front line.

The political move to the right in Britain had, thankfully, been less sudden and violent than in Chile; yet by the late Seventies and early Eighties the governments of both countries were united in their enthusiasm for monetaristic solutions to economic problems. In that sense, perhaps, Chile might once again have earned the sobriquet, 'the England of South America', except that, in this instance, it had got there first and become Thatcherite even before Mrs Thatcher.

Although I was by no means a Conservative, my radicalism, like Cristián's, had been diluted. Now that my son went to an independent school, I told him when I answered his long letter, I could no longer honestly call myself a socialist.

I'm glad your boy is going to a stimulating school [Cristián replied]. Does that really mean that your socialism has faded? All bourgeois socialists send their kids to the best schools they can afford. All of them, too, try to live as well as they can. Socialism, as a fine friend of mine says, is not *for* poverty but *against* poverty. We all got so fucked up with socialism in

Chile during Allende . . . Felipe González and Mitterrand
seem to me to begin to understand what socialism may be as a
'real' proposition. However, it's curious, I've ended up by
abandoning the use of that word. But, in using the English
language, too many things come back to me: in England I *was*,
I think, a socialist. Now I tend to think of myself as a 'liberal
leftist', as I recently said in a press interview. Soledad tells me
that I shouldn't fool around with words and [should] face up
to my present reactionary conservatism. I disagree with her,
of course.

Cristián was intrigued to hear that I had moved out of
London (though I still worked there part-time) and settled
in my native Devon. With some misgivings, I had gone
along with my wife's desire to live in the country; and now
that my mother was a widow, living on her own, her
village in Devon seemed the obvious place for us to go.

'The question of roots,' he wrote, 'remains for me one of
the big mysteries of life. I know that's what brought me
back to Chile in '66, what took me to farming in '68, [and]
what keeps me tied down in this appalling country under
a dishonourable government which goes against all my
traditions, habits and tastes.'

He was looking forward to coming to England but he
was worried about the cost of the trip. The British Council
would pay his fare and a lump sum of £3,000 for a three-
month stay, but he would have to find the money to pay
Soledad's fare and any extra expenses they might incur.
(A mutual acquaintance from Cambridge days, now a lecturer at the University of Essex, to whom Cristián had
written to ask if he might give some lectures there, had
come up to me at a party and asked anxiously if I knew
what Cristián's politics were nowadays – 'Students at
Essex are very left-wing, you know . . .') Prospects for the
forthcoming avocado harvest were not good: prices were
high but the crop did not look promising.

By the time he wrote again, in December, the harvest
was over and his forecast had proved only too accurate;
the excellent prices had failed to compensate for the
meagre crop. Cristián became unusually depressed.
Nothing like this had happened to him in sixteen years of
agricultural experience. Indeed, he had always regarded

farming as therapeutic. People he knew who had died on
the land, whether family or friends, had all died well,
their deaths fitting conclusions to lives that were at once
creative, successful and hard-working. His own life, by
contrast, now seemed to him 'a mess and a failure,
nothing to do with creation and imagination, only with
pretension and confusion'.

There followed a hint that all might not be well with him
physically, though he made so light of it that I missed its
significance: 'One of my brothers-in-law is a good brain
surgeon and he came along and gave me a big box of
heavy sleeping pills which have kind of made me, well,
sleep. Quite a lot.'

At first he was inclined to abandon the projected European visit (which now included a month in Paris as a
guest of the French Institute); but on second thoughts he
determined not just to go through with it but to bring it
forward to mid-March. That was the time he now
expected to arrive in Britain.

I had suggested in one of my letters that he make use
of his university connection in Santiago to help him get
accommodation in London. He answered that this might
no longer be possible:

A couple of weeks ago I was subjected – yes, this is my
country today – to a legal trick and made to resign [from] my
radio programme of interviews, for 'financial reasons'. I
expect they wanted me to get angry and resign entirely [from]
the university job, since the real, never-mentioned reason for
all this has to do with my articles in *Hoy*, one of them [dealing]
in an ironic way with the University of Santiago's anti-student
policies and another having to do with a recently censored
satirical novel by a writer I know. But I decided not to
resign . . . If they want to turn me out, let them do it.

After this letter I heard nothing. January, February,
March passed. By the middle of April, when there was still
no news, I was sufficiently alarmed to phone the British
Council. All they could tell me was that his date of arrival
had been postponed till the end of June; no one seemed
to know why. But the confirmation that he was coming
reassured me, even if it was rather later than expected.

At the end of May I at last heard from Cristián himself. He explained that two things had prevented him writing sooner. One was the Chilean earthquake, which had been 'violent and destructive all over the country': it had severely damaged the house in Valparaíso where he and Soledad had been staying, though their own house in Santiago and the farm buildings at Cabildo were fortunately unharmed. The other event was more ominous, though Cristián again made light of it. He had been suffering from a severe headache and loss of memory – names of people, plants, streets eluded him. Then, the day before the earthquake, he suddenly found he could neither speak nor write clearly.

'Though none of these symptoms lasted,' he recalled, 'I felt they meant something really wrong inside my head, so we came quickly back to Santiago, where my brain surgeon brother-in-law did not give me sleeping pills this time.' Instead, Cristián had to undergo a series of tests, as a result of which he had an operation for a brain tumour on March 14th. After its removal he was put on a short course of radiotherapy which, though it did him good, made all his remaining hair fall out – 'Today I'm as bald as a billiard ball.' Nevertheless, he seemed in good spirits and was looking forward to his trip to Europe, which the doctor had just sanctioned. The doctor had also encouraged him to start writing again.

He ended his letter saying that he would phone me the moment he and Soledad set foot in London.

Despite his warning, it took me a little while to adjust to Cristián's appearance. At first sight the hairless, shining dome of his cranium, above the line of his spectacles, gave him a severe, almost an inquisitorial look. I had forgotten how tall he was. There was something brooding, sinister, even menacing about him; fleetingly, it occurred to me that he could be cast as a Latin American dictator. But soon I began to descry the familiar features of my old friend under the distorting mask. He introduced me to Soledad, who was dark and beautiful – it was impossible to believe that she had had five children who were now all grown up – and the three of us left my office and went out to lunch.

There could be no doubt about the depth of their feelings for one another. They were so loving and considerate that I was tempted to remark upon it until I remembered my gaffe of twenty years before when I had visited Cristián and Paz in Spain. Nor could I estimate how far the intensity of their rapport was attributable to the trauma of Cristián's recent operation and their mutual delight at his survival.

It was a day or two later, when we met again for dinner, that I learned from Soledad how temporary a reprieve it was, that despite the operation and the radiotherapy Cristián probably had no more than three months to live. Once I knew this, it coloured everything. As a figure out of my past, Cristián was already to some extent a ghost. Now he seemed like a ghost in another sense as well: though he walked among us, he was not quite one of us.

Cristián and Soledad came to stay with me in Devon. On the train Cristián quizzed me about recent English fiction: who were the novelists to read now – what about Malcolm Bradbury, David Lodge, Martin Amis? He was arranging to have a number of paperbacks sent out to Chile, where he was thinking of offering a course on the modern English novel. He greatly admired Evelyn Waugh and was reading Christopher Sykes's biography of him. Perhaps I remember this conversation so clearly because of the unspoken question in my mind. Yet as I listened to him outline his plans for the future – what he would teach, what he would write, what he might grow on the farm – I found it impossible to believe that he would not live long enough to do any of these things. He was so alert, so full of interest and curiosity.

In Devon Cristián and Soledad met my wife and my mother. Cristián had met my mother before but he had never met Jenny, though he was predisposed in her favour because she comes from New Zealand. He had written:

When I went to Australia in '76, I stopped for a few hours at Auckland, and I was nearly left there for good, as something

[was] wrong with my ticket. The second reason for my love of New Zealanders – the first being Katherine Mansfield – is that they put me on an Air New Zealand flight, first class, and flew me all the way to Sydney eating scrambled eggs and drinking champagne. Then, in '80, I went to Los Angeles, Cal. to take a crash course at Riverside University on 'Avocados: from Soil to Marketing'. There I met a number of New Zealand farmers, one of [whom] was feeling very homesick. He approached me and said, 'So, you come from Chile.' I told him my NZ anecdote and the fellow [was] so moved that he [bought] a round of whiskys for all six of us Chilean avocado growers.

Cristián seemed very much at home in Devon. In the old days at Cambridge I had been impressed by his intellectuality; now I observed the country gentleman, a little old-fashioned in manner, courteous, charming and aristocratic. He was also happy. Despite the political ghastliness of his country, and despite the recent operation on his brain, Cristián expressed himself well content with his lot. As we walked together on Dartmoor, he reiterated his commitment to Chile, his passion for the farm, his love for his daughter, Daniela, for Soledad and her children – towards whom, he said, he felt more like an elder brother than a step-parent. With all this and his writing too – above all, his writing – should he not consider himself a lucky man?

On the Saturday evening we went out to a restaurant for dinner and Cristián and Soledad tried to give us some idea of what life in Chile under the dictatorship was really like. Cristián described a Military School reunion lunch to which Soledad had expressed a desire to go. They had sat at a table with some other civilians and, as the wine flowed, the idea took shape that they should confront, in the politest possible way, the two generals who were present and put forward their scheme for a return to democracy. If they all did it together, and stood by one another, there would be less danger of victimization. As they trooped over to where the generals were sitting there was a certain amount of jockeying for position and Cristián found himself being elbowed into the forefront and obliged to take on the role of spokesman. He began to put their case; but even as he was speaking he noticed out of the corner of his eye that his fellow conspirators were slipping away, one by one, until he was the only one left. The generals remained frighteningly impassive throughout. Only later, when he bumped into one of them outside the lavatory, did the general profess himself interested in Cristián's ideas and suggest that they discuss them one day over lunch. Cristián laughed. He was still awaiting an invitation.

I recalled the one Gurkha regimental reunion to which I had taken Jenny: the guest of honour there, too, had been a general but though Walter Walker's calls for the setting-up of vigilante groups throughout the country had earned him some notoriety in the early Seventies, his real influence on affairs of state had been negligible. The Chilean Walter Walkers, however, were no laughing matter.

Cristián told us that Pinochet had been an instructor at the Military School when he himself was a cadet there. He was the kind of man, Cristián said, who liked to creep up behind you at night, when you were on guard duty, and catch you smoking. A nonentity. It was Allende who had made him commander-in-chief of the army and the worm had turned.

That night at dinner, or the next day perhaps, Soledad told us the story of their epic drive from Valparaíso to Santiago immediately after the earthquake, when Cristián had to be rushed into hospital. They arrived at a bridge just as it was about to be closed because a crack had appeared in the middle of it. When Soledad explained the urgency of their mission they were allowed to proceed, but warned of the danger they faced. So they crossed the bridge like film stuntmen, holding the car doors open in case it gave way under them and they had to leap for safety. One way or another Chile sounded like an exceptionally dangerous place.

Back in London, shortly before Cristián and Soledad left for Paris, I went to dinner with them. The other guest, a descendant of Lord Cochrane, the British admiral whose exploits at sea made him one of the heroes of the Chilean War of Independence, along with San Martín and the

Liberator, Bernardo O'Higgins, failed to arrive. Once we realized he was not just inordinately late, but was not going to turn up at all, we settled down to enjoy a more intimate evening on our own. Cristián showed me an old Chilean volume he was reading in preparation for a novel he intended to write and talked about the railway line (now closed) between Santiago and Valparaíso and how it might feature in his projected novel. I treasure the memory of this evening as the last occasion on which we really talked; I felt closer to him then than at any other time during the visit.

For in truth our experience of life since the days of our intimate friendship in Cambridge had driven us apart, despite the common ground of failed marriages, death of fathers, and published books. While Cristián had lived in England long enough to have a thorough understanding of the country, its language and literature, and could comment on my writings, I had neither lived in Chile during two decades of violence and repression nor mastered enough Spanish even to read his books. No one else I knew had had the secret police knocking at his door. And as if that were not enough, there was now, in addition, the likely imminence of his death.

A month later, when they returned from Paris, Soledad phoned me in London to say that all had gone well except that Cristián had developed back trouble – nothing, she hastened to add, to do with the other trouble – which made it difficult for him to walk without her support. Nevertheless they insisted on coming to lunch with me one last time before they flew back to Chile. Despite our efforts to be cheerful, this was a melancholy occasion as at least two of us knew that never would all three of us sit down together again.

After that I heard nothing. As the months passed I lulled myself into believing that Cristián was still alive. Otherwise I would surely have heard. At the same time there was a sense in which he was already dead to me. Whether he survived two weeks or two years I would not see him again. So when Soledad phoned in the depths of winter and told me he was dead, had been dead three months, the shock was muffled – or, more accurately, delayed. The force of it did not finally hit me until I went back to Gara Rock in the summer and walked along the cliff path to the point where, if I looked in one direction, I could see where I had taken a photograph of Cristián and Soledad with their arms entwined and their backs to the English Channel just twelve months earlier, and, if I turned the other way, I could look across to Bolt Head, where Cristián had once photographed Paz and me standing below him, staring out over that same English Channel. Then I realized that when you mourn a friend you are also mourning that part of yourself, or your past, that dies with him.

PART II

Journey to Santiago

'We were talking at this meeting the other day about *transculturación*, which is an important concept for Latin America. It means that you lose a culture but you don't really lose it, and you acquire a culture but you don't really acquire it. You're always in the zone in-between. The strangest things happen in that zone in-between.'

Adriana Valdés,
in conversation with the author

'. . . a timely reminder: don't be too certain of learning the past from the lips of the present. Beware of the most honest broker. Remember that what you are told is really threefold: shaped by the teller, reshaped by the listener, concealed from both by the dead man of the tale.'

Vladimir Nabokov,
The Real Life of Sebastian Knight

1

I had to go to Chile. There was no other way of discovering the Chilean Cristián. I knew the English Cristiań, but in a language other than one's own one becomes a different person; and to present the man only as I knew him would be to offer a very partial and inadequate portrait. I needed to get the smell and the feel of the country he loved even while it exasperated him. I needed to see how he fitted into the landscape, how it felt to be a Chilean at a moment in history when it seemed, on the outside at least, to be more a matter of shame than of pride. As I summed it up in my application for a research grant, I wanted to study the 'dilemma of the liberal intellectual in Chile'.

Two acquaintances of mine went to Santiago within weeks of one another early in 1989; I asked both if they would try to contact Paz Errázuriz for me. I still had the address of the 'grand old house' which she and Cristián had bought together with such high hopes, but I was so sure she must have moved that I did not bother to give it to them. The first failed to make contact with her; the second succeeded, but only at the very end of her visit, and brought back a hastily written postcard from Paz, who was indeed still living in the house that she and Cristián had purchased nearly a quarter of a century before. After that, we were soon writing each other long letters.

I still found it hard to believe that I would actually go to Chile. It had been a dream for too long, and the reality (which involved long flights across the world and the seasons) terrified me. But my need to find answers to the many questions in my mind about both Cristián and Chile was even stronger than my fear of flying; so I had to make the journey.

I would leave at the end of October. That would give me six months in which to transform my rudimentary Spanish

– or *castellano*, as I was already learning to call it in deference to South American sensibilities – into something
more serviceable, and still get me there well before the
presidential election in December, the first in Chile for
twenty years. This was expected to endorse the result of
the previous year's plebiscite, in which a majority of Chileans had rejected the Pinochet regime and thereby opened
up the road back to democracy.

I bought tapes and grammar books and struggled through
the writings of Cristián and others, noting down and
trying to memorize vocabulary (a task I reserved for my
weekly train journey to London); and I had conversation
practice for an hour every week with a Venezuelan
woman resident in Exeter.

Through her and others I heard of a Chilean exile working in the computer unit at Exeter University, whom I also
began to see most weeks. Sergio Cornejo was a
Communist, who nightly recorded the broadcasts of Chilean exiles from radio stations in Moscow and East Berlin
and then listened to the tapes the following morning while
he was working. His was a working-class and trade-union
background and he came not from Santiago but from Ran-
cagua, some sixty miles to the south of the capital.

His wife, Ledy Castro, had been in exile with him
between 1974 and 1982, but had then returned to Chile
with their son, Julio. Two years later she was arrested by
the secret police, and she had been incarcerated ever
since, detained without charge. When she was finally
charged, she got a five-year sentence, which should have
meant she was free to go since she had already served
five years; the catch was that there were other charges
pending . . . She could not look after her son while she
was in prison and did not like to leave him in the care
of relatives who, though personally well-disposed, were
Pinochet supporters; so Julio was now back in Exeter,
living with his father.

I attempted to speak *castellano* with Sergio but, even
when he slowed his speech for my benefit, I had difficulty
understanding his Chilean intonation. For the most part
we argued about politics – in English. And he lent me

films and books which he hoped might enlighten me ideo-
logically.

Shortly before I left for Chile, Sergio asked me if I would
take some things to Ledy which he was reluctant to
entrust to the post. He gave me the name of her lawyer in
Santiago who, he said, spoke good English. He also
wanted me to meet Julio so that, if I got the chance to visit
Ledy in prison, I could give her a first-hand account of
her sixteen-year-old son. He came to lunch at my house,
bringing Julio with him, on the Saturday before I flew off.

Political as ever, he held forth on the evil purposes of
the Americans in extending the airport runway on Chile's
Easter Island which, he insisted, was part of the Star
Wars, rather than space landings, programme. Julio,
having lived more than half his life in England, is bilingual
and speaks English with a faint Devonian burr; he teased
his father about his accent which transformed the word
'beaches', for instance, into 'bitches'. Sergio had told me
that Julio had had some trouble at school, and had had to
defend his corner with his fists, but he must have been
provoked in some way; he seemed a well-adjusted and
agreeable youth. After lunch, Sergio handed over the
small bundle he wanted me to take to Chile.

That same day, Paz and Cristián's daughter, Daniela,
whom I had last seen when she was six months old,
arrived to stay for the weekend. She was on a European
trip, paid for by her mother out of the proceeds of the sale
of an antique wooden spiral staircase, *una escalera de cara-
col*, which was no longer required in the house in Santiago. Paz had written to me that she thought Daniela
would benefit from a spell away from Chile, though Daniela herself had not been so keen on the idea. But Paz had
prevailed and here was her daughter, whose resemblance
to Cristián, in her speech and her gestures, was uncanny –
the way she paused before agreeing or disagreeing with
you, her definite way of saying 'No' but softening it with a
little laugh, even her linguistic errors, as in the phrase,
'Thanks God': all these mannerisms revealed whose
daughter she was. In her looks, too, she was more

Huneeus than Errázuriz, more Scandinavian than Spanish.

Although she could speak English, Daniela was reluctant to speak it with me; so we communicated in a mixture of two languages, each for the most part speaking our own. In that way I learnt that Daniela had renounced her half-share in the avocado farm at Cabildo – 'I do not like the *campo*', she said. The property was anyway so submerged in debt that Soledad was having a struggle to keep it going. When Cristián died, Soledad had at first been reluctant to part with anything of his, but after a year she let Daniela have his books and papers, including the journals he had kept for most of his adult life. Daniela had done little more than dip into these but she had been shocked by the sexual revelations she discovered there, especially as Cristián had always tried to protect her from exposure to eroticism, whether it was his own (she had not been invited to the launch of his pornographic novel, *El verano del ganadero*) or D. H. Lawrence's *Lady Chatterley's Lover*. A Chilean woman Daniela had just been staying with in Paris had told her that yes, of course, Cristián had once tried to seduce her but she had resisted out of loyalty to Paz, to whom he was then married.

Daniela loved her father, but even as a child she had been amazed how childish *he* could be: he had to have his own way in an argument, even with her. He was the spoilt child of his mother and liked to seduce (or at least charm) everyone, not just women.

For those few moments when I was not overwhelmed with panic at the thought of the imminent flight into the unknown, I found myself wondering just where my obsession with Cristián might be leading me. How would I come to regard my old friend? Might I end up disliking him? Well, it was too late now for moral qualms. I was committed to making a journey, perhaps *the* journey of my life, in which my feelings for Cristián would be tested against the reality of his country. Exactly what part had he played in its grim recent history? Neither in his letters nor in our conversations during his last visit to England had he discussed his public activities in anything other than very general terms. He had identified himself with the opposition to Pinochet all right, but he had also shown a marked lack of enthusiasm for Allende. So might I end up having political, as well as personal, reservations about him? And what of Paz, whom I had not seen or heard of for so many years: how would we get along? Would Cristián's memory cement our friendship or come between us?

Then there was Chile itself, a frightening place it seemed from a distance, even in the dying days of the dictatorship, with its secret police and appalling record of violence. As an Englishman I did not feel I would be in personal danger, but would people – could people – talk to me openly, or would they be too afraid? Having never lived under a dictatorship, I had very little idea what to expect.

2

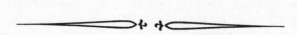

After a day and a night in the air – London to Amsterdam, Amsterdam to Toronto, Toronto to Santiago – I stepped out into dazzling spring sunshine, euphoric but woozy with the after-effects of Valium and sleeping pills, not to mention incipient jet-lag. Paz was at the airport to greet me. I had no difficulty in recognizing her; though the years had put flesh on her, she was as attractive as a mature woman as she had been as a young girl. Her eyes and her smile proclaimed the same person, yet I knew instantly that something about her was different, something I could not immediately identify.

She drove her little red Fiat fast and well, while I absorbed the novelty of my surroundings. We were in a basin encircled by hills, on one side the magnificent Andes, which I had already observed with awe from the air, and on the other the *cordillera de la costa*, a smaller range of brown, bare hills baking in the mid-morning sun. Santiago itself impressed me at first glance as a big and bustling city, but without particular architectural distinction. Paz's house was in the inner suburbs, in the Avenida Ricardo Lyon. It was, as Cristián had described it all those years before, big and U-shaped, built around a courtyard, inward rather than outward-looking, high-ceilinged but all on one floor, characterful in a way that most of the surrounding suburban houses were not.

I stayed in Daniela's room, since she was still in Europe, for the first fortnight I was in Chile. There I was surrounded by memorabilia of Cristián, his books and papers, some of them still in crates, as yet unpacked. I resisted the temptation to pry into his personal effects, feeling that it was Daniela's prerogative to decide what I might or might not look at. Of the many books on the shelves that bore witness to Cristián's love affair with

England and English literature, several had been bought during his five years there and seemed like a direct link with the past, rather sad relics of a life which had then seemed so full of promise, yet had somehow failed to come up to expectations.

Paz introduced me to her son by her second marriage, Tomás, a handsome youth of seventeen, and to the maid, Inés, who was engaged to be married to a man from her village in the south. Inés and I often had breakfast together, an occasion for me to practise my *castellano*; she did most of the household chores, cooking and washing-up, cleaning and washing clothes, while Paz did the shopping. As I knew from Cristián, as well as from her own letters and some exhibition catalogues she had sent me, Paz worked as a photographer; in fact, she had an exhibition on in Santiago (and in Sydney, Australia) right then: it was a series of photographs she had taken over some years of a group of transvestite prostitutes who had been forced out of Santiago by the activities of the police and had taken refuge in a male brothel in the southern town of Talca. Paz had been determined that this exhibition – which was, among other things, a mocking commentary on the *machismo* of the military – should be held before the end of the dictatorship.

Paz's husband, Tom Daskam, was away when I arrived, staying in the camper-van he kept down in the far south on the windswept wastes of *Magallanes*, or Tierra del Fuego; this, I soon discovered, was his favourite haunt, a genuine wilderness where, as in parts of New Zealand, the sheep outnumber the people and there are dozens of bird species for him to study and photograph. For in addition to being a painter – his pictures, including a huge and rich canvas of another favourite place, the port town of Valparaíso, adorned the walls of the house – Tom was a naturalist and bird photographer who, for more than five years, had a weekly column in *El Mercurio*, which in addition to being Chile's first newspaper claims to be the oldest Spanish-language newspaper in the world.

Whether it was because it was snowing down in the south, or because he was anxious to see for himself just what sort of fellow Paz's friend from the time of her first marriage was, Tom returned home within two days of my arrival. Paz collected him from the airport and left us together while she and her journalist collaborator, Claudia Donoso (who had tape-recorded the stories of the transvestites), went to their exhibition.

Despite thirty years' residence in Chile, Tom remains quintessentially North American; tall and rangy in appearance, he resembles one of the more exotic species of bird he himself might have photographed. Learned in the subjects which interest him – painting, of course, natural history, old furniture, country and western and, increasingly, classical music – he has an autodidact's passion for detail and comprehensiveness. He also has a dry sense of humour and tells a good story; but if he is bored with the conversation or the company, he will get up and leave the room without explanation or excuse. Within five minutes of our becoming acquainted he was telling me, bluntly, that when he first heard from Paz that some English guy was coming to study the life of her first husband, and *was going to be staying in their house*, he was not overjoyed at the prospect. 'I mean,' he had said to her, 'what if some guy – or worse, some *woman* – wanted to come into the house and do research on my first wife?'

Yet he did not seem unduly perturbed by either my presence or my project. He remarked of Cristián that it must have been awful for him to die so young when one of his more endearing qualities was not so much to assume as to *know* that the world had been specially created for his benefit. How could he possibly leave it so soon? How could it go on without him? He was a prince, Cristián, but what was it based on, this extraordinary self-esteem? His achievements scarcely merited it; but then regality is perhaps more a question of being than of doing. Tom had observed the same quality in Daniela ever since she was a small child, when he had teased her, calling her 'Princess'.

Tom himself might have followed Cristián into an early grave when he fell seriously ill about a year after the latter's death with a lethal combination of chronic ulcers, cirrhosis of the liver, hepatitis and peritonitis. Any one of this quartet of ailments, let alone all four together, could have finished off someone with a less robust constitution or less determination to survive. As it was, Tom had to spend some weeks in intensive care and give up alcohol for good.

Paz was under no such prohibition. She liked nothing better than to sit down at midnight with a bottle of wine and a packet of cigarettes and reminisce. On one such occasion she told me about her 'Dickensian' childhood and her life with Cristián.

The hate-figure of her early days was not her mother or her father – they were too distant for that – but her *mama*, her nanny, whom she thought of as her *real* mother (the word for mother and nanny is the same in *castellano*; only the accent falls on a different syllable). This nanny, who came of peasant stock and had Indian features, may have been jealous of Paz's beauty or her privileged background but – whatever the reason – she was crueller and more brutal towards her than to any of her siblings. At the age of seven Paz started to keep a diary-cum-scrapbook, *Mi diario* as she proudly labelled it, in a kind of code so as to make it incomprehensible to her nanny – who was anyway barely literate. She went first to a Montessori school and she was happy there, but before long she was removed to a convent, where she remained for the rest of her schooldays. By the age of thirteen she had had enough of both religion and the nuns, and she refused to attend Mass any more.

She was fifteen when she started to go out with Cristián, though she told him she was a year older; he was twenty. Her nanny, inevitably, disapproved, and so initially did her parents, on the grounds that, though he was from a good family, Cristián was of foreign stock (what kind of a name was Huneeus, for heaven's sake?), not Spanish aristocracy. But that only strengthened Paz's resolve; and Cristián was very supportive of her in her battles with her family and nanny. He even helped her run away from home. She stayed at a girlfriend's house, and her parents, much to her chagrin, did not attempt to contact her for a week. When she finally did go home, she gave them an ultimatum: either the nanny went or she did. Reluctantly, they let the nanny go, but she was soon re-employed by Paz's half-sister (Paz was a child of her father's second marriage) and remained a kind of family retainer even in her retirement: when Daniela was young and this nanny, now a harmless old woman who was nice to everyone, took her on her lap at some family gathering, Paz discovered such reserves of resentment in herself that she immediately called Daniela away.

Paz's father had wanted her to be a lawyer – 'Can you imagine?' she said. His distaste for the arts was such that she had to keep it a secret from him that she did ballet classes. So it was hardly likely he would approve of her marrying a writer. But they not only got married, they also escaped to Europe, where for five years they were blissfully free of family and social pressures.

Paz was devoted to Cristián. She believed in him both as a man and as a writer, and supported him with all the fervour of youth. When he felt increasingly miserable and out of place in Hull, it was she who insisted they leave, even though it meant forgoing his British Council scholarship. In London she worked as an *au pair* in a professor's household to facilitate Cristián's struggle to establish himself as a freelance writer and broadcaster working for the Latin American service of the BBC. And it was she who pushed him into going to Cambridge, though once again she had to go out and do menial work to keep them going until he acquired a Rockefeller research fellowship. In more trivial ways, too, she made him do things he would not otherwise have considered. Without her prompting he would never have dreamt of hitch-hiking, for instance; but then he would irritate her by hiding bashfully behind his umbrella while she thumbed a lift.

When things got rough in the Cambridge Latin American Society, of which Cristián was president, and some right-wing Puerto Ricans attacked him outside the flat in Fitzwilliam Street and broke his glasses, Paz, who was pregnant at the time with Daniela, picked up a milk bottle, broke it against the wall and threatened to kill them with it; but they jumped into their car and Paz could only smash it across their windscreen as they drove off. A few days later one of them tried to run her over in the Market Square and she had to leap for safety. Violence had always been part of her life, as she saw it: to take the most recent example, only that day she had been appalled to hear of the assassination of 'La Momia', a wrestler friend from one of her photographic projects; he had been acting as doorman at a pop concert and had been knifed to death by a couple of youths he had turned away for not having tickets. They had probably been taking drugs.

What was different about Paz, I began to perceive, was that she had acquired that purpose in life which she had seemed to lack in our Cambridge days. Iron had entered her soul, and her commitment to her family did not prevent her pursuing her own artistic career with the same dedication as she had once lavished on Cristián. But she had not achieved that degree of independence without suffering, and recently she had been undergoing psycho-analysis. This had forced her to recognize that there were things in her relationship with Cristián which remained unresolved. When they had separated she had not had the time to grieve properly, so his early death had come as a profound shock. She had gone to his funeral, despite misgivings about her reception there, and seen him lying in his coffin *como el rey Arturo* (like King Arthur), as a mutual friend had put it. She told me that I was the one person she would have liked to have got in touch with then, if only she had had my phone number; we had been such a threesome in those far-off days, had we not? Almost like *Jules et Jim*, was how she remembered it.

I had written to Soledad to inform her that I was coming to Chile and she had replied at length, telling me of the difficulties she was having keeping the avocado farm at Cabildo going. In addition to the debts she had inherited when Cristián died, the river in the valley, which was generally no more than a trickle, had unexpectedly burst its banks in 1987 and swept away several acres of avocados as well as the little house she had built in a spot favoured by Cristián. By way of compensation, however, there was a new man in her life: his name was Jaime, he was some years older than her and she was not sure what Cristián would have thought of him, but he had been very kind and helpful to her in her time of need, and he was a very lovable man.

Soon after I arrived in Santiago, Soledad invited me to dinner. She came to fetch me herself and I scarcely recognized her. The first time I had met her I had been impressed by her beauty and youthful looks, but now she looked even younger. Then she had had all the worries of living with a man who was about to die, but with whom she could not discuss this single, overwhelming fact. Now she seemed rejuvenated, radiating the well-being of a woman in love. It was impossible to believe that she was already a grandmother. She tested my Spanish as we drove along in her pick-up truck, the music on the car radio too loud to be ignored; then she asked me – in English – what I thought about the forthcoming election. I said that I could see evidence of it all around me, even on the surface of the road, where the names of the various candidates were inscribed in white like directions to slow down or stop, but that I had hardly been in the country long enough to have an opinion, beyond a general notion that a return to democracy must be a good thing. She, too, welcomed the end of the dictatorship but voiced fears for the future.

These fears found more concrete expression in the newly-erected fence and electronically operated barrier outside the high-rise apartment block where Soledad rented a flat. Here, as elsewhere in the smarter parts of town, one had the impression that the rich were barricading themselves in against the possibility of a siege.

In the seventh-floor flat, as in the car, there was music. A toy poodle, a fluffy little white thing the size of a kitten, gambolled between its master and its mistress. Jaime seemed ill-at-ease in this environment and made it plain that he preferred the country to the city. Polo was his passion and he said that, coming from England, I must know his friend Ronnie Ferguson. It took me some moments to realize he was talking about 'Fergie's' father, and my obtuseness must have baffled him. His recipe for improving Chile was to import more Germans – and English, he added as an afterthought, probably for my benefit. The great difference between him and Cristián, I found myself thinking, was that while Cristián played at being a landowner, and enjoyed the game, Jaime was more like the real thing. Soledad, he told me (and she agreed), had been too soft on the peasants at Cabildo and, predictably, they had taken advantage of her.

Another couple joined us for dinner. The wife, who was from Ecuador, was a distant cousin of Cristián's. The ensuing conversation was three parts *castellano* to one part English, and I had to struggle to keep up with it. Sometime after midnight the doorbell rang and a young man in a suit arrived. This was Cristóbal, Soledad's youngest son, who had come to collect his birthday present, a Walkman for two (having two sets of earphones); his girlfriend had been too shy to come up and was waiting in a taxi outside. Cristóbal was very affectionate towards his mother and I suddenly remembered how much she had missed her children when she came to England, how she had adopted my son Tom and invited him to stay with her in the flat she and Cristián rented in London.

Yet I still found it difficult to match the image of Soledad I retained from that visit with the woman now sitting beside me. It was not that she was a chameleon, adopting a new persona to suit the man she was living with; her own personality was too strong and definite for that. It was simply that I had seen her only in relation to Cristián, and at a time when that relationship was all-consuming. I began to understand that the very thing that had brought us together in the first place, our mutual love of Cristián, now stood between us and made us wary of one another, since she needed to forget what I was intent upon recalling. Perhaps it would be easier to re-establish our intimacy at Cabildo. She explained that they were building a new house there and when it was ready I should be the first to come and stay.

3

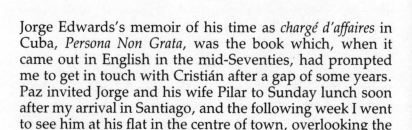

Jorge Edwards's memoir of his time as *chargé d'affaires* in Cuba, *Persona Non Grata*, was the book which, when it came out in English in the mid-Seventies, had prompted me to get in touch with Cristián after a gap of some years. Paz invited Jorge and his wife Pilar to Sunday lunch soon after my arrival in Santiago, and the following week I went to see him at his flat in the centre of town, overlooking the Santa Lucía hill.

The English name of Edwards is an important one in Chile; it is the name, for instance, of the wealthy proprietor of *El Mercurio*. Jorge comes from a liberal branch of the family and, up to the time of the military coup, combined a diplomatic career with that of a novelist. Aged about sixty, jolly, rotund and balding, he seemed very much a man of the world, easy in company and not dissatisfied with his own achievements. Though his books have not acquired as wide a readership as those of his Peruvian friend, Mario Vargas Llosa, among living novelists in Chile he ranks second only to José Donoso. As a political figure, however, he is more controversial: unpopular with exiles loyal to Allende's memory on account of his 'anti-Castro' Cuban memoir, he has his detractors at home, too. One of these, who saw *Persona Non Grata* as symptomatic of the self-importance of Chilean intellectuals during the Allende years, told me: 'He judges Cuba, not for whatever Cuba is, good or bad, but for the impact Cuba made on him. He was expecting this or that and he was not satisfied with it. That was the Chilean way in those days.'

The comment might, with equal justice, be applied to Cristián. Jorge told me that when Cristián phoned him from Santiago to say he was coming to Cuba, he had been taken by surprise because it was almost unheard of then for an *individual* to visit Cuba: either you came as part of a deputation or you didn't come at all; Cuba was definitely not on the tourist circuit. It was typical of the man, though, that Cristián should want to see for himself, since at that time many people saw Cuba as the model for Allende's Chile. But Cristián's appearance, his height and his fairness, made the Cuban authorities suspicious: they thought he was an American spy. Castro himself, in his last conversation with Jorge, referred to a party held on the visiting Chilean flagship, the *Esmeralda*, and told Jorge he had made a mistake in inviting that Cristián Huneeus. When Jorge protested that it was not he who had invited Cristián but the Captain, who was an old friend from the days when the two of them had sailed together in the channels of southern Chile, Castro was partially mollified. But he did not like writers and Jorge reckoned that Cristián would have made a better impression if he had introduced himself as a farmer whose sole interest was in visiting model farms.

Jorge spent far too much time for Castro's (and probably Allende's) liking consorting with 'dissident' writers, such as the poet Heberto Padilla, and might have been destined for some diplomatic Outer Mongolia after his time in Cuba had it not been for his friendship with the great Pablo Neruda. Despite his Communism, Neruda was no lover of Cuba. In 1966, when first he went to New York as guest of the PEN Club under Arthur Miller's presidency and then, to add insult to injury, accepted a Peruvian honour for his poetic sequence *The Heights of Macchu Picchu*, the Cuban Writers Association wrote a letter denouncing him; this Castro-inspired attack was also directed at the Chilean Communist Party which, up to the time of the coup, was very much a party of the centre-left, with groups of socialists well to the left of it. When Neruda was appointed ambassador to France by Allende, he wanted Jorge as his assistant and threatened to resign if he could not have him in Paris. Allende was reluctant to offend his personal representative, so he was obliged to let things be, though probably he would rather not have rewarded Jorge with such a desirable posting after the Cuban debacle.

*

Jorge recalled a conversation he had once had with Neruda about a literary critic who wrote under the pseudonym 'Alone' (pronounced as though it were a Spanish word, in three syllables, A-lo-ne). Alone was the arbiter of literary taste in Chile between the Twenties and the Sixties and, though they were at opposite ends of the political spectrum (Alone was an arch-conservative), Neruda admired him both as a writer and as a man. 'Who will replace Alone?' he had asked; then, answering himself, he said, 'Maybe Cristián Huneeus.'

Neruda might appear to be out of touch, but he could be very shrewd; and Jorge believed he might well have been right about Cristián, who was a very good critic. The trouble was, Cristián did not want to be a critic, he wanted to write fiction. He did introduce certain new tendencies into Chilean writing: in particular, an ironic stance in relation to the narrator on the part of the author. He was one of the first Borgesian writers in Chile; he was sophisticated where the older generation had been naturalistic. But he did not really develop as a novelist.

Jorge was on holiday in Spain when the coup happened. After Neruda's departure from Paris in November 1972 through ill health, he stood in as *chargé d'affaires* there until August 1973. If he had kept quiet, he might have been able to continue as a diplomat; but he wrote an article about the coup for *Le Monde*, which was like signing his professional death warrant. Even though he was expelled from the diplomatic service, he might still have returned to Chile had he wished, but he decided to stay on in Spain until the political climate improved.

When he came home on an exploratory visit in the middle of 1978, before returning for good at the end of that year, one of the first people to greet him was Cristián; and Jorge became part of a group which included Chile's two most distinguished poets following the death of Neruda soon after the coup in 1973, Nicanor Parra and Enrique Lihn, both of whom, along with Cristián, were regarded as collaborators by the exiles. Jorge saw his own exile (voluntary though it was) as a kind of double exile: from his country, because he was not sure how he would be received if he returned; and from most other exiles 'because I had allowed myself to criticize Fidel Castro'.

He sympathized with those like Cristián, Enrique Lihn and Nicanor Parra who had stayed in Chile after the coup, and when the group got together 'it was like the first Christians meeting in the catacombs'. They were all shocked by what was happening in Chile under the military but had no illusions about the old left. They wanted reform, not revolution, and as a result were regarded as being too bourgeois. When *Persona Non Grata* was first published, Cristián had written to Jorge in Spain to express his concern that Jorge had called him a Christian Democrat when he had never belonged to that party. Jorge corrected the error in subsequent editions of the book, but there was no doubt that he was close to the party. It was at Cristián's house, Jorge recalled, that he had met Jaime Castillo, the Christian Democrat president of the Chilean Human Rights Commission (*Comisión Chilena de Derechos Humanos*).

In his last years, Cristián had been beset by economic problems. He had made the mistake of taking credit, when it was all too readily available during the 'boom' years of 1978–9, in order to develop his farm. Unfortunately for him, a crash followed, the dollar doubled or trebled in value and Cristián, along with thousands of others, was trapped: his debt multiplied several times over and he spent the rest of his life indulging in *gimnasia bancaria* (financial gymnastics; shorthand for shifting funds and/ or overdrafts from one bank to another). The anxiety of these last years – in Jorge's view – may have contributed to his final illness, since he was 'a prisoner in a tangle of debts'. But he persisted in his belief that the farm could be made profitable.

Cristián's love of the land, his relationship with plants and trees and country people, was something Jorge envied but could not share. It was in the blood, of course, though among farmers of the old sort, who pretended to be very aristocratic but were in fact primitive and savage, Cristián's father had been exceptional: a genuinely cultivated man, with not only a fine house and good furniture but a library as well.

'In being so European,' Jorge suggested in a final paradox, 'Cristián was also very Chilean.'

The Cuban revolution had galvanized the whole of Latin America and provided at least the illusion of an alternative to American imperialism; Fidel and Che were legends throughout the continent even before Che's early death in the wilds of Bolivia, still in pursuit of the revolution. With few exceptions, leading Latin American writers and intellectuals in the Sixties were on the left politically; only later, in the Seventies and Eighties, did the cracks appear in what had seemed like a common front, and Cuba, once again, was the touchstone.

The 'Padilla affair', described at length in *Persona Non Grata*, alarmed leftist intellectuals throughout the western world, but nowhere more than in Chile, where socialist government was still a novelty. 'It would be difficult for me to comment on the Padilla affair,' Cristián wrote in the journal *Mensaje* in June 1971, three or four months after returning from Cuba, where he had interviewed Heberto Padilla along with several other Cuban writers, 'from any other perspective than that of a Chilean eight months after the electoral triumph of the *Unidad Popular* . . .'

Heberto Padilla was widely regarded as the outstanding Cuban poet. His revolutionary credentials were impeccable; he had held important positions in the early days of the Castro regime. The trouble started in 1967 with the publication of his book of poems *Fuera del Juego*, which, despite winning the national poetry prize awarded by the Cuban writers and artists union (one of the judges that year was the celebrated English translator J. M. Cohen), was seen as 'counter-revolutionary' and provoked official disapproval. Cristián hailed the book as a superb example of 'civic poetry' – 'one of the most luminous and brilliant examples that I know of socially responsible poetry, of poetry informed with a moral purpose, directed towards social life, towards collective life.'

The problem, as Padilla told Cristián, was that 'it is

expected of Cuban poetry, just as it used to be expected, and required, of Russian poetry and literature in general that they should reflect, not lived reality, but the projected reality which was being striven for'; and Padilla was not prepared to suppress such truths as, for example, that 'alienation persists during one phase of socialism'. In socialist society, he said, there was still no demand for popular participation in decision-making.

Jorge Edwards, describing his frequent meetings with Padilla, writes of the poet's excitability, his volatile nature, and suggests that he went some way towards provoking the authorities to act against him by his mixture of recklessness on the one hand and extreme wariness on the other. For instance, Padilla made a point of never letting his latest manuscript out of his or his wife's hands, as though the explosive nature of its contents demanded that it be protected in this, as Edwards calls it, 'ostentatious' way. But perhaps he had a premonition, or advance warning, that the authorities were about to pounce.

In his own account of the affair, written many years later and entitled *La mala memoria* (an apt title, according to Jorge Edwards in his recent memoir of Neruda, *Adiós, Poeta* . . . , since his memory is 'partial and incomplete, if in some ways revealing'), Padilla claims that 'when I want to learn something of the desperate and self-destructive being that I was then, I read a few chapters from *Persona Non Grata*, where I emerge as a stubborn Pulcinella from whom Edwards cannot separate himself'.

Padilla was arrested and imprisoned in March 1971, and on April 9th, *Le Monde* published an open letter to Fidel Castro in defence of Padilla, signed by almost the entire cast of European and Latin American literary heavyweights on the left. This 'letter from the hundred intellectuals' expressed anxiety that Padilla's arrest might mean 'the resurgence of a more powerful and dangerous sectarianism than that which you denounced in March 1962, and which Commandant Che Guevara alluded to many times when he denounced the suppression of the right to criticize in the bosom of the revolution'.

The letter continued:

At a time when a socialist government has been established in Chile and the new situation in Peru and Bolivia makes it easier to break the criminal blockade of Cuba by North American imperialism, recourse to repressive methods against intellectuals and writers who have exercized the right to be critical of the revolution can only have profoundly negative repercussions among anti-imperialist forces the world over, and most especially in Latin America, where the Cuban revolution is a symbol and a banner.

Castro was not impressed; he did not deign to answer the letter directly, but made slighting references to European intellectuals in a speech he delivered at the beginning of May. He talked dismissively of the *pájaros de cuenta* ('big shots') who had been the beneficiaries of Cuban hospitality and liked to pass themselves off as friends of the revolution, but were now more concerned about 'two or three stray sheep' who got into difficulties because they were not given the 'right to go on sowing poison and setting traps within the revolution' than with Cuba's serious problems. But he reserved his most scathing criticism for those Latin Americans who, 'instead of being in the trenches, live in bourgeois salons ten thousand miles from the problems, usufructing a little of the money they earned when they were able to earn any'. These 'bourgeois intellectuals and bourgeois liberals and agents of the CIA' would no longer be invited to judge literary competitions in Cuba, or even be allowed into the country again.

Padilla regained a limited freedom after performing the ritual self-abasement – 'self-criticism' – demanded of 'dissidents' by totalitarian regimes, thus silencing the likes of Simone de Beauvoir, Jean-Paul Sartre, Italo Calvino and Mario Vargas Llosa, and no doubt giving Castro himself some satisfaction. But he was not allowed to leave the country for another decade; he finally went to live in the United States in 1980.

In Jorge Edwards's memoir, Castro comes across as bombastic, but also as surprisingly naïve, sometimes forgiving, occasionally almost lovable. It is the machinery of State Security, the secret police surrounding him, that is the essential evil in Edwards's eyes. State Security may have found out in advance about the Bay of Pigs invasion;

it may have foiled various assassination attempts on Fidel: 'But an excess of zeal on the part of the security forces, or their uncontrolled growth, finally becomes a danger of another kind; they eat away at the Revolution in a different way.'

'Chile, meanwhile,' Edwards quotes from his Cuban diary entry for the day he met Régis Debray (whose revolutionary fervour, he notes in passing, seems to have diminished over the years), 'is trying to create its revolution without a police regime, without any more police than any normal state. I must admit that the term "normal state" does not mean anything, and that many militants of the *Unidad Popular*, if it were within their power to do so, would set up a secret police apparatus as sinister and powerful as they come . . .'

He worries away at the question, 'How can the Revolution be defended without falling into a rarified atmosphere of suspicion and generalized mistrust?' He reports rumours in Chile that certain Cuban diplomats have travelled there in order to set up for Allende a police system similar to Cuba's, and comments:

> . . . policemen everywhere feed off the existence of enemies, whether visible or concealed, and they are liable to invent them to justify and increase their own power. Police action brings about a polarization of political forces and leads to manicheism. It always proceeds by selecting and over-simplifying. For this reason the police, despite the firmness of their methods, are abstract and inhuman in their motivation. Their *raison d'être* is the enemy within [shades of Thatcher's Britain in the Eighties] and particularly the concealed enemy, who acts without the slightest scruples. Who could quibble with this *raison d'être*? The revelation from North American sources of the efforts to overthrow the Chilean Government constitutes an overwhelming argument. But how can the tentacular growth of the security apparatus be avoided?

The historical irony is that it was not so much under Allende that there was a 'tentacular growth of the security apparatus' as under the regime that deposed him. The military coup, however, could not have taken place so unopposed but for the fears of many, mainly middle-class, people that Chile's 'peaceful road to socialism' would end up in a Cuban cul-de-sac.

In an epilogue specially written for the English edition of *Persona Non Grata* in 1975, a year and a half after the military junta seized power in Chile, Jorge Edwards asks, 'Is it in the least bit strange that the neo-Stalinism . . . I came to know [in Cuba] at the beginning of 1971 should secrete neo-fascism as a reaction and antibody to itself? Is it not possible that, to some extent, one feeds off the other . . . ? Are they not both, despite the extreme differences in their aims, characterized by a similar attempt to depoliticize, and by a similar and fundamental mistrust of culture?'

4

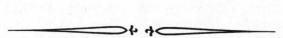

Paz had welcomed Allende's election. He was an attractive man, but he was inefficient: everything had been in short supply during his regime, even canvases for Tom to paint on. At the time Paz had been teaching infants in a private school and the staff were constantly having to send the children home early for one reason or another. There were so many false alarms before the coup actually happened that it was 'like the end of the world every day'. It became so bad that Tom persuaded Paz that they should emigrate to Australia; he had talked to the Australian ambassador, who arranged for them to be sent a form; but the coup put a stop to that, along with much else.

On the day of the coup they climbed on to their roof and watched the planes swoop down to bomb the Moneda. They could see the smoke and hear the military giving each other instructions over the radio. When it was over, some of their neighbours celebrated with champagne.

Immediately afterwards, one of these neighbours invited Tom into her house to warn him that the military might be paying him a visit. She said she had heard it from a general's wife who went to mass at the same church as she attended – in other words, Tom said, she had told the general's wife about the strange bohemian couple living next door; but as they were friends, she felt obliged to warn them too. Tom told Paz and together they burned Paz's old posters of Che Guevara and anything else they thought might be incriminating.

The doorbell rang – at least the door wasn't broken down – and the next moment there were young, trigger-happy air force troops swarming all over the place; they made everybody stand up against the wall while they searched the house. At the time, Tom said, he was not afraid, though he could feel the nervousness of these boys in uniform who never knew, from one house to the next, what kind of reception they would get: some people would blow themselves up, along with their attackers, rather than submit to being captured. It was only later, when he considered how narrow an escape they had had, that Tom felt at all frightened. But it was no big deal, he insisted. Everyone had such a story; it was part of the mythology of the time.

The question of servants had exercized Paz considerably after her return from England. In a country where all upper-class families employed maids as a matter of course, it would have seemed wilfully eccentric not to do so; besides, the girls from the south who made up the majority of servants needed the work. So in the end, Paz compromised: she employed a succession of maids but treated them, with varying degrees of success, as part of the family rather than as employees. For instance, the maid would eat with them in the dining-room, instead of in the kitchen. When one of these maids married, Paz invited her husband to live in the house as well. He came, but he was less comfortable with the liberal regime than his wife had been, so, by a tacit agreement, things reverted to a more traditional pattern.

This couple, Tom told me one evening, owned a black-and-white television set before he and Paz ever got one. On the night of the Muhammed Ali–George Foreman 'rumble in the jungle' Tom borrowed the set, and invited several friends and neighbours in to watch the fight with him. They were all sitting around, placing bets and generally enjoying the build-up, when the maid walked in and demanded the TV set back.

'But wait a minute,' they protested. 'The fight hasn't even begun.'

The maid stood her ground. She pointed out that the set was theirs; they were poor people; they had saved up for a long time to get it; and now they wanted it back.

The assembled guests were dumbfounded. But why *now*, they asked, just as the fight's about to begin?

The maid looked embarrassed and it was some time before she could be prevailed upon to answer. Eventually she admitted that her husband was worried that, with so many people watching, the set would wear out.

Nothing they said, no appeal to scientific logic or reason, made the slightest difference. The maid, acting on instructions from her husband, pulled out the plug, and Tom and his friends were obliged to go elsewhere to watch the fight.

Adriana Valdés, I was intrigued to see when she invited me to dinner, summoned *her* maid with a little handbell like a Victorian matriarch. But I soon discovered that Adriana's apparent formality masked a rebellious and independent spirit and an unusually sharp mind. She rented from Soledad the house in Santiago in which the latter had lived with Cristián for many years, a large, L-shaped suburban bungalow with a pleasant garden at the back; and it was there that Paz took me to see her. She was a tall, handsome woman in her forties, with shortish hair and commanding, clear blue eyes. Her name was already familiar to me from Cristián's books; she had written an afterword to one of his novels and a prologue to his autobiography.

Her friendship with Cristián had developed comparatively late. She had first known him when he was eighteen or nineteen, through his sister Veronica, who was a schoolfriend of hers. He had taken no notice of her then, which was not surprising since she was only fourteen, but she had been struck by the degree of respect, even reverence, shown him by the rest of the family and the servants – Cristián was the most intelligent man in the world; Cristián had a lot of reading to do; Cristián must not be disturbed. There was an aura about him. Only years later, when Adriana, who was by then the mother of three daughters and had left her husband to live with Enrique Lihn, did she and Cristián become at all close. But it might have been otherwise, since Cristián was at first disapproving of the relationship and thought her an unsuitable partner for his friend. That soon changed, however, and even after Enrique had left her (for Paz's collaborator, Claudia Donoso, so small is the world of the

Chilean *haute bourgeoisie*) she and Cristián remained good friends.

Coming from his background, Cristián was exceptional, Adriana explained, in wanting to be an intellectual – something which, in the highest class in Chile (as in Britain), was 'a bit suspect'. In general, the Chilean 'aristocracy' (Chileans themselves put the work in inverted commas) differed from the Argentinian in being less cultured, less open to European influences. But Cristián's father, in particular, was a cultured man; he read a great deal. As an intellectual, Cristián had been faced with a choice: he could either reject his class by becoming a rebel and being irreverent and eccentric, or he could identify with it. Since his early experience of family life had been so happy, he was more attracted to the latter course. 'I think he was too little frustrated for his own good,' Adriana said. 'He was the golden boy.'

His first book of stories, *Cuentos de cámara* ('Chamber Stories' – as in chamber music), was both successful and good; and if his decision to study literature (after an abortive year of studying architecture) was not a sound one for a man, he had redeemed himself by going to Cambridge. His marriage to Paz, too, had been right and proper. The flaw there was not personal but social, deriving from the institution of *pololeo*, a kind of pre-engagement between couples too young to become formally engaged. For instance, when you were *pololeando*, or going steady, you did not normally dance with anyone other than your *pareja*, your partner. *Pololeo* tended to be a long-term arrangement, often leading to marriage and involving a complicated mixture of class, morals and religion, which produced a certain rigidity, well described in Cristián's early stories. According to Adriana, who was also speaking from personal experience, it made people think of themselves in family terms too young: 'They become a prison to one another because of a set of expectations imposed on them.' Their fantasies were all invested in a single relationship that could not necessarily sustain them.

By the time Adriana got to know Cristián, his reputation was tarnished; he was divorced and was thought of as a womanizer – though that did not necessarily detract from his desirability. His father had died, and Cristián was running both the family farm and the Centro de Estudios Humanísticos, which was in the process of being upgraded into a university department. It was during Allende's presidency, when politics permeated everything: farms were being expropriated through the *tomas*, or takeovers, by people who simply squatted on a piece of land and planted a Chilean flag on it; and in the universities neutral or rightist academics were being subjected to 'a witch-hunt from the left'.

Adriana now sees this whole era in historical terms: since the Twenties and Thirties there has been an explosion of the middle classes in Chile, and in the time of, first, Frei and then Allende the country was opening up. Too many ideas were thrust on to a very fragile, old-fashioned structure; there was a demand for people's rights but no mechanism to support them. In the countryside relationships were strictly paternalistic: the peasants were both dependent and loyal – it was a very nineteenth-century situation. Adriana herself grew up feeling that she was the favourite child of the peasants on her father's land. Later, when she questioned them about this and they expressed their disappointment in their own children, she came to realize the extent to which they had imbibed the values of their masters. This changed in due course. In about 1958, long before Allende, or even Frei, Christian Democrats had been talking about the need for equality.

'In the city,' Adriana pointed out, 'opposition is faceless; in the country, it's people you've known all your life.' However feudal and archaic the system, what replaced it was no system at all, just a void. People were so used to being told what to do that, left to their own devices, they lost everything, had to sell the land they had been given and, as a result, were worse off than ever. A good idea needed to be properly applied, but in Chile everything was done the wrong way round, Adriana said, quoting from a book by Cristián's friend and colleague, Ronald Kay (the man who had pointed out to Paz the dead

Cristián's resemblance to King Arthur): 'Here we get all the answers before we have asked the right questions.'

Class was crucial to an understanding of what had happened. Too many upper-class young people, such as Carlos Altamirano (the ex-Secretary-General of the Socialist Party, blamed by many for provoking the military backlash with his rhetorical excesses during Allende's rule), had taken up the left-wing banner, and this had resulted in an 'unholy alliance of Marxism and classism'. People had followed these upper-class young men not out of commitment to the cause they espoused but because they were the natural leaders. If you were a Roman Catholic, 'the burden of guilt was such that you read Marxist writings and found yourself portrayed there – Catholics are conditioned to guilt and we were all Catholics'. The Nicaraguan, Ernesto Cardenal, was the perfect example of this: brought up in a devout atmosphere, he became both a priest *and* a Marxist. For such as he, Communism was a crusade of noble (in both senses of the word) people trying to help their neighbours.

Enrique Lihn had joined the Communist Party at the end of the Sixties. He won the Casa de las Americas literary prize and went to Cuba to receive it, and stayed on as a member of the jury for the following year's award. But like Jorge Edwards – and Cristián – later, he became friendly with Heberto Padilla and got into trouble with the Cuban authorities. When he returned to Chile, Adriana said, he was expelled from the Communist Party and became a pariah, just when Communism had come into fashion. Such bad timing was typical of the man, of whom Jorge Edwards coined a witty phrase: adapting the Chilean saying, *el no da puntada sin hilo* (he doesn't sew without thread), meaning someone is an opportunist – does nothing without a reason or purpose – he said that Enrique did not sew *with* thread (*el no da puntada con hilo*). Fortunately, Cristián took him on as a lecturer in his fledgling department of humanities, which had been set up partly in opposition to the Marxist-dominated Instituto Pedagógico. Nicanor Parra was another 'dissident' from the prevailing Marxist orthodoxy who found a niche in Estudios Humanísticos.

At that time Adriana was teaching at the Catholic University in Santiago (after the coup, she escaped from academic life into the United Nations Economic Commission for Latin America and the Caribbean, ECLAC or, in its Spanish version, CEPAL, where she still works). People were steeped in university politics and there were terrible constraints. She herself believed in Allende and because she was 'a prig about work', enjoyed teaching and was thought to be strict, she was elected to councils and generally used by the left as a presentable person. In the last days of Allende, she was one of those who struggled to keep the university going, continuing to give classes rather than going on strike. Yet one day she looked over the shoulder of a lefty professor standing beside her and caught a glimpse of a list of university lecturers, seventy names in all, her own among them; and next to her name she saw the words *'más o menos'*, signifying that she was 'more or less' to be trusted, come to the crunch. Cristián was bitterly opposed to all that. If he thought an intellectual was worthy, he backed him to the hilt regardless of his politics. For this he was called a *momio* (a very Chilean word for the hopelessly bourgeois; literally, a 'mummy'), and strikes and lock-outs were organized against him.

After the military takeover, which at first was expected to be short-lived, Cristián played an ambivalent role, on the one hand protecting people who might be threatened with dismissal in his own department, on the other acting as an *interventor* in other departments, mainly the Pedagógico, doing the dirty work of removing political undesirables. Having to take decisions about other people's jobs continued to haunt him. It was a hard time and feelings on both sides ran high. Cristián was never afraid to speak his mind and later he spoke out just as forcefully against the dictatorship. One of his great virtues was that he was always available for conversation; this was particularly valuable at a time when so many people were afraid to talk.

As a writer, Adriana thought, Cristián wrestled with self-doubt. She said that, in relation to Enrique Lihn and

Nicanor Parra, 'there was always something about Cristián which said, "You are the real thing; I may be a fake".' Enrique, who died not long after Cristián, always called Cristián a *pije*, a toff.

'In Chile,' Cristián himself had written in his diary when he was living in London (and recalled when he came to write his autobiography), 'one can still lead a nineteenth-century existence; one can still do many things in the course of a single life.' He certainly did many things in the course of his short life; but given that his supreme desire was to be a novelist, it has to be said that he may have spread himself too thinly to satisfy his ambition fully in that direction.

There is a phrase which often crops up in his writing, *botarse a artista* (to give oneself the airs of an artist; to claim to be an artist), and is always used pejoratively – in the same way that F. R. Leavis uses the expression 'being an artist' when discussing snobbish contemporary attitudes towards D. H. Lawrence in his book on that novelist. Indeed, it occurred to me later that this was probably where Cristián had taken it from, since he had been influenced by Leavis at Cambridge and had written a thesis on Lawrence; and I wondered if, in the opposition between Vronsky and Mikhaylov in Tolstoy's *Anna Karenina* – which Leavis cites as the *locus classicus* of this argument – Cristián did not, in his heart of hearts, identify more closely with Vronsky, the aristocrat who plays at being an artist to the accompaniment of flattery from a subservient critic, than with Mikhaylov, the gauche but talented painter who is patronized by both Vronsky and the critic (though Vronsky is honest enough in the end to admit that Mikhaylov is 'the real thing', while he himself is no more than a dilettante).

The big house and park of San Juan de Chena, on the outskirts of Santiago, belonged to Adriana's father, who no longer lived there though he often came to stay. He was not going to be there on the Sunday Adriana, Paz, Tom and I visited Chena, and Adriana suggested we took a picnic lunch and our bathers, so that we could also swim in the pool.

We drove along a dual carriageway, flanked by poor housing and large industrial estates, until we reached an old iron gate nearly hidden behind lush foliage. Turning off the noisy, glary, busy highway into the shady arboretum beyond the gate was like leaving the modern world for a more elegant and spacious past. We pulled up under a mulberry tree and helped ourselves to the fruit before turning to admire the browny-pink façade of this edifice, built for a president in the middle of the nineteenth century and then rebuilt at the beginning of the twentieth century. The faded magnificence of the place, with its splendid verandahs and bell-tower, its cracked walls and curious corrugated-iron roof, its feathery fountain and overgrown lime-walk, made it a film-maker's paradise; and indeed, Adriana told us, no fewer than two films had been shot there.

She unlocked the heavy door and the temperature dropped several degrees as we penetrated the dim interior. The hall was huge, overlooked by a gallery on three sides of the first floor, the fourth being taken up by the biggest stained-glass window I have ever seen, with the initials AV (Antonio Valdés) highlighted in the word SALVE. The walls of both hall and gallery were covered with a hotch-potch of genre paintings reflecting upper-class taste three-quarters of a century ago. Off the hall, there was a large dining-room, a billiard room, a kitchen and servants' quarters, all unused for many years but preserved more or less intact, and a suite of rooms in which Adriana's father camped when he came to stay. Upstairs there were a number of bedrooms and bathrooms, and a library with a balcony overlooking the lime-walk.

Adriana's father had been a typical Chilean landowner, spending much of his time playing bridge while his farm manager looked after the land, nearly 1,000 acres of it in its heyday. Now it was all gone, sold to developers of industrial estates, or expropriated in Allende's time; and outside the little oasis created by the house and its park there was a kind of wasteland where people were living – or squatting – in shabby wooden huts. Tom and I found ourselves wondering, as we peered over the wall by the disused stables, why it was that the house, which stood so invitingly empty much of the time, was not frequently burgled. Adriana's explanation was that the local people were too frightened to approach it, as it was rumoured to be haunted (a rumour she was not inclined to discredit, having experienced some ghostly intimations there). Despite that, a week or two after our visit there was a break-in, though very little was taken.

Since the dissolution of the big estates, landowners were no longer quite the bogeymen they had once been. Here were the trappings, rather than the reality, of wealth and power: it was all a front, like the stone façade of the brick-built house. As we picnicked on the verandah, and then swam in the shady pool surrounded by the blue-flowering plumbago, I felt like a visitor to a National Trust property allowed in on a day when it was closed to the public; this was a museum, not a working estate, and to get some sense of what it must once have been like, one had to people it in the imagination with a small army of servants – maids and gardeners – all long since departed.

Adriana admitted that for many years she had been reluctant to bring friends to her childhood home; though she loved the place dearly, she had come to regard it almost as a guilty secret. That she no longer felt this way was part of the long and painful process of coming to terms with her background.

Camilo Marks was the name of the lawyer acting for Ledy Castro, Sergio's wife. His manner on the phone had been off-hand, and when I arrived at his office nearly half an hour after we had arranged to meet – but scarcely late by Chilean standards – he told me brusquely that he had been about to leave, and ignored me while he gave his secretary lengthy instructions. Eventually he ushered me into his tiny office where, once we were seated, his tone completely changed and he became the soul of affability. I handed over Sergio's presents, which he undertook to deliver to Ledy in prison, and asked him if he thought I might be allowed to visit her. Lawyer-like, he was reluctant to commit himself either way. He was happier explaining the procedure, which was that Ledy would have to give my name to the authorities before they would even consider a visit, and then they might, or might not, let me in. When I told him that Paz would probably accompany me, he said that she, being Chilean, was unlikely to encounter any difficulty; but a visiting Englishman was another matter, especially as the British embassy had just made a public protest to the government on Ledy's behalf – the first time it had ever taken up the case of a non-national.

This protest got a mixed reception in the Chilean press – *El Mercurio*, the establishment newspaper, for instance, suggested in an editorial that 'British meddling' in this case was 'as unwise as it would be for the Chilean government to give an opinion in Great Britain on a *sub judice* case against an IRA terrorist for the sole reason that he happened to have lived for a time in our country' – but at least it succeeded in publicizing Ledy's case. The longest report, which included an interview with Camilo Marks, appeared in one of the opposition dailies, *Fortín Mapocho*, on October 19th, the fifth anniversary of her imprisonment, 'taking into account the eleven days of torture she experienced at the hands of CNI agents in the Borgoño Street barracks,' as the lawyer put it. He described his client's situation as 'Kafkaesque [he also writes book reviews for the other opposition paper, *La Epoca*] and incomprehensible'. Ledy had received her five-year sentence for 'breaking the arms control law' from a military court, but there were charges against her in the civil court over the kidnapping of a child of rich parents, known as the Cruzat child case, by members of the Manuel Rodríguez Patriotic Front (FPMR).

Marks went on to say:

The only scrap of evidence against her is an unlawful statement extracted under torture. As to the offence relating to the kidnapping of the minor, there is absolutely no connection whatsoever. She is charged with illegal association, but it has never been established that she is even a member of the FPMR; she is charged with theft, with intimidation, yet she doesn't even know the place where these deeds took place. Moreover, this last accusation was used as a means of charging her under the anti-terrorist law. This is an absolute denial of justice. By the logic of this, anyone accused of theft ought to be held under that law.

In a note smuggled out of jail to the *Guardian* correspondent Malcolm Coad, Ledy wrote that 'while held by the CNI, I was beaten, had electricity applied all over my body, was made to sign false confessions and lied to about the fate of my son'.

This sounded more like Pinochet's Chile, as described in countless articles, books, films and television programmes, than anything I had so far encountered in Santiago, and I wanted to see this other Chile for myself. So Paz drove me to the nondescript house in Santo Domingo Street, not far from the centre of town, where some thirty women political detainees were incarcerated. From the road I could see a solitary jacaranda tree, with its clusters of blue flowers. I could not make out whether it was in the courtyard of the prison or just outside it. I wondered what it might signify to those inside: did it mock their aspirations towards liberty, reminding them of all they lacked – access to nature, beauty and freedom itself – or did they, conversely, derive sustenance from it, seeing it as a symbol of what they must eventually regain?

On this occasion I had no opportunity to find out, as I got no further than the entrance lobby where a sullen doorman and green-uniformed warders of both sexes screened all visitors, removing their identity cards and frisking them before allowing them to proceed. I was told I would need a special pass from the chief of the *Gendarmería* and was made to wait outside, holding Paz's handbag and camera (which she had over-optimistically brought along), while she went in. She did not stay long, as Ledy had other visitors, but came away impressed with Ledy's cheerfulness and indomitable spirit. The message she relayed to me was that Ledy had received the radio and cassettes I had brought out from England and that she hoped I would persevere in trying to see her, as she longed to hear of her son. I could foresee a long struggle with the bureaucracy (*muchos trámites*, in the graphic Chilean phrase), but it had become important to me, as well as to Ledy, that I should get to see her.

5

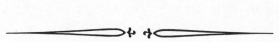

Felipe Alliende would have been more comfortable speaking German than English, but he was keen to talk about Cristián in any language; and his enthusiasm, which soon transcended linguistic limitations, was infectious. A heavily built man, he had 'teacher' written all over him, though he could also have been a priest. There was a purity about his regard for Cristián, which was enhanced by his lack of interest in me, or what I might be doing; he just wanted to sing the praises of the man who was the best chief he had ever worked for. He was impatient of interruptions, repeating in his Germanic English, 'Ja, ja, ja,' while he waited to resume his reminiscences.

He had begun working as a part-time lecturer at the Centro de Estudios Humanísticos in 1967. He had been recommended by Cristián to the then director, Roberto Torretti. Up to that point he had not seen much of Cristián since the time when they had both been students at the Instituto Pedagógico, but their friendship revived during Cristián's affair with the French woman Marie Claire, who was a friend of Felipe's wife. He remembered Cristián 'playing the charming host' in the house on San Cristóbal.

That affair had not lasted long. Soon afterwards Cristián had married his second wife Sylvia, and that had been big news in the exclusive seaside resort of Zapallar, where her family, the Erlweins, occupied a prominent social position. But it was her first name that mattered to Cristián. He made much of the fact that, as he told Felipe, she had 'the same name as my mother and sister'.

The dean of engineering, Enrique d'Etigny, had wanted to create a new faculty of letters; so the CEH was transformed into a department. In 1972, when Cristián was elected director, he made Felipe his second-in-command

and set about remodelling the place. Although it continued to take students from medicine, engineering and other scientific faculties, it also acquired its own students of philosophy, history and literature: twenty students for each of the new arts subjects. The faculty expanded from a core of half-a-dozen full-time staff to forty or more, and their main work was with the new students of the humanities.

Cristián was a very genial chief, but he was also a bold one: he broke all the university rules, selecting students on the basis of personal interviews when they had already been at the university for a year. They could be from any background, and they could be any age: Adriana Valdés, for instance, took some courses there, though she was already a lecturer at the Catholic University. Nor did it matter what subjects they had been studying as long as they showed an interest in the humanities. It was a genuinely *open* university.

The CEH had occupied eight or nine offices on the ninth floor of the engineering faculty building. For the new department, Cristián managed to buy the old Spanish embassy cheaply. This was more of a traditional house than an institutional building, and it was just the place for a humanities department. There was a big hall, for which Cristián purchased a piano, and a library and printing-room. The fourth-floor attic was converted into a theatre and projection-room for art movies. The department started taking its own students in March 1973, but the house was not acquired until 1974.

Since the building was so cheap, the faculty was happy to pay for furnishing it. Soledad was Cristián's secretary, and together they bought old furniture at auctions. Cristián recognized the importance of welcoming and tasteful surroundings for staff and students alike. He was still married to Sylvia, but Soledad was his mistress. Many people thought of him as a 'Satanic lover', and they were jealous of him, but he and Soledad were accepted as a couple even before he divorced Sylvia and married her. The house was their home and they took care of every detail, right down to stripping the paint off the doors. It was a beautiful and elegant house, where you were happy to pass the time even when you were not working.

Cristián was not the most distinguished academic in the department, but he was very much the director, the chief of a talented bunch, responsible for selecting staff in the first place. He took on people for academic, rather than political, reasons, though they were not all academics either, but included poets such as Nicanor Parra and Enrique Lihn. He had to fight the university authorities to be allowed to take on creative people, and Felipe found himself defending the poets against the academics. But they all worked well with Cristián; he was liked because he was so charming, and he was able to get the best out of people of all political persuasions.

One of the innovations for which he was responsible was the magazine *Manuscritos*. Felipe had edited an educational journal before he joined the full-time staff at the department, and he was keen to edit this one and make it a serious and traditional publication. So at first he was rather resentful when Cristián did not invite him to do it, but then he realized that Cristián had totally different, even revolutionary ideas about its function.

The editor of *Manuscritos* was the aforementioned Ronald Kay, a German-born professor raised in Chile who has since returned to Germany; and his then wife, Catalina Parra (daughter of Nicanor), was the designer. The first – and only – issue caused a scandal. The new rector (i.e., vice-chancellor) of the university, who was appointed by the military junta, took exception to the magazine on the grounds of both expense and content. It was a lavish production, and it was 'not serious': it contained irreverent jokes from Nicanor Parra, and a sequence of poems about cows called *Areas Verdes*, by Raúl Zurita, who became known as 'the poet of the cow' – Cristián and Ronald Kay discovered him and sometimes claimed they had 'invented' him. These were excellent poems, Felipe said, and Zurita has gone from strength to strength, but the authorities dismissed the whole enterprise as frivolous.

This was not the only scandal Cristián had been involved in. When he set up a disco, called *La Máquina*, and spent all his evenings there, people started saying: 'How can a director run a disco?' But while Felipe and others were interested only in teaching, Cristián 'wanted to live in every space: agriculture, business, art . . .' He became more and more adventurous. 'He was so successful he believed he could do anything. It was very dangerous for him.'

It was d'Etigny who had had the idea of having another department of philosophy in the first place because the Pedagógico was then submerged in politics and mediocrity, Felipe told me. But it could not have happened without Cristián: the DEH was his personal creation, supported by d'Etigny. D'Etigny was promoted to vice-rector of the university, but he was in trouble with the powers-that-be: the new rector, appointed by the military, wanted to dismantle the department he had set up and have only the one faculty of philosophy, as in the old days of the Pedagógico; and d'Etigny was obliged to remove Cristián from his post as director (this did not save him, though, as he himself was removed soon afterwards).

After Cristián went, there was no one to guide the department, 'and now we are dying'. Only a dozen staff remained: some had passed on, some had passed away. No new blood had been brought in; the courses had lost all importance: they were no more than options now. In Cristián's own field of literature, only three teachers remained – Nicanor Parra, who was seventy-five and often absent in New York or elsewhere, Jorge Guzmán and Felipe himself – and they were isolated, even from one another, 'not like in the old days when there was a real sense of a group'.

Felipe had never wanted to be the chief; he had felt honoured 'to be a good second to Cristián; he needed a good second'. Cristián was like 'another part of myself'. Felipe was not an outgoing type; he said of Cristián: 'He did what I was afraid to do.' But it worked the other way, too: 'I was his *alter ego*, quiet and solid.'

The whole enterprise had been permeated by politics. In the days of Allende's *Unidad Popular*, Cristián had had to fight powerful enemies. As he was a traditionalist, the left had seen him as a rightist. They had even taken over the faculty once. After the fall of the *UP*, he had to fight the military, who saw him as a leftist. His Military School background, far from helping him, probably worked against him since the military saw him as a renegade. When he went to a reunion dinner with other alumni of the Military School, the civilians were all placed at one table and the military at another. Cristián had tried to bring the two groups together to discuss the rights of the military in politics, but one of the generals who was present said: 'We don't speak to Communists.' Two days later, Cristián was fired from his job at the University of Santiago (*La universidad de los militares*, as it was known), where he got work some years after leaving the University of Chile. This must have been the same incident, I realized as Felipe was telling me about it, that Cristián and Soledad had described to me in Devon.

Several months after Cristián's removal from the directorship of the DEH, twelve men from the CNI, the secret police, arrived at the house Cristián had bought for the department and told the academics to leave since they now owned it. The surprised staff went to the rector, who admitted he had sold the building to the CNI but managed to obtain three months' grace for the department. New offices of a more institutional kind were found, and most of the furniture Cristián and Soledad had bought went into storage. But there was one relic from Cristián's disco days which, scandalously, found its way on to the inventory (before disappearing): twenty plastic models of nude girls.

Felipe was critical of Cristián's development as a writer. He said that Cristián had been very proud of going against the vein of naturalistic writing, in which he was at home, but he had not been successful as an experimental writer, however important it was to him to be part of the avant-garde. It was a case of interesting theory but poor practice. Although his novel *El rincón de los niños* was published in an inexpensive edition, it was still a failure. Felipe had read it out of the obligations of friendship, but had found it a struggle to finish. *Cuentos de cámara*, his first book of stories, was his best work. Contact with influential avant-garde critics like Kay and Guzmán had not been good for him as a writer: they wanted a new kind of writing and Cristián had tried to provide it instead of following his natural inclinations. Felipe had enjoyed *El verano del ganadero*, as it was the first occasion on which a young upper-class Chilean had revealed his dirty mind; such people were so formal and moral on the surface, but underneath they were very different. Cristián's aim in that book had been to be ironic about his own class and, at the same time, to parody the style of erotic writing.

He had had a good theme for his Cambridge thesis – not so much Lawrence as how Latin Americans reacted to, copied or imitated, English literature – and he had collected interesting material. But he had not followed it through; he was doing too many other things. Perhaps that was why Cambridge had not awarded him a doctorate, only an M.Litt.

In general, though he was an upper-class type, he was also highly self-conscious and critical. He was not a leftist – he hated blind Marxists and fought with them – but he could work with leftists. He was an excellent critic of his own class, Felipe thought, yet the way he lived and dressed – he was always discreetly elegant – marked him unmistakably as a *pije*.

The day I talked to Felipe Allliende I also moved out of Paz's house into a sixth-floor flat near the centre of town, with a view of the San Cristóbal hill, which rises steeply out of the plain of Santiago and has at its summit a huge, floodlit statue of the Virgin, to remind anyone who might need reminding that Chile is a Catholic country. I soon became accustomed to the sight of the cable-cars of the *teleférico* meandering across the horizon. But it took me some time to adjust to living on my own, as I had grown used to the relaxed sociability of Paz's household. Now days would pass without my speaking more than a word or two to a waiter or shopkeeper or the maid who came twice a week to clean my flat or the concierge on the ground floor, and my sense of isolation was compounded by my inadequate command of *castellano*. I was troubled, too, by doubts about what I had undertaken: was it not presumptuous to imagine that my ancient friendship with Cristián and Paz would open doors to an understanding not just of their lives, but of their country's recent trauma as well? Still, I had no alternative but to persevere in my search for enlightenment.

Prompted by Felipe's parting remark – that, despite its disappointing superficiality and exoticism, Cristián's *Autobiografía* pointed to several things worth studying – I reread that slender volume. And after discussing Cristián with other people, it was invigorating to hear, in my mind's ear, the ironic inflection of his own voice behind the words on the page.

The very first sentence – which so impressed Nicanor Parra that he later quoted it to me from memory – establishes the tone: 'I do not pretend to know who I am, nor am I under the illusion that I will ever come to know.' What anyone sees of himself will depend on how he looks and what he is looking for; so an autobiography is only one of several possible versions of the truth. Cristián, quoting Lampedusa, promises not to perpetrate any falsehoods, but reserves the right 'to lie by omission'. He suggests that it is virtually impossible to tell all, limited as one inevitably is by what one knows, or does not know, and by what one is prepared to make known, as well as by consideration for friends and relations. In addition, he reminds us that in Chile over the last eleven years (he was writing in 1984) everyone has had to watch his tongue.

He admits to making seven separate starts and offers what follows as 'the sum of these beginnings'. Whether this amounts to an admission of defeat or the achievement of a formal breakthrough is perhaps an open question. Is he generalizing about the condition of modern man in offering these disconnected, or loosely connected, fragments? Or are these several beginnings evidence of a personal failure on his part to fulfil his renaissance man ideal? With Cristián there was always an intimate relationship between creation and criticism; and what he actually offers is as much a critique of each beginning as the sum of them all.

*

The first two beginnings are concerned with horses, though Cristián is at pains to deny any professional interest in these beasts. In the second, he refers to the 'foggy days of August 1973, weeks before the fall of Allende', when Daniela, who was then seven years old, spent weekends with him and his second wife Sylvia – 'named the same as my mother and my favourite sister'. Sylvia took long siestas, sleeping away the hours of a marriage that was slowly unravelling. The house was as heavy with tension as the garden was with fog, and Cristián welcomed the opportunity to escape by taking Daniela out to look at horses.

His own anguish, however, was but a small echo of the misery engulfing the whole country: 'contemplating the horses' tall loveliness I discovered, like Gulliver on his fourth voyage, a serenity which had deserted human beings.' 'The horses,' he goes on, 'like the trees, did not have any part in the climate of those months; they did not arm themselves for what, by an historical perversion, all of us in Chile had come both to desire and, at the same time, to fear.' The horses would have no part either in 'the justice of the conqueror', which, Cristián remarks with a further reference to English literature, 'one could see coming round the corner, just like the Queen in *Alice* . . . dictating sentence before the trial'.

His next paragraph consists of a single sentence: 'Those were times for misanthropy.'

After that he returns with relief to Daniela and the horses, and to his own childhood recollections of them. But this beginning does not satisfy him either. With the significance of September 11th (the day of the coup) in the lives of all Chileans in mind, he asks himself the question, does one arrive at the social through personal history, or is it the other way round?

There could scarcely be a more extreme contrast, he suggests, than that between the socialist Utopia of the *Unidad Popular* and the restored capitalism of the Junta; yet a substantial portion of the population as a whole, not to mention each individual, had little difficulty in adapting to both systems. To see this solely as a matter of keeping one's head on one's shoulders, of equating life with opportunity or – worse – opportunism, is too Darwinian for Cristián. But where is the person, he asks, in this snare? How much real autonomy does he have beyond 'the dialectics of his situation'?

The third beginning closes with this suspiciously Marxist-sounding question. In the fourth, he examines the period of his life to which he admits that he returns obsessively in his writing: adolescence, the time of freshness and surprised discovery. What is the great virtue of maturity anyway, he asks defensively. Apart from horses and dogs, what he liked was the reflection of the mountains in the waters of a pond; he also enjoyed the geometrical lay-out of vines and fruit-trees, and the avenues of acacias so admirably arranged for strolling along and discussing literature with friends. But above all, as the eldest son, with only sisters until he was sixteen years old, he believed he was the centre of the universe (with apologies, he adds – a touch ironically – to feminists). He took it for granted that everything on his father's estate, Santo Tomás, down to the acacia walks, had been created especially for his enjoyment and would last for ever. Yet he spent his youth pursuing almost any goal other than that of preserving the estate. Indeed at university, in the Instituto Pedagógico, he became an outspoken critic of the agrarian system which supported his privileged lifestyle.

That was the time when he finally rejected the Church, too, though he cannot be sure whether it was because of the absurdity of its fight against the world, the flesh and the devil, or through his own intellectual difficulty in accepting a concept outside of history, such as faith. At any rate, after reading Nietzsche, he decided – 'with some fear and a great deal of joy' – that it was perfectly possible to conceive of a world without God. Despite that, he continued to experience, in moments of extreme anguish or awe in the face of spectacular natural beauty, 'intense bursts of nostalgia for God'.

The adolescent Cristián became a critical presence at the familial dinner table, making sarcastic faces whenever his father spoke in praise of liberals and conservatives, and maintaining a superior silence when he attacked the parties of the left. For the most part, his father succeeded in controlling his impatience, contenting himself with saying, over and over again: 'You have an obligation and a responsibility. And you will never fulfil them as long as you are disloyal to your class.'

This argument was not entirely lost on Cristián. In 1958 he wrote a story called 'The Bell', which encapsulated his dilemma. This was the year in which Allende lost by a narrow margin his second attempt to gain the presidency (and in which Cristián, having reached his majority, could have voted for the first time, but didn't; he abstained, though he accompanied his father on the night of the election to visit the right-wing President-elect, Jorge Alessandri, and offered him his congratulations).

The bell of the story was on the door of his father's office and was both an essential part of the daily routine of the estate and a symbol of the hierarchical divisions in society. When his father wanted to call the farm manager, he gave one ring repeated three times; for the watchman it was two rings repeated three times; and for the gardener three rings, three times. In Cristián's story a mob takes over the estate and rings the bell as a victory signal. So far so predictable, but he provided two alternative – and diametrically opposed – endings: in one, the young protagonist, the proprietor's son, greets the invaders with delirious enthusiasm, and it is he who celebrates their heroic takeover by vigorously ringing the bell; in the other, the same young man climbs on to the roof of the ancestral home and leads the farmhands in their armed resistance. It was a story he never dared show his father; and when he showed it to his Uncle Tomás, he got a long lecture on the necessity of taking sides in this world.

As a child brought up in the countryside and educated privately, first at St George, a Catholic school run by North American monks, and then at the Military School (and even after that at the School of Architecture in the Catholic University), Cristián saw the social hierarchy as part of the natural order of things. He never questioned it until he came up against a very different set of attitudes at the Instituto Pedagógico: there for the first time he was confronted by the idea of politics as an instrument of change rather than conservation. There was talk of injustice, exploitation, imperialism – all heady stuff. As Cristián recalls, 'This was the other face of the dance I had been dancing since infancy.' Until then he had accepted as his due the admiration his fair hair and skin, his upper-class way of speaking and dressing, even his name, inspired. Now he began to perceive that these might provoke a quite different reaction: 'It was a serious matter to be rejected because of one's skin, one's accent, one's clothes, or one's surname.'

Though it hardly affected his lifestyle, the Pedagógico influenced Cristián to the extent that he began to judge the world in terms of the success of the class struggle for justice, no matter how totalitarian the means. The social hierarchy, far from being part of the natural order of things, was now seen by him as a monstrous anomaly; the world was badly made and it was his honourable destiny to participate in the struggle to reshape it. From this point of view, 'my own past began to seem like a novel, a sublimely sweet romance'. The lure of the Communist Party for Cristián (as for so many others of his class and generation) was that it filled the gap left by the abandoned Church. In addition, it enabled him to transcend his class limitations and observe the world as if from outside. But he did not want to have anything to do with any other turncoats: 'What I wanted was contact with reality. But I wanted to be the only one to have it.'

This struggle culminated in Cambridge, of all places, where for the first time he seriously studied Chilean literature and history and became conscious of such issues as dependency and underdevelopment. He interested himself in Marxism and the Cuban Revolution, and 'came to maintain – today I admit it a trifle uncomfortably – that I was myself totally insignificant in comparison with the problems of my *pueblo*.' It was the study of D. H. Lawrence that brought him back to earth, in particular Lawrence's gloss on the commandment that one must love one's neighbour as oneself: first, one must learn to love oneself; otherwise, the love of one's neighbour will be nothing but an abstraction. Cristián could not immediately turn this insight to advantage; to do that, he says, he had to return to Chile.

So ends the fourth beginning of the *Autobiografía*. Several months would elapse before he picked up his pen for a fifth time.

When he did begin again, he plunged into family history, focusing on his grandfather's library and his own distant kinship, through that grandfather, Roberto Huneeus Gana, with the father of the Chilean novel, Alberto Blest Gana. His own father was a keen reader, especially of Chilean history – in *Persona Non Grata*, Jorge Edwards writes of 'that mania for history found among the greater part of the Chilean bourgeoisie' – but he confined his serious reading to evenings and weekends, when he would sit in his armchair with a glass of whisky to hand and classical music on the gramophone. During working hours he would never look at anything but *El Mercurio*. Cristián's maternal grandfather, on the other hand, gave up work as an engineer at the age of fifty in order to dedicate himself to his favourite authors, Darwin and Dickens. So, for Cristián, from the beginning there was an intimate connection between reading and ruin: 'The appeal of grandfather Roberto's library was always the appeal of the abyss.'

When he finally overcame parental opposition and went, at the age of twenty, to the Pedagógico, where he could spend all his time reading and writing, he felt the need to cultivate an anti-artistic persona. He found the perfect role-model in Thomas Mann's image of the bourgeois artist: one who adapts the rules and practices of the liberal professions to the pursuit of literature; one who has duties to perform, who cuts his hair short, wears a collar and tie – and not a flashy one either – and who, externally at least, seems just like every other bourgeois. Such sleight of hand suited Cristián perfectly: it meant that he could pass for either a lawyer, which was for his father the ideal mixture of the intellectual and the practical, or an architect, which was his mother's dream combination of the artistic and the presentable, without compromising his own ambition to be a writer. Thomas Mann's 'parachute', as he calls it, helped him 'descend into the abyss with the air of a perfect gentleman'.

Before long, however, he began to feel the constrictions

of the role. He thought of himself as more medieval than bourgeois: passionate, impulsive, unruly, eager for experience, unreasonable and full of aggression, 'saved from outrageous behaviour only by the intensity of my love for Paz, my first wife-to-be, and not by the straitjacket Mann's parachute had turned into'.

But he could not easily divest himself of the straitjacket. In England, in an effort to free himself, he read Chaucer and Rabelais, acquainted himself with Sterne and the picaresque novel, rediscovered Sancho Panza, and became a fan of D. H. Lawrence. For years after his return to Chile he kept diaries, made tape-recordings and left a trail of false starts and new discoveries ending in blind alleys. All to no avail. By 1970 he was on the point of subjecting himself to psychoanalysis, and was only prevented from doing so by his recollection of the – probably apocryphal – story of Freud's refusal to analyze Rilke for fear of meddling with the springs of his creativity and making him give up writing. Cristián continued to write – and make changes in his life, following the break-up of his first marriage in 1968: so many changes that his mother came to the conclusion that he was the latest in a long line of black sheep in the Huneeus family.

6

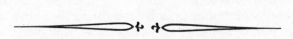

The sixth, and penultimate, beginning of Cristián's *Autobiografía* was prompted by a recognition that something crucial was missing: 'Today it is clear to me what was the problem: I had not yet said a word about how or why I began to write.'

He retraces his steps once more to his adolescence. Despite the fact that at St George, he tells us, there was the high-sounding *Academia Literaria del Joven Laurel* (The Literary Academy of the Young Laurel), presided over by one Roque Esteban Scarpa, it was not there that Cristián was bitten by the literary bug, but in the entirely antipathetic environment of the Military School.

At St George, his only writings, a diary, got him into trouble when Father Provenzano, 'a dreadful Sicilian from the Bronx', confiscated it during one of his classes. In this diary, Cristián had recorded details, not only of how many times he had masturbated (accompanied by gloomy prognostications as to the effect of this self-abuse on his life-expectancy), but also – and this was worse, as it involved others – the names of all the girls who had let him take their hand, kiss them on the cheek or the mouth, with or without inserting his tongue, and who sighed, even while they protested, when he touched their breasts.

Father Provenzano called him into his office and asked him what he thought the parents of these girls would say if they knew what he had so shamelessly written about them. As it had never occurred to Cristián to put himself in their position, he said nothing. So Father Provenzano asked him what he thought his father would say if he were aware of the brazen way he had indulged in such excesses and sinfully recorded them. Again Cristián had no answer. Finally, Father Provenzano asked him what he would say if his own sisters were subjected to such improper advances. Cristián had not considered this possibility either, since his sisters were still too young and, anyway, it seemed to him they would never allow so much as the hems of their skirts to be touched. Fortunately for him, his father took a rather more worldly view of his sexual peccadillos than the healthy and sporty American priests did, and only agreed with Father Provenzano on one thing: that the proper place for his son was the Military School.

Cristián was an army cadet between the ages of fifteen and seventeen (1952–4). His leaving home and entering the Military School marked a watershed in his relations with his parents. Until then he had been closer to his mother, with whom he spent all his time in the house while his father was out in the fields. Now he was entering man's estate and, more importantly, it was in his father's chosen arena, because his father had been the prize cadet of his era and had been commissioned into the cavalry. Whether crushed by his image or protected by his person, Cristián developed a sudden and not entirely comfortable closeness to his father: 'My invisible rivalry as the firstborn and only son now began to take shape.'

In any military contest, Cristián would always be the loser: he was hopeless at drill and his unusual height – he was the tallest cadet in his intake – drew merciless attention to his inadequacies. When he presented arms one second later than all the other 400 cadets on parade, the commanding officer gave him extra days' detention 'so that you learn who your father was!' Cristián could just about put up with that, but when he was falsely accused, along with other cadets who favoured a civilian, rather than a military, career, of stealing from the Quartermaster's store, he put in a request for his discharge, having first obtained his father's permission. But on discovering how disappointed his father really was, he changed his mind and withdrew his request. This was the zenith of his filial relationship: 'We became intimate friends, something we had never been before and would never be again.'

Despite his decision to soldier on for the time being, Cristián was not cut out for the military life. He had no understanding of institutionalized violence; wars – even those that were woven into the fabric of Chilean history: the Araucanian War and the War of Independence, the wars against Bolivia and Peru, the Civil War of 1891; not to mention the Second World War, in which one of his uncles had fought – might have taken place on another planet for all they meant to him. He could not take military discipline seriously. But, try as he might to laugh or shrug it off, he was so overwhelmed by it at the Military School that he began to lose all sense of his own identity. He had to construct a persona to help him survive a regime from whose rigours there was no escape:

> For the military world – it rapidly became clear to me – was nothing but a metaphor for the wider world. The army – and I soon understood this, too – was nothing but the brute reality latent in civil institutions, no matter how peaceful and well-balanced these might appear for miraculously long periods. A single breakdown of this delicate balance was enough to have the military world emerge from its barracks and take over everything, as the present-day history of the country goes to show.

Cristián discovered the persona he was seeking through writing. The world, he suddenly realized, had always seemed to him a chaos, which could only be put into some sort of order by invention. Religion and history, quite as much as fiction, were only convincing as works of art.

He recalls exactly how it began:

> I woke up one winter morning absolutely convinced that I must teach myself, without delay, to write with my left hand. That was the strange thing: it had to be my left hand. As if I was afraid of losing the use of my right. Perhaps it was lost already. With this injunction I think I was ruling out the possibility of direct action as far as I was concerned. For what action can be more direct than a bomb or suicide? Yet neither of these solves anything. So one should be trained for indirect action, oblique action, making use of unknown instruments, forging and occupying new territories.

The short, factual diaries which had so offended Father Provenzano at St George gave way to thick notebooks, painfully written in an ungainly hand and filled with ideas, feelings, memories, impressions, desires and projects for the future. Then suddenly, without knowing why, Cristián switched back to using his right hand and began to produce stories and one-act plays, which he gave to his friends to read.

From its origins in the misery of the Military School, Cristián's need to write was intimately connected with a sense of lost identity. Throughout his life, he found, the more lost he felt, the more he wrote. When he was happy, he did something else: taught in the university, tended the farm, took practical action of one sort or another.

He records his debt to the Military School, but doubts whether the army would see fit to include making him a writer in an inventory of its contributions to the welfare of the fatherland.

The remainder of the *Autobiografía* – except for the final section, which consists of a letter to a friend living in Moscow, on the other side of the political divide, and was written much earlier – concentrates largely on Cristián's experience of running the Santo Tomás estate, and includes the most revealing and lyrical chapter in the entire book. But it starts with his father.

Aníbal Huneeus was only fifty-seven when he died (Cristián, of course, did not even reach fifty), and it was said of him that he had missed his vocation: he should have been a politician, since he had convictions, natural authority, persistence and ability, as well as persuasiveness in putting a case; he respected, and was respected by, his opponents. But at the same time he was exasperated by opportunism, inefficiency and corruption. He spoke his mind and, in spite of a friendly disposition, could tread on people's corns. In his youth he had flirted with the Chilean version of fascism, the National Socialist Party, but had broken with it over a threatened coup. He gravitated naturally towards the Liberal Party, regarding radicals as corrupt and conservatives as backward-looking, though he was not averse to political compromise; in 1964, for instance, he voted, along with many other liberals and conservatives, for the Christian Democrat, Eduardo Frei, in order to keep the dreaded Allende out of office. The fact that the Christian Democrats chose to ignore this liberal and conservative support led to the fusion of the two groups in opposition in the National Party and thus contributed to Allende's eventual victory in 1970.

Cristián describes how, when he returned from Europe in 1966, he found his father had virtually given up politics, though he continued to oppose agrarian reform. From this sympathetic account you would never guess how contemptuously dismissive of his father's reactionary views Cristián had been at the time. Since then, of course, not only had agrarian reform come and gone – leading, as it turned out, to a capitalist rather than a socialist revolution on the land – but Cristián himself had stepped into his father's shoes and become a landowner in his own right.

It was university, rather than agrarian, reform, however – starting with a violent student takeover in the University of Chile, which rudely interrupted Cristián's courses on English writers, not to mention his thesis on D. H. Lawrence – that first made him question his leftist political position. In Chile, as elsewhere, participation was what the students were demanding in 1968, not just for themselves, but for assistants, drivers, waiters and cleaners, who would all have their say in choosing academics and administrators and in planning programmes of research and teaching. Cristián 'observed with astonishment the desires of a left that understood the university solely in terms of political power and wanted to eliminate every trace of the sovereignty of pluralism'. He began to ask himself how much intellectual freedom someone from the left would be allowed if the left came to power: 'And I think it was then that I reached the conclusion that the only possible freedom for an intellectual was to remain in opposition.'

He discussed these things with his father when he visited his sick bed, and listened closely to his comments. Cristián's growing disenchantment with the left was mirrored in his father's rejection of the right. And the fact that Aníbal was dying inevitably brought father and son closer together.

On the day of the military coup Cristián found himself thinking of his father. He had no doubt that, had his father survived, he would have enthusiastically supported

it and celebrated the resumption of individual land owner-
ship. But as an old-fashioned liberal he would certainly
not have approved of the abuses of civil liberties and
human rights that followed in its wake. Aníbal's own
father, who had been deported under the dictatorial
regime of Colonel Carlos Ibáñez in the Twenties, had sent
his sons into the army in the hope of influencing it from
within and thereby preventing further departures from
the traditional Chilean constitution. (In his last novel, *Una
escalera contra la pared*, Cristián attributes the blame for 'the
unfortunate events' of 1927–31, 'in the last analysis, to an
oligarchy which has lost the sense of its governing mission, turning its back on the armed forces in favour of
business, and, with a blindness more suited to moles than
to refined and educated people, allowing these forces to
be made up of a type of person with no sense of the
history of the country'.)

Now Cristián imagines his father trying to use his
influence to procure a restoration of democratic values and
then, when that failed, retreating into an eloquent silence
and dedicating himself to his business, his estate and agricultural affairs in general, doubtless concentrating – Cristián adds with feeling – on an attack on the excessive
interest rates charged by the banks. Perhaps he would also
have joined, or been tempted to join, the oppositional
Democratic Alliance. In other words, he would have
behaved in much the same way as his son and heir did.

Cristián's separation from Paz preceded his father's
death and, according to a favourite uncle, may even have
hastened it; but this is one of the subjects on which Cristián reserves the right 'to lie by omission'. There is, however, a curious passage in which he describes the view
from a small window above his bed in the studio on San
Cristóbal hill where he went to live with Marie Claire.
From this window he could see the tower of the church in
which he and Paz had been married seven years earlier.

'It had a strange effect on me, looking at it,' he writes,
'the oneness of past and present, a sense of harmony
beyond the break-up, something like a simultaneous feeling that it was right and proper to have loved her so much
and now to love again. And I was glad that we had come

back to Chile and, though separated, that we should live
in the same place where we had known one another and
shared much more than just our experience together'.

This is the nearest he comes to an expression of regret
that his first marriage, the great love of his golden youth,
ended as and when it did.

Like Oscar, the dwarf in Günter Grass's *The Tin Drum* (one
of the books Cristián insisted I read when we were at
Cambridge), Cristián never wanted to grow up. Returning
to Santo Tomás at the age of thirty-one he felt as though
he were recovering his youth. In the most lyrical chapter
in the book, he describes riding back to the house after a
day's cherry picking, being served dinner seated alone at
the head of the table, and then taking a book out on to the
terrace, sinking into a deckchair and resting his weary feet
on a green wrought-iron table. 'I must have that painted
white,' he says to himself, 'it will look better.' Then he
opens the book and tries to read, but he cannot concentrate, he is too excited. He contrasts his present life with
'my years as an intellectual in Santiago, in London, in
Cambridge, and in Santiago again'. Ah yes, but what is
the book he is reading, or *not* reading, as he sits and daydreams on the terrace at Santo Tomás? *Anna Karenina*, no
less, the great novel in which Tolstoy, in the person of
Levin, celebrates in similar fashion his discovery of the
joys of country living and estate management. Intellectuals are never so intellectual as when they are denying
their intellectuality.

Mention of London and Cambridge, perhaps, sends
him scurrying back to his English notebooks, where he
comes across a couple of pages he wrote when he and
Paz visited me at my parents' farm in Devon. In these he
ruminates on the differences between town and country
and remarks how his father, in particular, never seemed at
ease in their Santiago house in the way that he was at
Santo Tomás. He also notes his own characteristic of
'embracing several worlds at the same time and not being
entirely at the disposal of any of them'. He recognizes that
this is the antithesis of professionalism, but when he was
young he could not have cared less about success; all that

mattered to him then was style, and he cultivated the cool disinterestedness of the amateur. He is not at all sure, however, that he will be able to sustain such lofty detachment when eventually he returns to Chile . . .

Now, a decade later, he was celebrating his homecoming to Santo Tomás: 'The beautiful house, spacious and with a slightly English air . . . was the very embodiment of my Chilean past . . . I seemed to fall back into it quite naturally, and I watched myself growing with happiness and amazement. My nostalgia died the death, and gone was my melancholy: my past was transformed, by a rare alchemy of fate brought about by my father's death, into my present.'

But at the same time he recognized that this present was also, perhaps above all, a regression. He was intent on being a worthy heir to his father, brother to his sisters and son to his mother – particularly his mother, 'who has had a great influence on me', and who wanted him to take over the estate. As if to make up for the instability of his own family life, his desertion of Paz and Daniela, he was returning to the original fold and hoping to find acceptance there. 'But,' as he says at the end of the chapter, 'the marriage with the family, or more precisely with my mother, could never, to tell the truth (and to our mutual sorrow and salvation), be consummated.' What he does not say, however, is that he felt so strong a need for it that when he did marry for a second time he would choose a woman whose main qualification for being his wife, it seems, was that she had the same name as his mother and favourite sister.

Fruit-growing for export is big agribusiness in Chile now, but when Cristián's father began planting fruit trees in the Forties it was a new departure. Aníbal was a pioneer in the field and his management of the estate never entirely lost its air of experimentation.

In 1968, when Cristián took over the reins, Santo Tomás consisted of eighty hectares (roughly 200 acres) of land and employed fifteen men. Cristián could hardly tell a grapevine from a willow, because for years it had seemed to him more important to be able to distinguish between middle and late period Henry James. And even though he now set about remedying his deficiencies as an agronomist, characteristically he saw this not so much as a change of career as an expansion of his personality.

'For better or worse,' he writes, 'I was realizing, through this twist of fate, one of the aspirations that had brought me back to South America: to live many lives simultaneously.' He cites the case of 'one of my heroes in Europe', Vicente Pérez Rosales, author of *Recuerdos del pasado*, a nineteenth-century Chilean classic. Pérez Rosales, in addition to being a writer and a rancher, was – according to a Chilean cultural biographical dictionary – 'a businessman, a miner, a painter, a manufacturer, a civil servant, a country doctor, a mariner, a master chef, a hotel manager, a farmer, a mayor, a consul, a senator, a smuggler and a vagabond'. Cristián could scarcely compete with this, even if he did manage to combine writing with running his father's farm and advertising agency, starting up a disco and being director of the Departamento de Estudios Humanísticos. But the example of Pérez Rosales was what prevented him from specializing and settling for academic life, the idea of which had tempted him from time to time while he was still in Europe.

In the beginning, his activities on the farm were closely supervised by the family, who were reluctant to concede him autonomy until they were sure he knew what he was doing. His brother-in-law, for instance, remarked how effective his father's authoritarian approach to the peasants had been: 'When he was angry, guys trembled.' Cristián replied that his father, even though he was a liberal, had always liked the military, whereas he, who had barely survived his three years as an army cadet, could never come to terms with the system of giving orders. Besides, he argued, his co-operative style of management was better suited to an era of agrarian reform. His mother complained that he delegated too much; and when he told her that this provided fulfilment for fellow creatures, and contributed to job satisfaction, she dismissed this, saying that he had always been 'too much of an idealist'. It might work among enlightened people at the university, she conceded, but in the country a boss had to be a boss.

Between the Scylla of family pressure and the Charybdis of agrarian reform, Cristián had a difficult course to steer. In February 1973, he was summoned back from Lake Vichuquén, where he and Soledad had been on holiday, to head off a threatened *toma*, or seizure, of Santo Tomás. This was against the official policy of the *Unidad Popular*, which in Cristián's cynical account was to keep things quiet during the run-up to what turned out to be the last parliamentary elections in Chile for sixteen and a half years. But its supporters were less concerned with the processes of democracy, 'and in those days there were takeover attempts on all sides'.

Santo Tomás (which was half-owned by Cristián's uncle) fell within the size limit for individual property holdings allowed by CORA, the agency responsible since the early Sixties for implementing land reform. In addition, it exported virtually all the fruit it produced: 'And Allende in his three years was careful to keep exporting estates in private hands . . . partly at least in order to hold back the encroachment of want and inefficiency which nobody, friend or foe, could fail to detect in the burgeoning nationalization of land in the country.'

The trouble at Santo Tomás, such as it was, related to the employment of casual workers for fruit picking. An agitator challenged Cristián's right to employ these workers as and when it suited him, rather than all the year round. This man wasn't convinced by the argument that, by its very nature, this work was seasonal: it had nothing to do with the nature of plants, he maintained, but a great deal to do with the nature of capitalist exploitation. By the time the case came up before the local work tribunal, however, the accusation had been reduced to 'bad working conditions, characteristic of man's inhuman exploitation of man': the arrangements for changing, bathing and eating for casual workers at Santo Tomás were 'insufficient, unsatisfactory and typical of the contemptuous bourgeois attitude'.

The agitator's problem, Cristián explains, was that in order to make a more serious accusation stick, he needed the support of at least one of the fifteen full-time workers on the estate, and this was not forthcoming. These men knew that if the land were expropriated, they would then be at the mercy of the political machinations of the neighbouring communities, which was not a prospect they welcomed. So the takeover bid failed, but, as a face-saving device, the 'wise woman' (as Cristián calls her) chairing the tribunal ordered that conditions for casual workers at Santo Tomás be improved. She said she would come round after ten days to inspect the work and, if it had not been done, she would impose a fine.

The work was done. But she never came.

Cristián was not so successful in fending off the family challenge to his management of the estate. A large part of the argument was over expenditure. Cristián's view, which he maintains was also his father's, was that you had to spend money in order to make money; you could only get out of the land what you put into it, and many of the fruit trees were past their prime and needed replacing. His mother and sisters were in favour of reducing expenditure, though his mother's partiality for her firstborn ensured that she sometimes supported him not just against the rest of the family but even against her own better judgement.

At a family meeting following the thwarted takeover attempt, in which Cristián's role had earned him a measure of gratitude, he pressed for investment in the future: he wanted to plant more fruit trees and he suggested they tried plums and nectarines. His mother favoured raspberries, arguing that the canes would cost less and produce a quicker return. His sisters contented themselves with saying that if intelligent investment could bring back the quality of life which had pertained to Santo Tomás during their father's lifetime, then they too were in favour of it.

Cristián was touched. It was not the first time that his sisters had expressed such nostalgia, but their need was an impossible one for him, as estate manager, to satisfy. How could a single estate be expected to provide for five families – where in the past it had only had to support one, their own? He told them it would require much more than the replacement of a few old fruit trees to achieve that; nothing less, in fact, than the purchase of five new estates – not to mention the resurrection of their father and their own physical reversion to childhood. In that case, his sisters wanted to know, why was he talking of planting nectarines and plums?

Cristián conveniently forgets how he dealt with that question, but says that matters remained unresolved and a further meeting was fixed for three days later. It was at this second meeting that he put forward the possibility of poultry.

His sisters were appalled at the idea: one said how smelly hens were; another how ugly; and the third asked what purpose they served. But Cristián succeeded in persuading them, along with his mother, that poultry would be better business than, say, raspberries since eggs were in great demand during Allende's last months and prices were high.

There was no difficulty in obtaining credit, provided it was for the estate and not for his individual use. This meant that his sisters also had to sign the promissory note, which his mother persuaded them to do, though they took a highly critical stance on the whole enterprise. One of them spoke for them all when she said that Cristián had *yet again* managed to take advantage of his position as his mother's favourite.

Within months of the military coup, the bottom fell out of the egg market. Cristián was obliged to call another family meeting and confess that keeping poultry had ceased to be economically viable. After an initial silence, there was uproar, in which everyone blamed everyone else.

Cristián argued that, despite the failure of the poultry business, at least Santo Tomás was safe now that the right to private property had been re-established by the military government; and however unpleasant it might be, it would not be impossible to pay back the money they had raised on credit. He also defended himself by saying that if the *Unidad Popular* had remained in power – 'though we might like nothing else about it' – eggs would have proved a splendid investment. At the same time he was secretly asking himself why, since he had known perfectly well that Allende could not last, he had not taken that into account when he first mooted the poultry business. Such reasoning was elementary.

His sisters' main accusation against him was that in his personal use of the estate he had exceeded his function as manager: he was living in the ancestral home; he was making use of the family servants; he was inviting his friends there as if he owned the place; he was spending money on the park, riding the horses and generally living the good life.

Cristián does not deny these charges. But he does question their timing, since he had been behaving in precisely the same way ever since he had taken over the management of the estate, and nobody had complained before. He blames it on the failure of the poultry business, and on the changed political situation, because disputes among landowners, no matter how violent, no longer put the estates at risk of expropriation.

There was also his personal life. In 1974, he separated from Sylvia and was living openly with Soledad; the family did not approve. One of his sisters went so far as to accuse him of supporting three women with money made out of the estate, an absurd accusation since Paz had already remarried, and both Sylvia and Soledad came from wealthy families (and Soledad, in addition, was working for a living at the Departamento de Estudios Humanísticos). In other circumstances Cristián might have enjoyed his reputation as a Don Juan, but within the family it was accompanied by a growing animosity towards him.

By now, because of the poultry fiasco and his supposed misuse of the funds of Santo Tomás to support three women, his mother and sisters had come to distrust him to such an extent that they would not even listen to his proposals: 'It was as if they thought I was inventing everything and using Satanic powers of persuasion appropriate to literature, but not to farming.' The only way they could defend themselves against him was by blocking their ears.

'It became clear to me then,' Cristián writes, 'that, between hens and women, my choices had condemned me to the total loss of my old ascendancy in the family.'

Yet he kept on trying to persuade – or, as his mother

would say after the event – put pressure on his sisters. 'You seduce women,' she told him. 'It makes no difference whether they're your lovers or your mother or sisters. They're all obliged to follow you until you have sucked them dry. It's difficult not to end up ceasing to love you.'

Cristián had aroused his mother's anger by going to see each of his sisters individually and, as he thought, getting their agreement to bankroll the loan he needed. But for once his mother was not backing him. She also had a series of individual get-togethers with his sisters and these produced a very different result. They decided to sell Santo Tomás – and not to him. If they sold it to him, they (or their lawyers) argued, it would be like the poultry business all over again: they would all have to sign for the loan he would need in order to buy the estate. *His* lawyers disputed this, saying that only his signature was required. Subsequent experience showed him that a bank would have accepted either arrangement. But on this occasion he would not get his way. At a final family meeting, his mother formally announced that she had put Santo Tomás in the hands of an estate agent, an acquaintance of hers, who would be coming to value it the next day, and she asked Cristián to show him round.

'In spite of my age,' Cristián admits, 'I reacted childishly . . . Overcome with anger and sadness, I abruptly resigned as manager, stalked out of my mother's flat and went out to the estate . . .' From there he phoned Soledad. Then he loaded the car with his belongings and drove to Santiago, where he moved in with her and her children.

Ten months later, in May 1975, he bought the farm at Cabildo. He had not even waited to get his share of the proceeds of the sale of Santo Tomás, which came through a few days afterwards.

7

José Donoso, Chile's leading novelist, and his wife, María Pilar, invited me to lunch. The night before, I had been sitting at one of the outside tables at a restaurant in Providencia with Daniela, who had recently returned from Europe, and her boyfriend Alejandro, a political activist in the opposition to Pinochet, when a loud bang momentarily stunned us. 'Bomb,' said Alejandro, and the couple at the next table, who were just leaving, instantly blamed it on Patricio Aylwin, the presidential candidate of the *Concertación*, the centre-left alliance of Christian Democrats and socialists of many hues. The Donosos, who live in Providencia (described in José's novel *Curfew* as 'the green ghetto of the privileged classes'), also heard the explosion and their nephew Martín, a diplomat, said at lunch that the bomb had either been meant for Pinochet, who had been due to drive past that spot later in the evening – in which case some extreme left group would have been responsible – or was a scare tactic on the part of the right, who would put the blame on dangerous lefties and thereby hope to discourage people from voting for the *Concertación*. On the face of it, the latter explanation seemed the more likely, in that there would be little point in assassinating Pinochet at the very moment when he was about to stand down as President (though he intended to stay on as Commander-in-Chief of the army), but such uncertainties were commonplace.

José – or Pepe, as he is universally known – Donoso, like so many Latin American writers, lived for many years in exile, though in his case it was by choice. He left Chile in the Sixties and therefore had no first-hand experience of either Allende's regime or, until he returned in 1979, the military dictatorship. Yet in novels such as *The Obscene Bird of Night* (which pre-dates both: it was published in

1970, the year of Allende's accession) and *A House in the Country* (1978), a more self-consciously allegorical work, he explores the divisions both in individuals and in society that underlie Chile's unhappy transformation from what he remembers – as he described it to me – as 'the most benign country in the world' into the scary place he came back to at the end of the Seventies, when there were troops on every street corner and all the talk was of who had been killed or taken prisoner.

Adriana Valdés had told me, 'There are areas of darkness in Chile. The fact of domestic service is generally invisible, yet we would never live like we do if there weren't any domestic servants. It's absolutely fundamental, and yet it appears nowhere. Donoso concerns himself basically with servants, the master-servant relationship, the cruelty involved on both sides, and the terrible fact that everything that's clean and light and airy and intelligent is on one side, and everything that's the opposite is on the other; this implies sexual mutilation since people can never accept themselves as sexual beings, because that's on the other side . . . The only novel in Chile that really tells you from what zone, from what symbolic zone, the coup came, I think, is *The Obscene Bird of Night*.'

Donoso is a fastidious, some would say prickly, individual who perhaps suffers as much from under-exposure abroad, where he is less well-known than other big-league Latin American writers, as from over-exposure at home, where he is by far the biggest fish in a small pond. He told me an anecdote (and I came upon it again in *El Mercurio* a couple of months later, in a report of a writers' conference he had addressed), which suggests that he harbours ambivalent feelings about this. When he was living in Spain, he said, he entertained Carlos Fuentes with a story about Luis Buñuel and his sisters. A few weeks later, he was surprised to see the story appear in print under Fuentes's byline. He remonstrated with the Mexican, who brushed aside his objections, replying grandly: 'But Pepe, we are all writing different parts of the same great Latin American novel.'

Donoso is also ambivalent in his attitude towards Cristián, whom he does not rate highly as a writer: 'He was much more interesting as a person than as a writer,' he told me. He first met him when Cristián was a very young man, who wanted, 'as young men do, to pick my brains, not for ideas, but *how to do it*; he wanted of course to write the great novel . . .' Donoso remembers him then as tall, gawky and very elegant; he was particularly impressed by the way Cristián carried his duffle coat on his shoulder.

'We were very *cariñoso*, very friendly,' Donoso recalled. 'We assumed we would become very close, which finally we didn't.'

Perhaps each was a little disappointed in the way the other had developed. When he was young, Cristián had certainly admired Donoso's writing and he included a story of his in the issue of *Granta* he guest-edited at Cambridge (it is the outstanding story in the collection). But either because Donoso was an exile for so many years, and therefore did not share the experience of those crucial years of Chilean history, or because Cristián envied him his single-mindedness as a writer, if not his fame – according to Adriana, 'Everybody envies Donoso here in Chile' – his opinion changed and he used to dispute the value of his work with Adriana.

Donoso's view was that 'everything is *manqué* with Cristián . . . he didn't live to fulfil his promise. I think he was too much of a gentleman. It worked against him, the good life, this nineteenth-century life. In a way, it fostered many Latin American writers, who took it in their stride and made it work for them – like Borges, for instance. I think Cristián wasn't strong enough to put it to his own use: he always had to be doing too many things, cutting too many figures, seeing himself in the mirror, he was so insecure . . . Another thing I was careful with Cristián about: he was too well brought up to have strong feelings about many things. He was never rude, never annoyed, he always humoured people; he was always a nice guy – one has no business being a nice guy, really.'

Instead of the friendship that should have developed between these two well-born writers, there was a wariness based on mutual reservations. Donoso hardly needed Cristián's support, but he felt awkward when Cristián presented him with a copy of *El rincón de los niños* and he couldn't find anything nice to say about it. So they ended up seeing rather less of one another than they might have done.

Adriana Valdés, who cheerfully took on the role of being my mentor and guide to the Chilean social and intellectual scene, gave it as her opinion that Cristián envied Donoso his 'courage to be a writer, to really delve into his own most difficult and painful experiences.' Cristián was 'very true to himself erotically . . . The key to what he was, was in that sphere. He had to be true to his desire; I think he felt that his desire had a certain wisdom, which did not enable him to remain in a situation which was not a true one.' But 'he could not bring himself to deal with this in his work . . . it is one of the things that I miss terribly in his autobiography.'

Whether the reason for this absence is that he was, in Donoso's contemptuous phrase, too much the 'nice guy' or not is debatable. He does not spare his mother's or his sisters' feelings in his autobiography, when he takes them to task for selling Santo Tomás over his head. But in that particular fracas, he sees himself as the victim, more sinned against than sinning, whereas in his relationships with wives and lovers he could hardly lay claim to the moral high ground. Being true to oneself erotically has a Sixties-ish appeal but it may not be the best recipe for emotional stability or personal happiness. *El verano del ganadero*, Cristián's semi-serious attempt at an erotic novel, fails to engage with the complexity of his actual relationships with women and is, in Adriana's words, 'a silly erotic story' (she is equally scathing about an erotic novel Donoso wrote, also as a kind of *divertimento*).

To some extent, Adriana agreed with Donoso that Cristián had what an editor I once worked for called a 'niceness problem':

'He never really came to terms with a good many things because of his personal relationships. To be a writer, there has to be a very cruel being inside you whom you must unleash; all kinds of presentable beings may be there too, but there must also be this cruel person. That was why he needed a split personality: he was so polite that, after a while, he had to leave a situation very violently. He could not remain the gentlemen and still be true to this eroticism of his . . .'

After the break-up of his marriage to Paz, Cristián – as he had told me in the letter he wrote to me at the time – fell in love with Catalina, a woman he had known, and desired, when he was first in love with Paz. 'He was very much in love with her,' Adriana recalled, 'and it was a quite terrible relationship. He suffered a lot for her. I think she scared him to death . . .' It was partly in order to escape from this disturbing relationship that Cristián went to Cuba.

In the circumstances, his marriage to Sylvia seemed 'a very wise thing'. He was intent upon establishing a family. As Adriana saw it, 'Sylvia was, in a sense, Cristián's transaction with his mother'. She came of a good family; she was pretty, like all his wives; they got on well together; she was neither an intellectual nor sexually threatening. Adriana met her once, 'and all the time she was talking about how she didn't become pregnant, didn't become pregnant, *all* the time. It was quite an obsession with her. I think she rightly believed that unless she had a child or two of Cristián's they would never be a family.'

It was through Sylvia that Cristián met Soledad. Soledad's marriage had recently broken up and she was in a difficult position, having so many children and no work, so Cristián employed her as his secretary in the Departamento de Estudios Humanísticos. When they became lovers, they scorned to hide the fact, but Cristián was reluctant to end a second marriage: perhaps he felt that whereas to lose one wife might be regarded as a misfortune, to lose two would begin to look like carelessness. So, 'in his high-handed way', he tried to solve the problem by insisting on his need for both Sylvia and Soledad – a solution that was not likely to appeal to either of them. It infuriated Adriana, too, though she understood that it was his way of attempting to come to terms with an impossible situation: 'That is the sense in which I think eroticism was so important, the sense that it is something you can *never* wholly come to terms with.'

The trouble was, he could not make clean breaks, so he

left a trail of wounded women in his wake. No doubt he was to blame, but Chilean social attitudes did not help either. 'Friendly divorces are very uncommon,' Adriana said. 'Women's self-esteem depends wholly on this family thing; it's very hard for women here to get the idea that when a man leaves them he is not utterly destroying them. My experience of most women my age, school friends, etc, is that they value themselves only in terms of husbands – whether or not they have them, whether they have them now or had them once.'

In one of his essays, Max Beerbohm categorizes people as either 'hosts' or 'guests'. I asked Adriana into which category she would put Cristián.

'He was a host. To me, he was a host; when he was a guest he always arrived late and he always overstayed' – she laughed – 'whereas when he was a host he came into his own. Wherever he was, even in the tiny house he rented in the *pueblo* of Cabildo, he could be lord of the manor. It made other people very comfortable and gave him a role. He seemed to live both for himself and for the people around him; he was a very agreeable person.'

His love of conversation was one of his most endearing characteristics; but more than once it could have landed him in difficulties.

One day in 1975 or '76, for instance, when he and Soledad were driving north, they picked up a couple of young Dutch hitch-hikers. They all got on so well that they stopped and had lunch together. They talked quite openly about repression and censorship. But a private conversation is one thing; writing it all down on a *postcard* – which was what the Dutch couple, in their innocence, then did – is quite another. In those days all Chileans believed that their mail was being read; there may have been an element of paranoia in this, but the Dutch couple's postcard could easily have harmed Cristián and Soledad.

Sylvia got into trouble, serious trouble, for much less. Her only crime was to be visiting the house of a family which had a connection with Andrés Pascal Allende, nephew of the late President and leader of the *Movimiento de Izquierda Revolucionaria* (MIR), and very much a wanted man on both counts. Sylvia's wealth and privileged social position counted for nothing in prison, where she was given a hard time by both the authorities and the inmates, who instantly recognized that she was not one of them. When Cristián heard she had been arrested, he went to see all the people he knew who had any influence with the military and begged them to use it on her behalf. 'He was terrified,' Adriana remembered, 'absolutely terrified.' Sylvia was freed after a couple of months, but Cristián, who already had a bad conscience about leaving her for Soledad, was severely shaken by the whole grisly affair.

William Beausire was an Anglo-Chilean businessman, a young man far more interested in girls and sport than in politics, but it was his tragic fate to become a pawn in a deadly game of hide-and-seek.

He had three sisters, the youngest of whom, a ballet dancer called Mary Ann, was the common-law wife of Andrés Pascal Allende, by whom she had a daughter in January 1973. After the military coup the couple were obliged, like thousands of other opponents of the new regime, to go underground. By October 1974, the secret police, the infamous DINA, had become aware of the relationship between them, and agents started visiting the home of the widowed Mrs Beausire (her English husband had died in 1958) and interrogating her and other members of the family. That same month Mary Ann arranged with her eldest sister, Juana, to take her one-and-a-half-year-old daughter into asylum in the Italian embassy, while she remained in hiding with her lover. Juana herself sought asylum, along with her niece; and William decided to look for work in Europe so that, once he was established there, he could send for his mother and get her out of danger.

As an Anglo-Chilean, he had dual nationality and a British, as well as a Chilean, passport. On November 2nd, 1974, he flew from Santiago to Buenos Aires, en route for Paris. His mother accompanied him to the airport and then returned home, where she was promptly arrested by a number of DINA agents, armed with machine-guns. They searched the house and demanded to know the whereabouts, not only of her youngest daughter, but also of her son. As soon as they heard he had departed that afternoon for Europe, two agents started rummaging through Mrs Beausire's handbag, looking for the flight number and the name of the airline he was travelling on, and when they found them they left precipitately.

At Buenos Aires, William was requested over the loud-speaker to go to International Police Control. In his inno-cence he could not have suspected that the long arm of the DINA would reach out and pluck him off a perfectly legitimate flight to Europe and detain him – apparently in a lavatory cubicle – destroy his passport, remove his money, spare clothes and personal belongings, beat him up and virtually starve him, and then, days later, fly him back to Santiago as a prisoner in a military aircraft.

This was the beginning of a nightmare that only ended with his 'disappearance' eight months later. In between, according to the careful documentation of his story by Amnesty International in 1981, 'El Gordo', or 'Fatty', as William was contemptuously called by his interrogators, was subjected to the whole gamut of horrific tortures – 'electric current in every part of his body, sticks thrust up his rectum, suspended for long periods, etc.' – until his health was shattered and he shed so many kilos that his nickname became a mockery. He also suffered the atten-tions of a 'doctor', who tried to hypnotize him and brain-wash him with drugs; though when he resisted, this treat-ment was suspended. But still he was unwilling or, more likely, unable to reveal the whereabouts of Mary Ann and Andrés Pascal.

William's middle sister, Diana, was arrested a few hours after her mother. In her testimony, she states that at the time she was with a friend who was working for the Chi-lean government in the Diego Portales building (Diego Portales was made the seat of military government after the bombardment of the Moneda Palace, and it soon became a hated symbol of repression). This friend was Cristián's estranged wife, Sylvia. She was arrested with Diana and they were both taken out to a Chevrolet van, where they were blindfolded. On their way into deten-tion, Sylvia produced an identity card which established her credentials, but it made no impression on the DINA agents. The two women were put in separate cells at the detention centre known as Cuatro Alamos, but at eleven p.m. they were taken out – along with Diana's mother and the mother of Andrés Pascal, Laura Allende, the late President's sister, who had also been arrested – and driven elsewhere.

Their destination was a house in José Domingo Cañas Street that was used as a torture centre. Still blindfolded, they were taken into a room where they were ordered to lie on the floor and kept awake by guards who shouted obscenities at them. Eventually, Diana was summoned to interrogation. She was taken into what seemed like a large room, with many people talking and the clatter of typewriters. They sat her front of a desk and questioned her, gently at first, about her sister and Andrés Pascal. But when her answers failed to satisfy them, they started to scream at her, beat her and kicked her all over her body; they even threatened to torture her mother in front of her to get the information they wanted. It was some time before she was allowed back to the cell where, throughout the night, the women could hear the screams of other prisoners being tortured.

After that, Diana was shunted back and forth between Cuatro Alamos and the interrogation centre at José Domingo Cañas, or in the aptly named Villa Grimaldi. Once or twice she saw, or rather, since she was generally blindfolded, heard her brother, but she had no opportunity to communicate with him directly. An 'unnamed witness' – who could be Sylvia, since she states that she was arrested along with William's mother and sister – was able to exchange a few words with William once while she was washing dishes (for that she was allowed to lift her blindfold, so she saw how thin he had become).

Diana, her mother and Sylvia were all eventually released, and in June 1975 Mrs Beausire flew to England for safety on the advice of the British ambassador. William continued to be held hostage until July 2nd, when some DINA agents came to the prison to take him away. He had formed a close liaison with another detainee, Adriana Borquez, who was with him when these strangers arrived.

William told her he had no idea where they were taking him. She helped him pack his few clothes into a paper bag; then he kissed her goodbye, saying: 'Shit . . .' That was the last anybody saw or heard of him.

Two other witnesses, an architect and a lawyer, suggest one powerful motive the DINA would have for doing away with him: that officially he was not even in the country. The military had brought him back from Buenos Aires illegally and there was no record of his re-entry; that was the reason the authorities had denied that he was under arrest. In such circumstances, it was but a short step from being a non-person to ceasing to be a person at all.

The Chile Committee for Human Rights and the British Section of Amnesty International kept up the pressure to discover what had happened to William Beausire, and in 1979 a British solicitor, Geoffrey Bindman, went to Chile in an abortive attempt to find out. Meanwhile, the British ambassador had been withdrawn from Santiago in December 1975, following the more widely publicized torture of another British subject, Dr Sheila Cassidy, and two successive Labour Foreign Secretaries, Tony Crosland and David Owen, had made strongly worded protests. But in 1980, with the change of government in Britain, diplomatic relations with Chile were resumed and human rights issues no longer gained ministerial support.

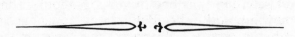

8

I arranged to meet Jorge Guzmán on the morning of December 4th, ten days before the elections. By now I was familiar, from watching television, with the three presidential candidates: Patricio Aylwin, the elderly, often rather mournful-looking – though constantly smiling – Christian Democrat leader of the *Concertación*, who was favourite to win; Hernán Büchi, the young technocrat who had resigned from the government in order to mount his campaign and had the dubious distinction of being Pinochet's man (perhaps that was the subliminal message of the slogan that adorned his posters: '*Es el hombre* – 'He's the man'); and Francisco ('Fra-Fra') Javier Errázuriz, who – without the aid of Tim Bell's minions, who were working for Büchi and monetarism – had come up with the best jingle of the campaign, 'No more blah-blah; vote for Fra-Fra', but was still very much the outsider in the contest.

Alywin's concerned grandfatherly image contrasted effectively with the Pinochet persona of the stern father, though Pinochet himself was busily projecting a more relaxed, smiling and grandfatherly image in keeping with the changed political situation he found himself in. Büchi, in contrast to these two old pros, was plainly ill-at-ease with the role assigned to him by the image-makers, that of a latter-day Beatle, long-haired, youthful and zappy. No matter how excitedly gangs of middle-class teenyboppers squealed whenever he appeared, Büchi still couldn't quite conceal his known preference for the loneliness of the mountaineer or the long-distance runner. He was like a startled rabbit dazzled by lights, an ascetic invited to an orgy.

He was easily upstaged by Fra-Fra, who was the joker in the pack, presenting himself as a self-made man penalized by the Pinochet regime for his honest endeavours – self-made? A man who shared the name Errázuriz with two nineteenth-century Presidents? His was the voice of sanity and independence, the charm and good looks of affluent and youthful middle age. But he was up against the big battalions: on one side the repressive forces of law and order, and on the other a – for once – united opposition intent on suppressing political differences at least until a workable democracy should be re-established. Fra-Fra was not going to win this time round, that much was clear, but next time maybe . . .

It had to be Aylwin. Most people I spoke to agreed on that, though few were wildly enthusiastic. Büchi, though personally by no means unsympathetic, was tainted by his association with Pinochet and the unfair advantage that gave him when it came to choosing sites for rallies and so forth. Yet, unpopular as the dictatorship might be, most people did not have any illusions about the likely effects of a return to old-style politics; a victory for Aylwin was a symbolic, rather than a practical, necessity: it would express the national desire for unity, a yearning to heal the wounds of two decades of undeclared and shadowy civil war.

From that point of view Aylwin was the ideal leader. His partial responsibility for the coup – as party president of the Christian Democrats he had rejected the possibility of an eleventh-hour agreement with Allende and initially had supported the military – and his subsequent *mea culpas*, enabled him, as it were, to purge the national guilt by taking it on his own shoulders. An awareness of this burden gave dignity to his performance as President-in-waiting even before his election.

Jorge Guzmán had suggested that we met at his office, so I made my way by taxi to a dilapidated building in an anonymous street where the remnant of the Departamento de Estudios Humanísticos was housed. When he saw that I walked with sticks, Guzmán apologized for dragging me out so far and worried that I might not be able to manage the two flights of stairs up to his room. The interior of the building was as bleak as the exterior and it brought home to me, more than anything Felipe Alliende or Guzmán himself might say, the moribund state of this once-thriving department. Yet Guzmán was a stimulating talker, and he soon made me forget these depressing surroundings as he evoked the glory days of the DEH.

He had given up university teaching to concentrate on writing novels when Cristián invited him to join the staff of his new department in March 1973. Jorge was very poor then, so he readily accepted; and he had never regretted his decision. The university at the time was in a state of upheaval because of the reforms: 'It was all meetings, day after day after day: something which did not happen in this department.' The DEH was a haven in which it was possible to 'study and discuss things and lead a university life in the traditional sense'. It was also a refuge for people who were at odds with the prevailing political orthodoxy, and though Guzmán himself was an *allendista* – 'I was for Allende, I voted for Allende and I supported Allende to the end' – he did not participate actively in politics and welcomed the respite the DEH provided. Cristián was 'the best chairman I have worked for in any university, and I have worked for some good ones . . . working with Cristián as a head was a pleasure at all times and in all senses. He was respectful, cordial, so refined.' But was he democratic? 'Not quite, no, he used to have things his way. Charmingly, but he did.'

Jorge had had considerable experience of teaching at the Pedagógico, 'and that really was a horrible place to be in . . . there was violence everywhere, insolence and even worse. It was part of the political outlook of the whole country.'

Even before the coup, 'life was very unpleasant in Chile for everybody', not just through shortages, though 'there were those queues for blocks and blocks'. 'Put it this way,' he said. 'You had to go and pick up your wife *every* day in the midst of tear-gas, bombings of all kinds, blood (not in the sense that later on there was blood, but people being hit, mugged, mistreated). You never knew whom you were talking to. There were all kinds of disorders . . . It was the atmosphere, the daily atmosphere, I mean, you woke up in an atmosphere of violence. You felt it to be violence. Later on, we found out that was not real, the real violence came later . . . [But] the atmosphere was very unpleasant for a person like Cristián, or myself. I was very displeased to be living in a country like that.'

What they didn't realize at the time was the extent to which they were being manipulated by hostile media, as subsequent research published in Canada has shown. 'If you look at the newspapers of those days,' Jorge said, 'on the front page of *El Mercurio*, for instance, in the upper half you will see a big photograph of somebody very prominent in the regime, and in the lower part a dog, teeth bared, with a policeman holding it – and that was *every* day, things like that, an association, something violent, a threat to the reader.' There was scaremongering; rumours were fostered that people were eating human flesh: a man had been dismembered and pieces of his flesh turned up in different parts of the country, that was the story; the implication was that you might be eating part of it. Such things became the subject of ghoulish jokes.

It was not surprising that Cristián was deluded, that he became so critical of the Allende regime at the end of those years: 'so much so that he participated in some initiatives sponsored by the military in the university, which he later regretted, but he did'. This was when he was called in, with one or two others, to 'clean up, politically speaking' the Department of Philosophy, his own *alma mater*, the Pedagógico, where he and Guzmán had first met.

'Now I must say that Cristián never persecuted anybody,' Jorge insisted. 'He went there in that capacity, but he went mostly to help people save themselves, or have a less rough time – in other words, he didn't take *any* personal advantage of *any* kind. He helped people who were interesting to me at the time, and to many other persons. But he was one of the men of the military. We talked about it because he was quite upset about this problem, and his view was that he was going to see that nobody was persecuted for reasons of politics, and if somebody was removed it had to be for academic reasons. I don't think he had any hand in removing people at all. Some had to flee the country – and of course he had no control over anyone's freedom or detention, nothing of that sort. No, he had only to do with the problem of who stayed at the university and who didn't stay. But he helped some people he knew avoid political persecution by personally recommending them and saying they were politically reliable.'

There was, for example, 'a professor here who was rather hated because he had participated in the Allende regime with some enthusiasm, and Cristián took him aside and told him, "Stay here, sit down, be quiet, don't teach, don't appear, don't publish, don't speak, don't think . . ." He was kept, I think, one year in silence and retirement, still getting his salary, which was quite something at the time. One of the worst ways the military had of persecuting people was to deny them work.'

Cristián made the same mistake that many, from Aylwin down, made at the time, and that was to think that he was collaborating with a regime 'which would hold power for only a few months and then go away and leave the thing to the civilians'. Jorge Guzmán (like Jorge Edwards) saw Cristián as 'a Christian Democrat at heart . . . an atheist Christian Democrat!' He was against dictatorships of any sort, and as first the months, and then the years, went by, he became increasingly critical of the military regime. He had never imagined such brutality, such violence and such repression and neglect of ideas would be possible. His way of distancing himself from the regime was to take risks to ensure that the people who worked under him enjoyed real academic freedom. Guzmán remembered a seminar they had all taken part in – he, Cristián, Enrique Lihn, Ronald Kay, and others – in 1974, in which they had discussed Marxist writers. Someone who came to that seminar had said, 'I don't know why you aren't in jail, the whole lot of you.'

To some extent Cristián was protected by being a member of 'the so-called Chilean aristocracy'. His ambivalent relationship with the military, his Military School past, also perhaps gave him a certain immunity: 'He was not *against* the military; I mean, he was not perceived by the military as an enemy, but rather as a sort of friendly fellow who didn't agree with them, that was all.' Then, 'his personality was nice, and he was always ready to serve his friends', which was another sort of protection as the repressive apparatus of the state worked through denunciations and 'nobody would ever have thought of denouncing him'.

The magazine *Manuscritos*, to which Guzmán contributed an essay, was another way of cocking a snook, not just at the military authorities, but at the older generation of teachers as well. They objected to something 'so free and so unacademic', but there was an underlying seriousness in the attempt to make widely available, through newsagents' kiosks as well as bookshops, avant-garde art, epitomized by the *Quebrantahuesos* of Nicanor Parra, an irreverent series of collages, or *happenings textuales*, made up of newsprint and pictures. These were not, in fact, new: they dated from 1952. But in reminding people of another Chile, 'a Chile where Communists and conservatives had dinner together and attended the same clubs and were friendly with each other, a Chile in which nothing was really dangerous', they performed an important function.

Jorge was out of the country when Cristián resigned as chairman of the department, or was forced out: 'I had been going to the States for quarters, or semesters, to breathe because here the air becomes unbreathable . . . I wrote him a letter and advised him not to resign. The rightists began to spread rumours about him never being available, his neglecting his duties and things of that sort. But I think it was political. D'Etigny was also losing power very, very fast.' Pinochet himself wanted to destroy the university; he did not approve of a state university. So he always appointed as rectors people he thought unlikely to oppose its destruction. It was also rumoured that he had a personal grudge, that he had failed to complete the requirements to be a lawyer. Whether or not that was true, 'the military have always disliked the University of Chile'.

They destroyed the Pedagógico, they 'didn't want first-class work in the humanities to be done in any university, they didn't like it. They knew that eventually we would begin teaching Marx and Bertold Brecht again, and they wanted especially to take away from the University of Chile the capacity to teach humanities. So they used any argument to deny us the right to teach what we wanted to teach. First, they said, no, you cannot be two departments [the DEH and the purged Pedagógico, the Department of Philosophy] because that would be a duplication of activities and that is not permitted in this country – which is absurd, I mean, do you have to take away the planes from the army and give them all to the air force? Then they took away from the University of Chile the capacity to teach teachers, which was traditionally something the university had done . . . You can do nothing in Chile if you are a Doctor of Philosophy; you can't teach anywhere, you can't even teach in secondary schools because they ask you, "Where is your professional title?" "I'm a doctor." "Well, you may be a doctor, but you're not welcome here." '

Jorge was becoming impassioned; he asked me if I had visited the Faculty of Philosophy and, when I shook my head, he said: 'Well, don't. It is pitiful: they have almost no students; they have no assistants; there are no young people doing any work there; the classes are sometimes taught, more often they're not. That's because everyone is apathetic. I mean, you know you are teaching something nobody needs and nobody can make any use of. No professional historians, think of that, in Chile. No experts in literary theory: what would they do? No professional philosophers, to go and think in their homes without any money for the rent? It's part of the persecution that the whole Universidad de Chile has suffered. All the other universities can train teachers, graduate teachers; we cannot.'

Because of this, many of Jorge's friends who had recently returned from exile had been unable to get work. They were not being discriminated against, as some were inclined to think; it was just that there were no positions and no money. Jorge hoped that, after the election, things might improve.

The subject of exile was beginning to strike me as crucial to the intellectual debate about opposition to Pinochet. To stay or not to stay, that was the question.

'In the very beginning,' Jorge Guzmán recalled, 'those who stayed, myself among them, were hated by those outside. Not only that, we were slandered. We were called traitors, collaborators and many other things. That was quite understandable. Then it changed, and we became small heroes for having stayed . . . When I went to the States in '75 for the first time [after the coup] I had to prove I wasn't a fascist, which was rather unpleasant. They looked at me incredulously and said, "Are you staying there?" If you said yes, you had to follow up with an explanation, which I didn't . . . The real stupidity was cleaving the country in two, the good ones and the bad ones; with the good ones being the ones who had left.'

In his own case, Jorge felt that the advantage of having stayed in Chile through the Pinochet years was that 'I have become reconciled to reality'. Before the coup, he said, 'I lived among dreams, historical dreams, political dreams. I thought we could do anything. I mean, we were such fools we thought this country was independent. That is really to delude oneself to the point of lunacy. We thought we were independent. Now I live in reality and I have found out that I have to work with it, in it, for it, from it, and I think that's the main difference between us who stayed and those who went.'

Another thing he had noticed about the people who stayed was that they had ceased to be interested in themselves. 'If you had come to Chile, let's say, in 1970,' he told me, 'you would've found us very passionate in political matters, but at the same time you would have detected that all of us were linking our personal bourgeois development to whatever was going to happen. So it was *me* who was so important, *my* personal development needed a change of politics. Not any more. I don't think any of us gives a damn about ourselves. I have heard with these ears a Communist in 1972 say, "How come the government doesn't take good care that we, the intellectuals of the regime, are supplied with cigarettes? They're so scarce we have to queue up and lose our precious time. They should make sure we have our cigarettes every day . . ." That was the Chilean way in those days. We all thought first of ourselves, our development: we were going to be perfect, we were going to be brave, we were going to be beautiful, we were going to be intelligent, therefore we needed a change in Chilean politics . . .'

An obvious focus of attention was intimate relations: ' "How interesting are the problems I have with my *pareja* [partner]." It was normal for someone to say, "I have this horrible problem" – and the wife was right there – "but we're working on it and . . ." As if it was of any interest to you. But it was – that was the odd thing.' The attraction of the Allende years, and the five or so years before, was their sense of freedom – not just sexual freedom, but the feeling that 'the world was there waiting for new initiatives, that you could change and turn yourself into something you never dreamt you could be'. Jorge was affected by the spirit of the age to the extent that he seriously considered moving into the wilds, to the south perhaps. Some people he knew actually did it. There was the son of a well-known psychiatrist, for example, who fell in love with a married woman and whose story, as Jorge told it, sounded like a parable:

'They ran away to an island in the southern part of Chile where they led a beautiful life. He had everything: a little hut made of logs; with his hands he carved the cradle of their first child. And then the coup came, and one day she said, "I think I'll go back to Santiago for a few days," and she did. She didn't come back when she said she would, though. Months went by, then she came back and said, "You know what, I met my ex-husband and he's very rich now. He's become the director of a bank and I fell in love with him again, so I'm going back to my old life." I think that is very typical of what was happening in those years: you went out into the wilderness and began living with nature, and then, when the coup came, you realized your limits were narrower than you thought. Her reality was the reality of wealth and influence and power . . .'

The coup split up many families, whose different members, even husbands and wives, found themselves on opposite sides of the political divide. Jorge himself was divorced then. 'Most of my friends are divorced,' he told me. 'Most of their marriages are from after the coup.'

It changed lives in other ways, too. Jorge had been, on the one hand, an academic who specialized in medieval Spanish literature and had published a book on the subject; on the other, a novelist. And he pursued these two interests quite separately. Now he thinks that you cannot, or should not, do that; also, that you have to belong where you belong: 'Here in Chile you must be interested in Chilean history, in Latin American history and in Spanish history, with a view to knowing who you are, and to seeing the reality that surrounds you daily, humbly. We have been living for centuries trying to hide the fact that we are descendents of Indians and Spanish. The Spaniards and the Indians who are our grandparents are denied by us; we don't like that. It is crazy but Chileans, and Latin Americans in general, despise, with equal force, the Spaniards and the Indians – '

With equal force?

'Not equal, no,' Jorge admitted. 'More the Indians, but also the Spaniards. If you are a Chilean and your name is Jorge Guzmán MacPherson, you never forget the Mac-Pherson, but if you are called Jorge MacPherson Guzmán, you surely forget the Guzmán! [In Spanish the mother's surname follows that of the father but in practice it is often dropped.] I think this is one of the things that is characteristic of Latin Americans, the fact that we are all half-breeds. Maybe some of us are pure Indian or pure European as far as genes are concerned. That we are both things is cultural; these are the remnants of the Indian past in ourselves.'

The point, as Jorge has come to see it, is that Latin Americans are *different* – hence the title of his latest critical book, *Diferencias Latinoamericanas*, which has two pictures of himself on the cover: in one he is bearded and wears a conquistador helmet, and in the other he is clean-shaven, in a woolly hat with earflaps.

'Everybody perceives us as different,' he said. 'You would see us as belonging to a different culture, wouldn't you? We don't want that; we want you to see us as English. It is stupid; I mean, how could I be British? But we want the Germans to see us as Germans, the Americans to see us as Americans, and so on. Also the French: there are quite a few of us who are French at heart. Well, this is what I don't like. I want to see myself as different, I want to be perceived as different, and I want to study that and to write about that and to deal with Latin American texts as different.'

This recognition of difference was the first step towards establishing an identity, and it was in ways like this, Guzmán believed, that 'we have reaped enormous bene-fits from Mr Pinochet: people work better now; we have been silent for a number of years and people have been working . . . I think we will have profited from these years of silence and violence and all that.'

We had been talking for over two hours and I had switched off the tape-recorder when Jorge suddenly said something that had me reaching for the machine and asking him to say it again.

'I said,' he duly repeated, 'that nothing has really hap-pened to me during these sixteen years: I've not lost any-body, any relative or friend; one or two friends are now living outside the country but that's all. I never suffered anything. I've not been persecuted, nothing. Only once, I was under arrest for eight hours. Those eight hours were because I was visiting a friend who had been taken to jail and I was retained there for a little interrogation – quite cordial and friendly and respectful. So nothing has hap-pened to me. Yet I don't think there is anything in my life that is half so important to me as the coup. The one thing that has changed my life is the military coup; the rest is nothing compared to that. Up to that point I was interested only in medieval Spanish literature; now I cannot understand it, how could I?'

9

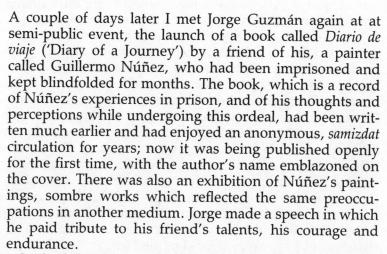

A couple of days later I met Jorge Guzmán again at at semi-public event, the launch of a book called *Diario de viaje* ('Diary of a Journey') by a friend of his, a painter called Guillermo Núñez, who had been imprisoned and kept blindfolded for months. The book, which is a record of Núñez's experiences in prison, and of his thoughts and perceptions while undergoing this ordeal, had been written much earlier and had enjoyed an anonymous, *samizdat* circulation for years; now it was being published openly for the first time, with the author's name emblazoned on the cover. There was also an exhibition of Núñez's paintings, sombre works which reflected the same preoccupations in another medium. Jorge made a speech in which he paid tribute to his friend's talents, his courage and endurance.

In the following Sunday's *La Epoca* he mentioned Núñez in an article in which he analyzed the continuing popularity of the low-life drama *La Negra Ester*, based on the vernacular verse of Roberto Parra, another member of that extravagantly talented family which includes Nicanor and the singer, composer and folklorist Violeta, who committed suicide. After its initial run, the show had been on a European tour and was now being staged again on the Santa Lucía hill in Santiago.

Guzmán attributed its success in part to the contrast it afforded to the stream of North American films and soap operas shown on prime-time television over the past sixteen years, in which the worst thing that could happen was that the central heating broke down or some-one had a headache. The power of television was such, he argued, that it did not matter if the viewer was poor, an Indo-Spanish half-breed, didn't speak English, and hadn't enough money even to make a trip out of his neighbourhood, 'he still feels that he belongs to the wonderful Anglo-Saxon, prosperous and cosmopolitan world, to the international jet set'. That this feeling was only skin-deep, however, was triumphantly established by the audience's enjoyment of the authentic and vital, if delinquent, world of *La Negra Ester*.

But more important was the fact that, in *La Negra Ester*, 'no one judges, no one is judged'. In contemporary Chile, according to Guzmán, 'a Manichean discourse has sought to impose on us an ideological terrorism in which dialogue is impossible. One is either a *patriot* or a *traitor*, a fully paid-up member of the human race or a *humanoid*'. (The habitual use of this last word to describe the left by the navy's member of the Junta, Admiral José Toribio Merino Castro, had become a grim joke.) Works of art such as *La Negra Ester* or the paintings of Guillermo Núñez resisted this simple-minded, black-and-white vision of the world. When Núñez's pictures were exhibited in Europe, particularly in Germany, people were puzzled: they wanted to know which of the two tensely opposed figures featured in so many of his paintings represented the good, and which the bad. Núñez replied that he did not know; he could not even say which he identified with.

At the book-launch Jorge told Adriana, who had taken me there, how surprised he had been to find himself talking to me about things he had never spoken about to anyone else. Later, Adriana teased me about my role as catalyst. It was a great advantage being a foreigner, she said, since 'we Chileans are flattered that someone from abroad should take an interest in our country'.

That same evening she introduced me to a friend from Uruguay who was staying for a few days in Santiago. Germán Rama was a colleague as well as a friend, since he was director of the Montevideo office of CEPAL. The three of us had dinner together in a restaurant and conversed in a mixture of Spanish and English. It was the first time, Adriana said, that she had heard Germán speak English; his French was fluent but his English was more or less on a par with my Spanish. With Adriana's help, however, he tried to dispel my profound ignorance of his country: he told me, for instance, that up to the Second World War

Uruguay had been virtually a British colony, made up mainly of sheep farms. But many things had changed since then. As in Chile, there had been a military dictatorship from 1973; but democracy had been restored in 1984, five years earlier than in Chile.

Given the position of this tiny country, hemmed in by two politically impossible giants, Argentina and Brazil, it had done well to maintain its independence – there was a saying, 'When Argentina sneezes, Uruguay catches pneumonia' – but as a trading partner Argentina now came well down the list, after Brazil, the EC, the United States and China. Most Uruguayan immigrants from Europe over the last century had been of peasant stock: Germán's own forebears were poor people in the province of Galicia in north-western Spain. But Uruguay prided itself on its education system and Germán and his brothers all became writers and intellectuals.

When he and Adriana first met, there had been considerable mutual misunderstanding: Adriana could not make out why Germán was always talking about 'the nation' and 'the state'; and Germán just laughed when she described herself, using a phrase of Cristián's, as a '*bala perdida*' (literally, lost or stray bullet, but more colloquially perhaps, 'oddball') of the aristocracy. In Uruguay, there was no aristocracy, not even a 'so-called' one because, as Germán put it, 'there are no grandparents'. Hence the importance of the state, or nation, which was the equivalent of the family in the less egalitarian Chilean society.

Germán felt that Chile had changed dramatically over the last two decades. Intellectuals, he said, had more influence in Chile than anywhere else in Latin America; but, whereas in 1970 they were all spouting ideology of one sort or another (mostly one sort), now there was a much more realistic and conciliatory spirit abroad. He was impressed by Büchi, but agreed that Aylwin had to win the presidential election since Büchi was fatally compromised by his connection with Pinochet.

The election was now only a few days off and the candidates were holding their final rallies in Santiago. Aylwin's was on Sunday, December 10th. Paz, who attended it, phoned me afterwards to say how moved she had been;

and what I saw of it on television certainly made it look impressive. That night the moon was almost full and, as I walked back from the Chinese restaurant where I often ate, I enjoyed the carnival atmosphere in the streets: boys and girls in T-shirts leaning out of the windows of cars and vans and waving *Concertación* flags; a veritable cacophony of hooting and tooting, despite the presence, albeit low-key, of *carabinero* vans with letters and numbers stencilled in white on their sides, reminding me of the ammunition boxes we used to have in the army; and the roads and pavements of Providencia littered, but *littered*, with leaflets flung from passing vehicles with gay abandon.

But this was nothing compared to the aftermath of the big Büchi rally the next day, when the several lanes of traffic in the main avenue ground to a halt and the non-stop blaring of car horns competed in decibel level with the songs pumped out of the loudspeaker vans at full volume. It was like a cavalry charge, momentarily halted, with a sea of Büchi flags fluttering from those car windows which were not filled with the buttocks of youngsters jammed so tightly together that there was nowhere else to put them. This fervent display did not, of course, mean that Büchi would win, merely that Providencia was his stronghold; 'the green ghetto of the privileged classes' was celebrating its man – in the awareness, perhaps, that it would have less cause to do so after the election.

On December 14th, I wrote home:

Tonight, as they say in old newsreels, there is dancing in the streets of Santiago: the election is over; Aylwin has won. It's after 11 p.m. and I've just been out on [Avenida] Providencia. The noise is deafening: the usual beating out of a tattoo on car horns, flag-waving, etc. But there's also a huge sense of relief. You really do feel that it's the end of an era; it's as if people still don't quite believe it, as if they are coming out of a long, dark tunnel and blinking in the unaccustomed light. I guess the celebrations will go on most of the night. Yet most of the day the place was deserted. I walked out to post my last letter and everything was shut up. Later, too, when I went out again to buy a newspaper, nothing but the kiosk was open, not even the restaurants and bars which stay open all weekend . . . But now the noise is constant; even up here in the flat, which, fortunately, faces away from Providencia, I can hear it quite plainly . . .

The next day was unusually cloudy, so perhaps the gods were unimpressed with the People's Victory – *Gana la gente*, 'The people will win', was the Aylwin slogan. I went to a restaurant where, earlier in the week, I had met the poet Diego Maquieira and a young novelist called Carlos Franz; they had suggested we foregathered again on the Friday to celebrate what they were confident would be a triumph for Aylwin. Diego, a gregarious soul with wild black hair and granny glasses, told me he did not enjoy work and was appalled by the Anglo-Saxon need to be working all the time: he preferred wine, women and . . . poetry – and he didn't believe in taking the last of the trio too seriously either. As the son of a diplomat he had spent the years of his boyhood in New York and Mexico; he also went to English and American schools, from all of which, he proudly told me, he had been expelled. He spoke good English, liberally sprinkled with 'fuckings'. Despite misgivings about the sincerity of his professions of friendship, I liked him; his evident enjoyment of life was infectious.

Carlos Franz had a more serious mien, in keeping with his training as a lawyer. Both he and Diego had known Cristián, and Carlos, who in some ways reminded me of the young Cristián, still gratefully remembered the good advice Cristián had once given him: to stop writing book reviews for *El Mercurio*. A third man present at this gathering was of an older generation. Ernesto Rodríguez had hardly known Cristián, but he had been a close friend of his second wife, Sylvia, whom he described as 'a tall beauty with long, straight, black hair'. Ernesto, who seemed to have fingers in several pies and contacts in several worlds, had been headmaster of a private school and now taught part-time at the Catholic University.

Then there was a good-looking, globe-trotting German called Günther, with blue eyes and long, dark, hippyish hair. His revolutionary world view prevented him from welcoming either the demolition of the Berlin Wall – which had had as huge an impact in Chile as elsewhere,

vying with the election for top billing on the TV news – or
the electoral success of the *Concertación*. Whereas in Chile
the freeing of Eastern Europe from the tyranny of Communism was seen as the mirror image of the defeat of the
dictatorship at home, Günther could only see the dangers
of a reunited Germany, so little faith did he have in his
own countrymen; and as for Aylwin's victory, well, he
could not applaud anything that reduced the possibility of
revolution. In his politics, as in his personal style, Günther
was locked in a Sixties time-warp.

Our oddly assorted lunchtime gathering failed to produce much in the way of a celebration. But then, as everyone said, this election was something of an anti-climax;
the real excitement had been the previous year's plebiscite: that had been the decisive victory over Pinochet, this
one merely confirmed it.

The election, however interesting in itself, obstructed my
research; few people were free to talk about Cristián while
crucial matters of state were being decided. Forced inac-
tivity increased my sense of isolation and I was more than
ever dependent on two friendships, one old and one new.
The new one, with Adriana, was uncomplicated by a past;
but this was not the case with my friendship with Paz.

Rightly or wrongly, I began to suspect that Paz felt burdened with a responsibility she had not sought and
resentful of either it or me. When she dropped by with a
pair of my trousers which Inés had washed for me, I taxed
her with this, saying that I thought she had me bracketed
with Cristián and for that reason, unconsciously or otherwise, she resented me. Paz denied this, but admitted that,
by a strange chance, my arrival had coincided with a painful stage of her analysis, when she was obliged to relive
the happy period of her life in England. She also admitted
to some lingering resentment towards Cristián, but
claimed that it was mainly in relation to Daniela. So we
moved on with some relief, on my side at least, to talk
about Daniela and never again referred to any feeling of
resentment that might have built up between us. After
that, indeed, there was no occasion to: whatever obstruc-

tion there had been to the re-establishment of our old intimacy vanished in that instant.

Gradually, too, I was making new friends. Ernesto Rodríguez, whom I had met at the café with Diego Maquieira, visited me and talked about Sylvia, who had apparently married again after the divorce from Cristián and now had a daughter; she was living with her second husband in the United States. When she had been in prison, Ernesto had done what he could to help her. 'We all have some rightist friends,' he told me. About Pinochet, he said it was impossible to understand his hold over the *haute bourgeoisie* unless one was aware of the tremendous importance of family in Chile. Pinochet was a father-figure, capable of kindliness but also terrible and vengeful.

After we had drunk two glasses of beer, Ernesto suggested I accompany him to a farewell party for an English adviser to the Büchi campaign, which was being given by a wealthy young Cuban expatriate called Mario Lobo, who had been brought up in London but now lived in Santiago. As Diego had also mentioned this party the week before, I was curious to go. Ernesto phoned from my flat to ask if I might come and Mario said, 'Sure, bring him along.'

The party had evidently been going on for some time when we arrived. Diego was having an intense conversation with a young woman on the stairs; other couples were dancing. Mario, the host, seemed slightly detached, in a Gatsby-like way, from the proceedings; but then he had only flown back from New York that morning. Neat and dapper in appearance, the most striking thing about him was the pair of red canvas shoes he was wearing. He described himself to me, in his exquisitely enunciated English, as 'happily divorced'. Certainly, he was surrounded by young and beautiful people of both sexes, among them one of Soledad's sons, who welcomed me with great friendliness, and his tall, blonde girlfriend. The guest of honour, the English adviser to Büchi, was a young giant of a man whose precise role in the Büchi campaign I never discovered. Büchi himself was nowhere to be seen, but then conspicuous consumption was hardly his style; he was famous for the frugality of his personal habits.

A few nights later, I took some other new friends, the *Guardian* correspondent Malcolm Coad and his Chilean wife 'Coca' Rudolphy, the daughter of a retired admiral, to the Chinese restaurant I frequented, which was owned, it transpired, by friends of theirs. We ordered a special dish, to which only Malcolm did justice since Coca eats little and I had lost my appetite. I was already suffering, though I did not yet know it, from an attack of gastro-enteritis that would confine me to bed over the Christmas holiday. Coca, *petite* and lively, is an actress; she had met Malcolm in London, where she was in exile for several years following her capture, torture and imprisonment by the military regime. That evening she told me the story of her arrest, a grim story but with an element of farce which the actress in her exploited to the full.

Coca lived in a rented flat in Providencia. In the immediate aftermath of the coup she provided refuge for an ex-priest, who was a leader of the revolutionary left, but he had already moved on by the time the secret police, having got wind of his whereabouts, raided the flat. So they had to be content with arresting Coca. They marched her down the four flights of stairs, one big man on either side of her, holding her under the elbows; she was so small that her feet, she said, barely touched the ground. Then they shoved her into a car and drove off with a lorry-load of troops in attendance.

Her one thought was that she had in her bag a slip of paper with the address of an elderly woman who was offering a 'safe house' for people on the run, and that she must somehow destroy it before the secret police discovered it. She remembered from films she had seen that the way to do that was to crumple it up and swallow it. So, very slowly and without looking down, she eased her hand into her bag and, by feel alone, identified the scrap of paper; but, just as she was pulling it out, one of her captors ordered her to hold out her hand. All she had time to do was to slip the paper between the top of her jeans and her knickers.

When they arrived at the detention centre, she was

taken in for questioning. She was not afraid, because she was sure that her name would protect her: all she had to do was identify herself as the daughter of Admiral Rudolphy and no harm could possibly come to her. Her interrogators, however, were uninterested in her antecedents. They began by asking her gently where the ex-priest was; then, when she refused to tell them, they turned nasty and ordered a guard to bring a blindfold. She told them she wore contact lenses, and they said they didn't give a damn what she wore; but one man took pity on her and provided the cap of an aspirin bottle for her lenses, and it was he who, when they took her into another and, she sensed – for she could see nothing – smaller room and tied her on to a slatted frame, fastened her right ankle loosely.

Before that, however, they had ordered her to take off her trousers, the first stage in a ritual of humiliation that was quite lost on Coca, who was so intent on not revealing the piece of paper with the address on it that she removed not just her jeans, but her knickers as well. Her persecutors were astonished at her apparent forwardness; then, when she pointed out that her right ankle was loose (she did it for fear that they would discover it for themselves and over-compensate by tying it too tightly), they said rather huffily, 'We're not going to rape you, you know.'

What they did next was no joke, of course: after mocking her exposed body, they set about torturing her with electrodes attached to her genitals, nipples, earlobes, gums, temples. But though it went on for hours, she did not break. She decided to die rather than talk, and once she had made that decision she knew she could resist, no matter how great the pain. When it was over, she was in no state to care about anything; she had to be dressed and helped to a cell. She had a vague memory of overhearing the guards say something about finding a scrap of paper; but they must have thought it unimportant and thrown it away because the woman was never visited or raided.

Coca was kept in solitary confinement for a month and in prison for over a year, but she was never tortured again.

I asked her if she thought she could have endured another session without breaking.

'I don't know,' she said, 'I really don't know.'

10

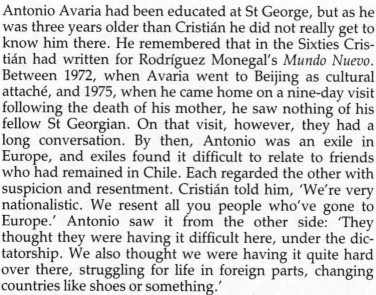

Antonio Avaria had been educated at St George, but as he was three years older than Cristián he did not really get to know him there. He remembered that in the Sixties Cristián had written for Rodríguez Monegal's *Mundo Nuevo*. Between 1972, when Avaria went to Beijing as cultural attaché, and 1975, when he came home on a nine-day visit following the death of his mother, he saw nothing of his fellow St Georgian. On that visit, however, they had a long conversation. By then, Antonio was an exile in Europe, and exiles found it difficult to relate to friends who had remained in Chile. Each regarded the other with suspicion and resentment. Cristián told him, 'We're very nationalistic. We resent all you people who've gone to Europe.' Antonio saw it from the other side: 'They thought they were having it difficult here, under the dictatorship. We also thought we were having it quite hard over there, struggling for life in foreign parts, changing countries like shoes or something.'

Adriana had introduced me to Avaria at the book-launch we went to. After that I had phoned him, only to be told he was in hospital. So I waited another week or ten days and phoned again. This time Antonio himself answered; he told me he had suffered a minor heart attack, but now he was home again and I was welcome to come and see him. We met one morning soon after Christmas.

'For me,' he said, 'the coup destroyed my future, my life – luckily, it didn't destroy my family, like so many others. I always thought it was a good answer of Che Guevara's when he said, "I used to be a doctor", because now he was something else. For several years after 1973, being in China, in Portugal, in Germany, in Switzerland, I would have answered, "I used to be a writer".'

Now that he was back in Chile, had been back for two years, he wondered whether he would not have been wiser to have stayed, or at least come back sooner, even if it had meant taking risks. He reckoned he would have written more, 'would have developed myself more, and my duty towards my country more here than outside, though there was not a day when I wasn't thinking about Chile, or dreaming of Chile, or trying to do something for Chile'.

The outside battle was important from the point of view of propaganda and information, not to mention such practical initiatives as the collection of money in Europe for the families of victims of the regime. The economic boycott might seem unpatriotic in Chile, but in Europe it was seen as part of a life-and-death struggle. Now Antonio was inclined to feel that exiles like himself had suffered from an *Altona* complex, by which he meant that they were like the elder son in Sartre's play of that name about a family of rich German industrialist collaborators with the Nazis, who emerges from hiding after years of believing – wanting to believe – that Germany has been reduced to a wasteland, only to discover that it is rich and thriving. In Chile there might be more poverty than ever, but the country had been modernized and, 'although I still think it was a puppet regime and these people just shot their way to power', that was the reality now. The coup was already a generation, two generations away, and the majority of people who had voted in the elections were too young to remember it.

Psychologically, one of the hardest things for a returning exile to get used to is what might be called the Rip Van Winkle effect. In Avaria's words, 'People here had got used to living without me – this "me" of course is a plural "me". Even best friends. They have got on with their professions. Then of course new generations were taking over . . . If you came back after so many years, you were out.'

Antonio remembered St George with affection. It was not the sort of Catholic school where there was compulsory Communion every Friday and Mass on Sunday. The

American Fathers took their pupils to the beach and were themselves quite happy to be seen in their bathing costumes; the boys considered them friends, though perhaps these friendships were superficial in the way South Americans and Europeans thought quintessentially North American. The Fathers certainly simplified things: the Holy Trinity, for example, was an aeroplane with three engines . . . 'But we loved them because they were free, so free that unfortunately they didn't force us to speak English; and we loved them because they didn't care about a student's background, how rich he was, or how aristocratic – that was the American democratic way.'

The school had outstanding teachers in the historian Mario Góngora (who later taught in Cristián's department at the university) and Roque Esteban Scarpa, founder of the Literary Academy of the Young Laurel, a kind of creative writing course which many students, including the young Antonio, continued to attend after they had left the school. Scarpa had such influence that none of his students was ever failed by the examiners; and he did not just teach what was on the syllabus, but included writers such as Proust and García Lorca.

But for Antonio, as for Cristián, it was the Pedagógico that revolutionized his political outlook. There it was not a case of visiting *poblaciones* and doing good works among the poor, as the priests in their paternalistic way did, but of forming friendships with poor people, discovering they too could be poets, visiting their homes and learning about their problems at first hand. The Fifties were not as political as the Sixties became, after Cuba; but the Pedagógico was full of exiles from the dictatorship in Venezuela, and from elsewhere. Students there became conscious of their heritage for the first time; at secondary school they had devoted six years to the study of European history – *six years* – whereas they had spent just two seminars on Chilean history, and none at all on the history of Latin America.

Another link with Cristián was the literary workshop at the University of Concepción (set up by Fernando Alegría, a Chilean-born writer and professor of Spanish American literature at the University of Stanford, and funded by the

Ford Foundation), which both aspiring writers attended in the early Sixties: Cristián had been on the first-ever course – where he had met and become friendly with Enrique Lihn – and Antonio, who went to Germany on a scholarship after graduating from the Pedagógico in 1957 and returned to Chile in 1961, was on the third. 'It was like Scarpa when we were teenagers', Antonio recalled, 'but with real professional writers: for example, in my case, we had José Donoso as one of the team.'

Cristián often invited friends home to Santo Tomás, and Antonio went there one day with a girlfriend. He still had a photograph, probably taken by this girl, who also, no doubt, penned the ironic inscription: 'In those days the famous writer, Antonio Avaria, used to spend some time in the house of the famous writer, Cristián Huneeus'. 'We were not children,' said Antonio, laughing at the memory, 'but we did those childish sort of things.' Yet there was also a sense in which they took themselves quite seriously, feeling that they belonged to a talented generation of intellectuals and writers, people such as Poli Délano and Antonio Skármeta.

Avaria was reluctant to criticize Cristián's writing, taking refuge in the first person plural: 'We always thought that something was lacking. The first books were well written, intelligent, but lacking in dramatic force, let's say.' He thought of Cristián 'as someone who was preparing himself, who hadn't given what he might have given'. Had he lived, he might have produced memoirs like Pérez Rosales or a big novel like the Sicilian Lampedusa.

But Antonio did not sound convinced. Perhaps he was too burdened by a sense of his own failure to live up to high promise – in his case intensified, if not caused, by sixteen years of exile – to sit in judgment over someone else. 'Lack of commitment,' he said, 'is a problem for all upper-middle-class Chileans. One of the few to have surmounted it is José Donoso. It's a kind of malediction of the Chilean twentieth century. Being privileged, with a secondary education in a private school, you really feel, when you are sixteen or so, you can try anything with some success; you don't admire effort too much. That's really stupid, of course. It was typical of many of us that we didn't bother with academic qualifications; when something didn't interest us, we neglected it: if you didn't get a degree, well, you didn't get a degree. It was more interesting to lead a bohemian life than to get a doctorate – because everything was possible: even without those things, you could become anything here. In Cristián's case, of course, on top of that he had land.'

If the combination of privilege and dilettantism – success too easily achieved and contempt for hard work – was deleterious for writers and artists, in the political arena it was fatal. As Antonio put it, 'Maybe we deserved this Pinochet. It's very hard to acknowledge, but he brought to the surface something that was very Chilean, but was very hidden: this brutality, this anti-democratic society. This society was officially very democratic, but it wasn't, huh?'

At the end of our interview, Antonio told me that before I had arrived that morning he had spoken on the phone with Armando Uribe, a poet and international lawyer, who had been the Chilean ambassador in China when he was cultural attaché. Uribe had expressed interest in what I was doing and would be at a certain café in Providencia from midday if we cared to join him there. I accepted the invitation with alacrity, as I was already curious about Uribe. He had returned only recently from exile in Paris, where he had taught international law at the Sorbonne; and he had been extensively interviewed in the Chilean press following the publication of a new volume of poems. Only the day before, Paz, who had photographed him for the magazine *Reseña*, had suggested I contact him; she was sure I would find him intellectually stimulating.

We took a taxi and arrived at the café before Uribe. Antonio ordered coffee, while I sat at a table and kept an eye on the door. I recognized Uribe the moment he walked in; this was not difficult since his appearance was both distinctive and already familiar to me from photographs. To start with, he was always impeccably turned out in a suit, collar and tie in a country where conventionality in dress was not usually taken to such dandyish extremes; then he sported a long cigarette-holder, through which he chain-smoked Kent cigarettes (a surprising lapse, this, for someone so fiercely anti-American). But these were externals. His photos made him look deeply melancholic: he had a long, lugubrious face, reminiscent of an old-fashioned Spanish grandee, with hair parted in the middle and brushed back firmly on either side of his head. Here was a man who – far more than Cristián, I felt – had taken Mann's image of the artist as bureaucrat as a model.

Yet the moment he opened his mouth he was transformed. He spoke with such humour and vivacity that all traces of melancholy vanished; he became a kind of sprite, twinkly, malicious and very entertaining. The man whose photographs had reminded Malcolm Coad (who had yet to meet him) of a Victorian undertaker turned into a schoolboyish prankster, trying, for instance, to force cigarettes on Antonio, who had been obliged to give up smoking after his heart attack. And that was not the only way he teased his old friend and colleague.

'Now,' he said, as soon as the three of us sat down together, 'I'm going to say things about Cristián Huneeus that Antonio said I shouldn't say: one, he wasn't a real writer, he was *hechizo*: you know what *hechizo* means?' (*Hechizo* carries the double meaning of 'manufactured, made' and 'artificial, false, fake'; in this context it was the equivalent of 'being an artist', *botarse a artista*). I was intrigued that Uribe should come up with this idea right off, but I was a little wary since he was so clearly a hostile witness. Well, I had listened to enough encomiums of my friend; I should also be aware of the case for the prosecution. According to Uribe, not only was Cristián not a good writer, he was none of the other things he claimed (or didn't claim) to be either: not an aristocrat – 'there's no such thing as a Chilean aristocracy' – not English: that too was an affectation, a very Chilean affectation; he was a *criollista*, a countryman, a landowner. In fact, if Uribe was to be believed, he was nothing more than a poseur.

Uribe apologized – quite unnecessarily – for his English, which, he said, he had given up speaking sixteen years ago because of the American involvement in the Pinochet coup. That had incensed him to such an extent that he had written a book about it, *The Black Book of the American*

Intervention in Chile. He was both a Catholic and a leftist, but not a Marxist. He was careful to point out that he had not been Allende's ambassador to China, but the ambassador of the Republic of Chile.

We arranged to meet again in a couple of days. He told me to phone him that Friday morning before nine o'clock – 'I'm always up by seven', he added, suggesting a rather un-Chilean eagerness to be up and doing. Then, brisk and businesslike, he departed.

I was impressed.

I phoned as we had arranged, and Armando Uribe suggested we met at the Café Santos, which was in a basement in the centre of town.

'It's very quiet,' he said, 'and I like it because it's exactly the same as it was when I first knew it forty years ago.'

I was there on the dot of ten, and Armando swept in shortly afterwards, striding purposefully towards the table where I was already seated. It was the very one, he recalled, at which he and Cristián had once held a conversation – the longest they ever had – about the Congress for Cultural Freedom. Perhaps this was when Cristián was writing for *Mundo Nuevo*; if so, he ignored Armando's advice, which was to have nothing to do with a magazine that was an instrument of US influence, to say the least. This was before the revelation of CIA involvement, and Uribe's anti-imperialism was then as much a question of identity as of politics. He, too, had been at St George, but when he first went there the school had belonged to the diocese of Santiago; and neither he nor his parents had approved of its sale to the Americans: 'My family looked on Americans as imperialists, as foreigners who wanted to make us as they were. We didn't want the American way of life; we were profoundly irritated when the Americans called themselves American: they were North Americans and we were not *Latin* Americans – absolutely not – we were *South* Americans . . .'

He remembered that he had had one other long conversation with Cristián, and that was when Cristián had sought him out in Paris shortly before he died. Armando had been surprised to hear from him, since they had never been close. Soledad had been with him, looking and behaving like his nurse. For the first hour Cristián had sat on a chair, but then he'd had to lie down on a divan, 'So the rest of the conversation was dominated by this figure with his eyes closed talking agonisedly and telling trivialities in his agony. That is the image that I have of him.'

The waiter came over to our table and greeted Armando – I was about to say 'familiarly', but that would imply the intimacy of the *tu* relationship in Spanish, rather than the formality of *Usted*; and one of several things that Armando deplored about the new Chile was the immediate assumption of the *tu* mode of address: it was almost as bad as the way people who scarcely knew one another – if at all – had taken to kissing like old friends when they met. The waiter was friendly but formal, his attitude of a piece with the old-fashioned and dignified atmosphere of the Café Santos. Armando ordered tea and, after the waiter had gone, handed me a scrap of paper on which he had scribbled a comment on Cristián's autobiography, which he had taken the trouble to read before coming to meet me:

> A Paradox: what is interesting in his book is that he gives enormous importance to an object which lacks interest, which is completely uninteresting: namely, himself. He treats himself as if he were a celebrity, a very modest celebrity revealing that he is, after all, only a human being like anybody else.

Still, this was the only book of Cristián's that Armando had read right through. It revealed, he thought, 'enormous insecurity . . . But he treats his insecurity as if it were a virtue'. It used some of the same methods – in particular, ending with a letter – that Uribe himself had essayed in an autobiographical work, *Caballeros de Chile* (published in 1978 in French under the title *Ces "Messieurs" du Chili*), though this was probably less a question of influence than a coincidence: the form of Cristián's autobiography, with its several beginnings, reflected the uncertainties of a generation. That it was no longer possible to write a linear autobiography such as González Vera's excellent *Cuando era muchacho* ('When I Was a Boy'), which was published in the Fifties, was 'a matter of identity and the disintegration of society'.

Cristián's concluding letter to Hernán Rodríguez, who was an exile, was an apologia, an *apologia por vita sua*. 'The interesting thing about those who remained here,' Armando said, 'is that, whether or not they were guilty of connivance with the Junta, they feel guilty. I'm sure, though I don't remember Huneeus's words in Paris, that what he gave me were explanations of the reasons why he remained.' In Uribe's view, the people who remained, like Cristián, were just as exiled as himself: 'At the beginning, for them, we were the guilty ones. With the passing of time, and with the atrocious conduct of the Junta, things changed and they began to feel guilty. Because they felt guilty, and because they had thought we were guilty, they finished up thinking they were the wronged ones and not us, who were the victims who survived.'

Armando was scornful of the argument that the economic boycott of Chilean goods could be seen as unpatriotic or harmful to Chile. According to him, it didn't take place: 'There was no boycott. It was purely rhetorical.' Far from feeling, like Antonio Avaria, that he should have come home sooner, he professed a certain 'arrogance', a sense of superiority – 'because the people who stayed were more or less accomplices of the regime'. But then Armando qualified as a succesful exile: he admitted to being part of 'a very privileged group from an economic and social point of view'.

What angered him most in Cristián's autobiography was the claim that only thirty per cent of the population supported Allende's government and seventy per cent opposed it.

'Huneeus is very wrong, maliciously wrong about thirty per cent and seventy per cent. At the beginning, Allende was chosen by thirty-six per cent, thirty-five per cent, more than thirty per cent in any case. Then he was ratified by Congress, by more than fifty per cent of Parliament. In the municipal elections in March '71, the majority was over fifty per cent. In the parliamentary elections in 1973, the *Unidad Popular* had forty-five, forty-six per cent. It was never a case of thirty per cent and seventy per cent, no. The problem for the right and for the United States was that his support might have increased to over fifty per cent during '73–'74. That was the main reason for the coup d'état. Normally, they would have waited until '76 and the new elections. They could at least have waited until after September 11th, 1973, when Allende was going to offer a plebiscite over the crucial points under discussion. They didn't want that because he might win. One doesn't know. But it was not thirty and seventy per cent. From my point of view that's the worst of the ethical attitudes that Huneeus takes in the book.'

Armando had not been predisposed in Allende's favour because his father had a low opinion of him. He met him a few times in the course of his diplomatic career between 1968 and 1973. His first impression was of a very sociable man – in a high-society sense. Allende had the reputation of liking women. He was a shrewd politician; he only vacillated when he had no alternative, and he knew how to manipulate things internally. But he had no room to manoeuvre against the will of a great power like the United States. He was 'absolutely non-charismatic: in that sense he was a very old-fashioned Chilean politician. But he had a profound sense of history. He knew he was fated. Several times he repeated, "I will not leave the Moneda except" – I will give you the phrase, a bit vulgar, in Spanish – *en piyama de madera* [in wooden pyjamas]. Not a bad image. He said that several times; so unconsciously he knew he was fated.'

He saw himself – according to Uribe – in the context of the historical and literary traditions of the country: 'Now the main heroic tradition is a tradition of defeat. You've probably heard of the naval hero of Chile, Arturo Prat: well, he was defeated! Allende acted as Arturo Prat. Also, if he did commit suicide – and there will always be a doubt – he acted as Balmaceda, the defeated President in 1891. And so on. The principal heroes in the *Araucana*, the epic poem by Ercilla, are defeated and tormented, and die in torment.'

Uribe also had theories about Pinochet. In his *Black Book*, he had likened Pinochet and the Junta to *dueñas de casa* – mistresses of the household. To explain this, he proceeded to give me a history lesson. Chile, he said, had always been a *tierra de frontera* (frontier state) in two senses: first, there was continuous war with the Indians in the south; and secondly – or was it thirdly? ('Having lived in Paris,' he said, 'I have this habit of numbering my points, but because I am South American I always get the numbers wrong') – it was the frontier defending the heart of the empire, Lima in Peru. The cradle of Chile was not Santiago; it was the southern part as far as Concepción that gave the country its character.

'There,' he went on, 'the men of the household went to war, so the household was dominated by women, the woman, the mother – better, the *materfamilias* – who had to control everything: the behaviour of the family, the economics of the family, the prestige of the family. So this type of woman was obliged to acquire a sadistic quality. In this there is also an element of mixed race, the mixing which took place in the sixteenth century. Now, sadism was used by women to control households made up of people who were not entirely loyal or trustworthy because of mixed blood and the appalling conditions in which the society was being born. This sadistic archetype is much more important in Chile than it appears. Some writers have said that Chile is a matriarchy, mainly in the upper classes, but also in the lower classes. Well, even today the man of the house frequently disappears, to look for work. That's the reason why I think the military acted as *dueñas de casa*.'

Armando claimed to have been one of the more impartial Pinochet-watchers; he had shocked the left by his insistence that Pinochet was both an intellectual and a consummate politician. Of course, he said, 'to be an intellectual in the armed forces, one doesn't have to be an intellectual in the wider sense of the word, just as you don't ask a geologist to read Hölderlin'. Pinochet was an intellectual in the sense that all officers who passed through Staff College were; but he was exceptional in having written – and published – two books, one on geopolitics and the other military history. When the former was assessed in an article in a French magazine, the writers concluded that Pinochet was rather well-informed on matters of geography and that, though his ideas might be repugnant to a contemporary readership, they were perfectly orthodox up to about 1940 and were currently being revived by reactionaries such as Le Pen in France and Enoch Powell in Britain. At least there was a conception of the state in the book and that, Armando said, was *de rigueur* for someone ambitious for power. What other twentieth-century Chilean President, he liked to ask, had written two books before he came into office? Only one – Frei – and one of his was a book of speeches.

Pinochet was also 'the best political manager this century'. He had 'a profound psychological penetration, *conocimiento de hombres*, and a capacity to manipulate particularly those layers of Chilean society which have been political agents during this time: that is to say, the military itself, the armed forces, and the caste – not class – that has profited from the regime. With them he has acted extremely well.'

It seemed to me that Uribe was in danger of overestimating Pinochet, just as the left in Britain had overestimated Mrs Thatcher when she was at the height of her power and popularity. For instance, he had written an article, a sort of mock-obituary of Pinochet, published in *Le Monde Diplomatique* in August 1986, in which he put forward the theory that Pinochet had 'a profound dilemma' in that he could not be less than Allende: because Allende had died in an armed struggle, defending his legitimacy, Pinochet might one day be obliged to defend *his* legitimacy to the death.

No sooner had Armando aired this idea, however, than by an extraordinary coincidence there was an assassination attempt – the *atentado* of September 7th, 1986 – in which militants of the Manuel Rodríguez Patriotic Front ambushed Pinochet's motorcade and killed five of his bodyguard. Uribe was of the opinion that 'if the *atentado* had been successful everything would have been different. I am absolutely in agreement with what the bishop said after the *atentado*; he said, "These people will be considered heroes in the history of Chile." '

He added that it was still impossible to say such a thing publicly; it would be politically untimely for, despite the elections, 'the dictatorship continues'. But it was what many people thought.

*

The puzzling thing about the Huneeus family, for Armando, was its links with the Military School. Between the years 1850 and 1950 roughly, army officers by and large were recruited from the older provincial families. So what was a family of relatively recent immigrants of some intellectual standing doing, sending two generations of male offspring to the Military School? The explanation that Cristián offered in his autobiography, that – in Uribe's words – 'this class saw the need to enter the Military School to protect itself from the social and political dangers it faced' struck Armando as a good one, though rather far-fetched. It might apply in the case of this particular family, but it was not generally true.

Genealogy, Armando said, was as essential to an understanding of Chile as history. The role of family was a tremendously important one. From the time of the *Conquista* almost down to the eighteenth century there was in Chile a nobility, not an aristocracy. But with immigration in the eighteenth and nineteenth centuries this nobility was transformed into a *proto*-bourgeoisie (Armando apologized for the pedantic term), nostalgic for nobility. There still remained the older families imbued with the standards and outlook of nobility but without means – *venidos a menos* (come down in the world) – that provided many of the leaders of the left, including Allende. Armando could trace his own ancestry back to the sixteenth, seventeenth and eighteenth centuries, and contrasted his lineage with that of Cristián, whom he characterized as 'a real scion of this proto-bourgeoisie, immigrants in the nineteenth century mainly'. In Chile, he said, 'nobody speaks of these things, but everybody knows them'.

Later, Mario Valenzuela, another international lawyer and diplomat well versed in such matters, put this in perspective by telling me that in Chile, unlike in the United States, say, each new wave of 'aristocracy' displaced the old. Rather than acquiring additional status through longevity, old families – like old people – were simply pensioned off.

Before we parted, Armando Uribe expressed a desire to meet Paz again. He had liked the photos she had taken of him. So I arranged a small drinks party at my flat, to which they both came, along with Adriana Valdés, Malcolm Coad and Coca Rudolphy. Armando dominated the conversation, which was in *castellano*. Even though I could not understand everything that was being said, I sensed the mounting tension between Adriana and Armando when the latter spoke slightingly of Nicanor Parra. Because he was more famous than Cristián, or even Enrique Lihn, Nicanor Parra was a controversial figure whose outspoken opposition to Allende and initially enthusiastic welcome to the military has earned him considerable enmity on the left.

But this was not just a political argument; it had a literary and a religious dimension too. Adriana's critical writings identified her with the avant-garde in Chile, the kind of thinking that had produced the magazine *Manuscritos*, for instance, and many experimental works, particularly in the visual arts; but in politics and religion she was a sceptic. Armando, by contrast, however radical his politics, was a traditionalist in literary and religious matters. He was a friend of the priest and member of the Vatican Council and *Opus Dei*, José Miguel Ibáñez – another contemporary at St George, who wrote under the pseudonym 'Ignacio Valente' and was the country's most influential book reviewer, the Cyril Connolly, say, of *El Mercurio*; and Valente had not endeared himself to Adriana by his consistent hostility to the work of Enrique Lihn. In the small world of the Chilean intelligentsia, political, religious and literary arguments inevitably became personal.

Armando visited me again the following morning after I had phoned to tell him he had left a bundle of notes and addresses in my flat. He stayed for a cup of coffee and paid me a backhanded compliment by attributing to me 'a diabolical curiosity'. To others he put it about, more whimsically, that I was a 'spy'. But then, according to the great Neruda, whose early diplomatic career had been spent in such outposts of the British Empire as Ceylon and Burma, all Englishmen belonged to the Secret Service.

11

Like Armando Uribe, who had suggested he contact me, Mario Valenzuela had pursued a successful career abroad and had only just returned to Chile. He was far from certain that he would remain: he had given up a good job in the United Nations Maritime Agency in Greenwich; he and his wife Milka had a daughter married to an Englishman and living in London; and there was a possible post in Cambridge in the field of international law . . . It would depend on how the Aylwin administration regarded former diplomats who had been in exile. Valenzuela had been the top official in the Foreign Service during the period of the *Unidad Popular*; he had been director-general. He had never been able to make up his mind whether or not he'd *had* to leave the country following the coup, but after a few weeks of uncertainty he had gone anyway, initially to Sweden, where he remained for almost a year, until he got a short-term teaching contract at a college in the United States. With the money he earned there, he came to the United Kingdom, where, after an unhappy interlude in Cardiff, he got the United Nations job in London.

Chubby-faced and bespectacled, Mario Valenzuela looked younger than his grey hair indicated. From 1959 to 1961, he had been third secretary at the Chilean embassy in London; then he had got a scholarship to do research at St Antony's College, Oxford, where he and Milka were living when Cristián and Paz were first in London, and then in Cambridge. Mario's relationship with Cristián at that time was not a good one. He admitted to me that he had been 'very much prejudiced against the social group Cristián represented', which was the class to which all the people in the embassy belonged. 'It was a time,' he recalled, 'when the government was very right-wing – not compared with the present one, of course! Now I think I'm probably completely in agreement with it, but then I thought it was very right-wing. One changes with experience.'

Mario found the young Cristián very arrogant. He said, 'When I am with an arrogant person I become arrogant too. So it was not a very successful friendship. When we parted after one meeting, I thought, "Why am I playing this game, when really I want to be with friends . . .?" One of our characteristics, in my experience, is that we treat life as a game; even after this experience [of the dictatorship], we Chileans are frivolous, show-offs. Maybe Cristián thought I was a show-off; I thought he was – at the beginning. Thirty years ago, with Chileans he was very much in competition, so I didn't feel very comfortable. "Why am I competing with Cristián?" I'd say. It was a competition in all fields. Probably at the time I had read more than he had read. I also thought that his experience was very limited. For me at the time it seemed almost childish to write those little stories about the high bourgeoisie at the seaside or in the countryside; it was of no interest whatsoever. But afterwards he changed . . .'

As I listened to Mario, I was reminded of nothing so much as what Cristián himself had written to me in that far-off time when he described the London he knew – 'that microcosmos of Chilean life' – as 'a most depressing pit of jealousy, competitiveness and envy' (envy, Mario told me later, was 'the Chilean vice') and went on to say: 'We Chileans are petty and provincial and savage. One sees a bit of them, just a bit, and leaves them exhausted by the amount of emotional energy spent in coping with them . . . And this kind of thing brings out the worst in oneself and one becomes another of them. The trouble is that one *is* one of them. By this I mean that I am by no means free of our kind of animosity and aggressiveness . . .'

When Cristián returned to England in 1985, he visited Mario and Milka, 'and we understood each other much better', Mario recalled. 'When he was well, which was most of the time, he was a very mature character. I realized that for him the period when we had both been living in England was very important; he remembered things I had said at the time which I had completely forgotten. I very much appreciated this historical pilgrimage; I think it was the beginning of wisdom.'

The rapport that developed between Mario and Cristián, despite their very different experiences, reflected a consonance of thought which had replaced the rivalry of their youth. Both had become political sceptics; Mario, when he talked to me, had been reading a book of interviews with the ex-Secretary of the Socialist Party in Allende's time, Carlos Altamirano, which had just been published in Chile, and he was moved to comment: 'All these socialist politicians: ambition and posturing – a good word, posturing. I don't believe in politicians. I consider myself more conservative now than I've ever been. At the same time I think that everything I feel is more genuine.'

Despite his years abroad, Mario had kept in close contact with Chile, obsessively following all that was happening there (through the UN he had been able to visit the country once every two years). The biggest change he saw was in the way that money had become the sole measure of success.

'Cristián was not typical at all,' he said. 'Neither are we. It's our tragedy, Cristián's and ours also, that we are in some way exiled in Chile. Because this is not a white country. The European element may predominate in the world the foreigner sees; but if you go to Valparaíso, well, it's Third World, completely Third World, with very primitive mixed blood. Or the countryside.' That was where Cristián's experience as a landowner was valuable: his recognition 'that all these literary things were useless if they were not rooted in real life, the life of work and contact with real people.'

The morning after our conversation, Mario phoned to say that he had been re-reading Cristián's autobiography, which he had described to me the day before as 'the only good book he wrote', and he had one question and one further comment. The question was: 'Why did he not write in his autobiography of the years *after* 1973?'

The obvious reply would be because of censorship, or at any rate self-censorship, given that the book was written during the darker days of the dictatorship. But I am inclined to think there was an even more compelling reason, and that Mario himself unwittingly provided the answer in his comment, which was that 'the purge in the university haunted Cristián'.

Hernán Rodríguez had been Cristián's friend since the Fifties. (Mario Valenzuela had known Rodríguez in Washington in the Sixties: 'He arrived at the embassy as a Christian Democrat, though a very left-wing one. No one knows why he became a Communist'.) It was to Rodríguez's family estate in southern Chile that Cristián had gone to write a novel after he had dropped out of the School of Architecture at the Catholic University in 1956. Two decades later, when he was at the University of Columbia in New York in 1976, Cristián heard that Hernán was in Rome on a visit from Moscow, where he had gone at the time of the coup, and wrote to him there. Rodríguez's reply, he tells us in his autobiography, was affectionate but rather disparaging about 'my bourgeois condition, transcended by him, or so he supposed, in Moscow'. Cristián was stung into writing a lengthy reply – the letter with which he concludes his autobiography. It concentrates on his conduct as director of the Departamento de Estudios Humanísticos up to the fall of Allende. He describes the exercise as 'a sort of examination of [my] political conscience'.

He became director in August 1972, he explains, as a result of a stalemate between the supporters of the *Unidad Popular* on the left and the people of the centre and the right, who were united in their opposition to the *UP*. In order to avoid a bitter and self-destructive electoral battle, the left had offered to vote for him *en masse*, knowing that he would also be acceptable to the centre and right. So he was elected unanimously. His line was that it did not matter to him whether lecturers were Marxist or conservative; what mattered was their academic ability and the quality of their writing. When he took over, he tells Rodríguez, the department returned to work with some relief.

He asserts that many people would have been hard

pressed to say which side he favoured. But *he* never had any doubts about his role, which was to maintain the same thirty per cent – seventy per cent political balance in the department as existed in the country (figures that aroused Armando Uribe's fury), to try to achieve a measure of agreement between people and to reconcile conflicting interests: that was the most effective way of opposing 'Allende's totalitarian programme'.

But the years 1972 and, still more, 1973 'were not times for words or persuasion'; people were already accumulating sandbags, helmets and firearms in their homes, their factories, offices and estates. Nevertheless, in the DEH they stuck to words and persuasion; at least, Cristián did. It was, he says, a curious experience. Engineering students, 'who couldn't always manage dates', accused him of seeing himself as 'Louis XVI, monarch of the fifteenth century'. They also characterized the DEH as an 'ivory tower', something that Cristián did not dispute: 'In a certain way, that is what intellectual life always is.'

As director, his most provocative gesture was to remove a librarian, who was a *UP* supporter, at the same time as he got rid of a book-keeper of the opposite persuasion; in the new, expanded department he was running, neither, he felt, was up to the job. He was not sacking these people, who were anyway on attachment, merely returning them to the central university pool. The book-keeper accepted his fate with a good grace; not so the librarian, who had hysterics and locked herself inside the library with a kettle, a mug and a jar of Nescafé. For the time being, Cristián did nothing; he just waited. Then, one evening after the woman had gone home, he summoned a locksmith and had the locks changed.

When the librarian arrived the next morning and could not get into the library, she had a tantrum. But that was merely the beginning. Some 300 employees of the university marched up to Cristián's office on the ninth floor of the faculty building, demanding to know why he was getting rid of her. Cristián listened patiently to the deputation of twenty who squeezed into his small office, while the remainder crowded the corridor outside, and then explained that the expansion of the DEH meant that it needed a librarian and a book-keeper of its own. The deputation wanted to know why he would not appoint the present incumbent. Cristián asked if they were referring to the book-keeper or the librarian, or both, or to some third party perhaps. Taking advantage of the confusion caused by his question, he went on to say that the DEH required an experienced and skilful book-keeper and a librarian with a background in the humanities rather than in mathematics and physics.

In the ensuing argument, every time the deputation spoke in defence of the librarian Cristián expressed puzzlement over why they did not also take up the case of the book-keeper – until he began to wonder if he was not over-doing it. He was saved by the arrival of lunch hour, at which both his office and the corridor suddenly emptied. After this skirmish, he felt a certain pride in seeing his name appear, misspelt, on the walls of university buildings: 'This is not your country estate, Uneus, and we officials are not your farmhands'; and, more threateningly, 'Landowner and bourgeois prick – watch out for the passing of the plough, *gringo* Hunneus.'

For a day or two nothing happened, then early one morning the *UP* took over the faculty and would not allow anybody in. Hanging from a tree just inside the main gates was a rag-doll with Cristián's name on it, which was set alight and burned. The rector summoned Cristián and asked him how he saw the situation developing. Cristián replied that, no matter what, he was not backing down. The rector supported him and said, 'Let's see what happens then.'

'What happened,' Cristián tells Hernán Rodríguez, 'was strangely prophetic.'

The *UP* – students, academics and civil servants – staged a sit-in at the faculty and told both Cristián and the dean, Enrique d'Etigny, that they would not budge until the librarian had been reinstated. In the subsequent negotiations, Cristián decided to avoid all theoretical discussion and not even to raise the issue of the book-keeper, which would only infuriate the *UP*. It would be better to concentrate on the librarian's lack of qualifications for the post, and at the same time express disbelief that such a small matter should paralyze an entire faculty.

The two sides confronted one another across a table, and neither was prepared to give way. It might have gone on like that indefinitely – with the participants repeating their roles with minor variations, as in a long-running play – if the *UP* contingent had not suddenly taken off in the middle of one morning and left the faculty building eerily empty. The sit-in ended on the last day of the month: why?

The reason was that the computer which processed the payslips of the entire university was housed in that building. If the *UP* had continued to occupy it under the pretext of fighting on behalf of one well-connected librarian, nobody, not even *UP* supporters, would have got their month's salary. Cristián could not suppress a smile at the thought. After that, he writes, 'everything went smoothly. Not for Allende, however. Nor for the opposition. At bottom, not for anyone or anything except the daily routines of Estudios Humanísticos.'

The lesson of the episode, as Cristián spells it out for Hernán Rodríguez's benefit, was that in any contest between the political and the disciplinary a militant Marxist had no alternative but to choose politics. The only possible – if not the only desirable – end was to obtain absolute power, in the university and elsewhere. The political struggle within the university was a microcosm of the larger battle going on in the country as a whole. As long as there was a Congress and a private sector of the economy, the *UP* government would do its utmost to destroy both, while those who were anxious to uphold liberty would be bound to defend them. 'It was not relaxing,' Cristián recalls. 'And curiously, all this violence was between people who knew each other and bumped into one another daily.'

Shortly after the fracas over the librarian, Cristián was invited to the birthday party of a relative, whose wife's younger brother had been one of the leaders of the takeover of the engineering faculty. As soon as Cristián set eyes on this youth, whom he describes as 'timid and at the same time pedantic', he demanded to know exactly what role he had played in the takeover and, more particularly, in the occupation of his office (where Cristián had discovered a trail of minor destruction and disorder, and mounds of dog-ends on the floor). He wanted to know how many nights had been spent there, since he had also found the tank of his paraffin heater empty. The young man coloured with embarrassment and swallowed his words, but Cristián would not let him off the hook until his relative came up and separated them, putting an arm around each and reminding them that they were there to celebrate his birthday.

'For Christ's sake, knock it off,' he said to Cristián. 'Don't forget that if the talks that are now going on between Patricio Aylwin and *el Chicho* [Allende] fail, if the Christian Democrats don't come to an agreement with the *UP*, then the military will move in and this brother-in-law of mine is going to have to get out of Chile.'

Though Cristián is intent on giving the impression of having been above the fray – of holding seminars on Henry James while Santiago burned – stories like this, which he cannot resist telling Rodríguez, undermine his credibility. But then Rodríguez was no longer the friend he had once been, and in Cristián's fictional portrait of him in *El rincón de los niños* (written at much the same time as he was writing his letter to him) the mask of irony slips and reveals a much rawer feeling. According to Gaspar's (Cristián's) mother, 'Martinez' would go far in life:

> What the good woman perhaps failed to take into account in her prediction was the infinite gamut of possibilities contained in the notion of distance . . . on September 10th he left on a journey of rapprochement with the brotherly peoples of the Soviet Union, on the 11th he signed a contract with Radio Moscow, and to this day that libertarian station broadcasts nightly on the airwaves of the world *the irascible and desolate evacuations of his bowels* [my italics] . . .

A large man, both physically and in terms of presence, Enrique d'Etigny chain-smoked throughout our conversation. I went to see him at the Universidad de Humanismo Cristiano, of which he was rector until he was appointed to a higher post by the Aylwin administration. This university was one of many private universities to have mushroomed all over the country in recent years. As far back as 1981 legislation had opened the way for the creation of private universities, but until 1988 they had to have the approval of the Ministry of the Interior, which – unlike the Ministry of Education – could reject proposals without explanation. As a result, only three new private universities had started up before 1988. After that, when the Ministry of the Interior was no longer involved and the fate of the government itself hung in the balance, the number rapidly increased to around forty. 'So we are educating the rich,' d'Etigny said. 'The universities were free until '73; they started charging after that and now, I would say, are more expensive than public universities in the States.'

D'Etigny was happier talking about university structure and reform than about individuals. Though he had been close to Cristián (Soledad told me later that Cristián had regarded him as a second father), he was rather vague about both Cristián's elevation to director of the DEH – 'I don't have a very clear idea of that particular moment, whether this was an election or an appointment' – and his departure – 'I don't remember it in detail'. Had I asked him about Cristián's stint as an *interventor* he probably would not have recalled that too clearly either. But he gave me a full and exact account of university politics and administration throughout the period.

'I was dean of the faculty of mathematics and physical sciences,' he said. 'The school of engineering was the popular name for the faculty, just as the faculty of philosophy and education was traditionally known as the Pedagógico. Our main school was engineering and we developed, first, science within the faculty, then we considered that it was important to have people in the humanities trying to understand what science was and what engineering technology was. This was in the Sixties. The curriculum then, alas, was very rigid, so we created a space for students to take courses in the humanities. We started with philosophy as the central idea; and the first director, Roberto Torretti, actually moved to philosophy of science. Then we expanded to other areas, literature, history, and Cristián came into this group . . .'

What was the motive, I asked d'Etigny, for transforming the centre into a department?

'Well,' he replied, 'it was under all the reform programmes in '68 to '70. At that moment there were great discussions about the future of the university. Expansion had been very rapid: we'd been growing at a rate of about thirteen per cent a year, which is quite fantastic. First, there was the development of centres outside Santiago, *colegios regionales*, and then *sedes* [seats; headquarters] – all part of the University of Chile network. In Santiago the idea was to create four campuses, based on the model of the University of London: integrated campuses which would each have humanities, physical sciences, biological sciences and a medical school. And we created the *sedes*, North, South, East and West. In medicine, for instance, there actually were four hospitals working, so we immediately created four faculties of medicine – one for each campus. In the *Sede Occidente*, where we were, we gathered engineering and sciences, the whole faculty of mathematical and physical sciences, as the core, and there was part of the faculty of economics as well as medicine, and part of the faculty of architecture and applied arts. We used the Centro de Estudios Humanísticos as the basis for a faculty of humanities, and then we created the department directly under the *sede*, and started to take students.'

D'Etigny made it all sound like an academic, rather than a political, decision, whereas my understanding had been that the creation of four independent *sedes* was a deliberate attempt to make centralized, political control of the university more difficult, and that the DEH was set up in direct opposition to the *UP*-dominated Pedagógico. D'Etigny agreed that there was a political aspect to these decisions: in the case of the four *sedes*, the argument between the left, who wanted subject-oriented *sedes*, and the Christian Democrats, who favoured a broader approach, was settled by a plebiscite. The broader approach won by fifty-five to forty-five per cent, 'a significant majority, considering the number of lecturers and students who were leftists and that the Federation of

Students, whose president was a Communist – he's no longer a Communist, like many others – strongly supported Allende.' There was, in d'Etigny's view, a 'generation problem' behind the movement for reform of 1968–70. The massive expansion of the University of Chile had resulted in the employment of a large number of young academics, mostly with PhDs, who had trained abroad; many of these were impatient with the older and less qualified – though not necessarily less able – university teachers, and they supported, if they did not actually instigate, the students' demands for participation in decision-making.

D'Etigny saw salaries, rather than differences in political outlook, as the main bone of contention between the Pedagógico and the DEH. At the time salaries in the university were related to those paid outside: lecturers in medicine received the same salaries as doctors, and engineers got the same as civil servants in the Ministry of Public Works; but the equivalent for lecturers in philosophy and education was a teacher's salary, which was very low. So the lecturers in the Pedagógico resented the fact that those in the DEH were paid the higher salaries pertaining to the school of engineering. An additional grudge was that, because of this advantage, the DEH could pinch the best teachers from the Pedagógico. On top of that, an independent DEH raised the spectre of an alternative, conservative humanities. That was the ideological aspect. 'But the basic dispute was about salaries, as it always – or usually – is,' said d'Etigny, with a laugh.

After the coup, everything changed. The *Sede Occidente* escaped relatively unscathed; 'the main changes were in the *Sede Oriente*, where they fired all the directors of the department of philosophy – the vice-rector, the deans of faculty, everyone. For directly political reasons, yes.' The military government set about destroying the University of Chile and appointed rectors with this in mind; but because these rectors were military men, who were trained to look after their people, they ended up defending the university and had to be replaced. There were two different rectors in the first two years, then a lawyer was appointed, 'a lawyer in uniform', who was more actively destructive: 'But he only lasted eight months, and then they put another one in.'

D'Etigny himself, despite having been promoted to pro-rector of the university, did not survive beyond January 1976. After that, the military government set about dismantling the whole university system. The intake of students dropped dramatically: in 1986 the number of students in higher education, in all universities, was less than in 1974. The *sedes* were eliminated: the four faculties of medicine were reduced to one; the faculty of social sciences disappeared altogether; and the DEH was another casualty, reverting to being a centre servicing engineering students. Intellectuals in Chile became increasingly isolated. D'Etigny recalled, 'It was very diffi-cult to get an intellectual from the north to come here, even if you were clearly oppositional. They said, "How can we go back to our university? They'll say, 'You're coming back from Chile, you're supporting Pinochet.' " '

Did d'Etigny see any connection between his own and Cristián's departure from the university? He laughed: 'No. Yes and no. But I don't exactly remember if he resigned or was . . . It was then that the magazine *Manuscritos* was published. That was one of the issues. I thought it was an excellent magazine, very original, very interesting. But the reactions of the government were not so good. Most criti-cisms were of the amount of money it cost – at least, that's what they said. There were other problems to do with the administration of the department. But I was not directly involved . . .'

Marcos García de la Huerta, who preceded Cristián as director of the Centro de Estudios Humanísticos, was an *allendista*; he invited Cristián to take over his job after the *UP* candidate for the rectorship of the university had been defeated. This was the second time a *UP* candidate had lost an election, and the oppositional *Frente universitario* had a comfortable majority, as the results of the plebiscite d'Etigny had mentioned showed. For *UP* supporters in the university, as for the *UP* goverment itself, the writing was on the wall; and in order to defuse a tense situation in which there was talk of getting rid of lecturers in the social

sciences, Marcos took Cristián aside and offered to dele-
gate the directorship to him, as it was in his power to do,
provided Cristián gave an undertaking not to persecute
the social scientists. Cristián readily assented and
d'Etigny, who as dean of the faculty had to ratify the
appointment, gave his approval, as Marcos had known he
would. That was how Cristián got the job, though some
months later, to conform with current practices, an election was held; the result was a foregone conclusion.

In his fifties, lean, grey-bearded and soft-spoken,
Marcos García de la Huerta gave an impression of kindliness and loneliness, of a herbivore in a country of carni-
vores. Whereas many Chileans were only too ready to
practise their English on me, no matter how inadequate it
might be, Marcos was reluctant to speak it except to help
me out or give me some respite from my struggles to make
myself understood in *castellano*. I sensed at once that he
could be relied upon to do what he undertook, unlike
some who, in their enthusiasm to be of assistance, promised more than they delivered. Though he had a wife and
a young daughter, there was an air of bachelordom about
Marcos, as though marriage and fatherhood had come too
late to alter his lifestyle. He did not smoke, drank little and
kept himself in shape by playing tennis at the French
Club, which he still did well enough to win a contest, the
prize for which was a trip for two to Buenos Aires. His
academic discipline was philosophy and (like the Centre's
first director, Roberto Torretti) he had made a speciality of
the philosophy of science, as I discovered when I helped
him translate a paper he had written into English for an
American publication. Through this and our conversations about Cristián, we became friends.

Marcos's background was not dissimilar to Cristián's
but, unlike Cristián, he had no yearning for the life of a
rural landowner. As he saw it, nostalgia was a potent force
with Cristián: it was there in his taste for the patriarchal
life, in his reverence for his father, his love of the countryside and fascination with his childhood there, his 'desire
to be master of something, a world which was like a
kingdom'.

They had met at the Pedagógico, where they both

studied literature and philosophy. They also came across one another at social gatherings, though they did not immediately become friends. They grew close only when they started going out with girls; Marcos approved of Cristián's *pololeo* with Paz, whom he had known before he met Cristián because they had spent their summers in the same place. Paz was then 'very young, very pretty but very shy'; Marcos had not been impressed by her taste in boys before she got together with Cristián: they had seemed to him rather worthless – playboys, ordinary, run-of-the-mill types. Cristián was not like that; he had a worldly side, but he had very definite tastes, strong likes and dislikes, and he was then in conflict with his family and his social circle. 'Chilean society is tremendously conservative, agrarian and patriarchal,' Marcos told me. 'When a son of a landowner studies drama, let's say, everyone knows that he's in for a difficult time because what it actually means is a lowering of status.'

(When I mentioned Armando Uribe's characterization of Chilean society as matriarchal, and Pinochet and the military junta as *dueñas de casa*, Marcos said, 'But that was in the south, Concepción, a long way from Santiago, which never had anything other than a civilian life. They talk of a history of war, but in reality it was marginal to the political and civil life centred in Santiago. The rest is marked by the patriarchal relations on the land.')

In 1961, when Cristián and Paz escaped to Europe, Marcos went to Paris, where he remained for three or four years. Cristián and Paz once came and stayed a week with him there. He remembered it as a very pleasant visit, in which they had many stories to tell each other. He thought that contact with Europe changed Cristián for the better: before, there had been something at once hedonistic and a little indolent about him; that disappeared and he became more conscious of his own country and his responsibility towards it. At that stage, he and Marcos were politically closer than they had ever been before or would be again; that was the only time Cristián voted for Allende, whereas Marcos voted for him every time.

Back in Chile, Marcos went to work at the Centro de Estudios Humanísticos. He and Cristián had an informal agreement, a pact, that if either of them got into a position of power, he should use his influence to help the other. So, when Cristián came back to Chile looking for work, Marcos mentioned his name to Roberto Torretti. At first Torretti had not been interested, saying that he did not have an opening for a literary man, but later, after others too had spoken to him about Cristián, he agreed to see him and was sufficiently impressed to take him on.

As Marcos explained it, the programme of the *Unidad Popular* divided the economy into three areas; one public, one private and one a mixture of the two. The private domain had nothing to fear; it was in the other two areas that problems arose. 'It was said that this was what the people had voted for,' Marcos told me. 'In fact, some thirty-six per cent, or thereabouts, had voted for it. Still, it was a legitimately elected government, so it had the responsibility of implementing its programme.' *Interventores* (inspectors, supervisors) were assigned to businesses that were not working properly and given powers of management and the task of sorting them out – or that was the theory. In practice, they did nothing to improve the smooth running of these enterprises; instead, they became a hated symbol of political interference and were partly responsible for producing a reaction against Allende. Yet the military regime also found a use for *interventores* – in banks, for instance (it was one of the proud claims of the presidential candidate, Francisco Javier Errázuriz, that his bank had been subjected to this kind of political interference), and in universities.

Cristián had been one of a three-man *comisión interventora* (two of whom, Cristián and Renato Espoz, came from the DEH), set up soon after the coup with the express purpose of weeding out politically undesirable elements from the Pedagógico. I asked Marcos if many lecturers were dismissed as a result of this intervention.

'In the Pedagógico, yes,' he replied. 'This faculty was virtually swept away. I couldn't give you exact figures, but I can tell you that it was enough to change the face of the institution beyond recognition; the Pedagógico could never again be what it had been. And today the faculty –

the old Pedagógico that is now known as the Metropolitan University of the Science of Education – is as right-wing as you could get. It is a college totally supportive of the regime; in other words, the old Pedagógico was destroyed.'

This did not happen all at once, Marcos conceded, but over a period of time; yet the initial responsibility for the destruction of the Pedagógico had to be laid at the door of the *interventores*.

'You have to consider the political climate in the country,' he said. 'The military coup has just taken place, the University of Chile has been the scene of internal struggles, the rector designate realizes that the University of Chile is a centre of power, and that the Instituto Pedagógico, where teachers are trained, is a stronghold of the left. They have to put an end to that. They have to eradicate the cancer of the left once and for all. It is all part and parcel of the brutality which characterised the early days of the regime. They appoint as *interventores* two lecturers who are conservatives, or liberals but antagonistic, strong opponents of the Pedagógico, who were themselves educated there but in some ways feel that they are in competition with the Pedagógico. People in the Pedagógico were critical of Estudios Humanísticos not just because of the higher salaries paid for the same work, but also because they saw it as elitist, full of well-connected people, et cetera, et cetera. So there was a social thing – mixed up with discrimination over salaries was a social thing: they'd say, "There go the *pijes*, the toffs." In addition, there was an undercurrent of resentment that these were people who got their doctorates in Europe.'

When I said that others had told me that Cristián saw his role as being to protect deserving cases, Marcos was sceptical, pointing out that the whole purpose of the commission was to get rid of people: 'In other universities, such as Valparaíso, from which I was dismissed' – Marcos had taught classes there in addition to his work at the DEH – 'the *interventor* was himself one of the military, and he held consultations. Those who were consulted acquired a reputation for protecting the ones who were

allowed to stay on. Cristián did not acquire such a reputation.'

Marcos's view was that, whether or not d'Etigny was
responsible for the composition of the commission, it was
through his influence that Cristián was involved. Something would have been said along the lines of: 'The Pedagógico can't go on as it has been going; we must preserve
the genuine teachers and academics and remove the political ones.' Whereas d'Etigny himself gave the impression
of being a very correct man, with considerable objectivity
of outlook – not the type to look for revenge, or to conduct
a vendetta against the Pedagógico – Cristián was much
more easily swayed by his emotions and was, according to
Marcos, capable of serious errors of judgement, especially
in areas outside his speciality, areas about which he himself freely admitted he knew nothing.

This was the nadir of Marcos's relationship with Cristián. Although they were old friends, they scarcely spoke
to one another for a long time after the coup. Playing
devil's advocate, I put it to Marcos that it was surely quite
natural that someone so bitterly opposed to the influence
of the organized Marxist left in the university, someone
who had been on the receiving end of its hate campaigns,
should seek to purge the university of this kind of political
pressure – especially as he would have thought that the
military involvement was transitional and democracy
would soon be restored.

Marcos replied, 'The fact that the question of power in
the university was raised at all was enough to enrage a
person like Cristián, used to exercising power, and these
people were fighting to maintain control of the university.
There were Marxist groups who were struggling for control by putting up highly respected candidates for the rectorship, truly distinguished intellectuals. At the same time
there were groups of student radicals who were also
applying pressure. But the nature of what was going on
was of a completely different order to the political
repression that followed the military coup, in which lecturers were dismissed, the *sedes* of the university dis-
banded, departments reorganized, faculties abolished. It
was never like that.'

For Marcos, this was an 'exceedingly black' period of his life; he was producing nothing. He read a great deal, but he had trouble concentrating and sorting out his ideas, he was so full of rage. The university was being torn apart, the country destroyed – he was overwhelmed with indignation at what was happening. If he had been sacked from the DEH as well as from the University of Valparaíso, he would have been forced to go into exile, and then he would have gone to Mexico, where he knew people. But it was not an appealing prospect.

There was an element of roulette in all this, he said. The left was not universally or indiscriminately persecuted; it was strategically weakened, its strongholds – such as the Pedagógicos in both Santiago and Valparaíso, and the Technical State University (which later became the University of Santiago, the 'university of the military', where Cristián would one day return to university teaching) – decimated. In the school of engineering, many socialists and Communists survived because they came under the protective umbrella of science and technology. In the DEH, only the social sciences went by the board. When Marcos discussed tactics with others on the left – some of whom had been dismissed from their jobs and were obliged to leave the country – they agreed that the best policy was for those who could to remain and try to prevent the university falling totally into the hands of the fascists. It was a strategy of survival in the hope of better times to come.

Nobody in Chile would ask the question, 'How can you be here?' Only certain exiles, who for reasons of their own tended to see the situation in black and white, put it about that remaining in Chile was tantamount to supporting Pinochet. 'These people did not understand,' Marcos said, 'that when, for example, someone like Federici [the dean of the school of economics] was nominated rector, the entire university was paralyzed for months. It was completely inexplicable to them. According to their Manichean view, anyone who was at the University of Chile was a *pinochetista*. In this way they revealed their ignorance of the actual situation here. It was a very abstract judgement.'

The first years after the coup were particularly bitter,

not just because people could be picked up in the street and condemned to death supposedly for carrying a bomb or a grenade when all they were actually doing was lighting a cigarette, but also because the left felt so isolated; their natural allies, the Christian Democrats, seemed to support both the coup itself and the politics of the military. This did not last; after two or three years a majority of people in the university at least were united in opposition to the dictatorship.

One day, during those critical years, 1973–5, Cristián had arrived at the DEH in some excitement, clutching a bundle of papers, and told Marcos: 'This has come to me from a friend in the navy; it is a dossier of the judgements passed on members of the navy who were supporters of the *Unidad Popular* – I am going to make of it the novel of my life!' In the end he never wrote it, but Marcos was shocked that at a time when the country was going through such a trauma, Cristián should be contemplating the novel of his life.

The military regime produced in Marcos two contrasting reactions: one was an abiding hatred of fascism; the other was a more critical attitude to the left – 'because dictatorships have so much in common with one another; there is a symmetry about *glasnost* happening in Eastern Europe at the same time as the defascization or redemocratization of Chile. So I hate dictatorships in general, as much of the left as of the right.'

Adriana Valdés's initial response, when she heard that Cristián had been made an *interventor*, had been: 'Why on earth is this man allowed to decide the fate of these other people?' They were not yet friends and she saw him simply as the scion of a rich family – 'like myself, in fact! But I didn't like that about myself, and I didn't like people like me getting into power again. And I thought, Why on earth . . . ? I thought it was vain of him, but I didn't think it was wicked; I thought it was ill-advised. And I think he always felt that way too. That letter to Hernán Rodríguez is full of guilt; it's even badly written. It's so full of guilt it's badly written. I feel that he never really resolved it.'

Vanity, she felt, was Cristián's Achilles' heel; he was

very susceptible to flattery and in this case, she was convinced, he had succumbed to it and lived to regret it. But he had suffered considerable abuse from the *Unidad Popular* and though, with hindsight, the threat of the *UP* might be dismissed as empty, that was not how it felt at the time.

'I really want to get this across to you,' she insisted. 'The feeling at that time was that there were two equivalent forces, even in the sense of power structures, and you never knew what was going to happen because these people had an inflamed rhetoric. The military didn't say anything; one of Pinochet's great acts of intelligence was making you feel that the military were stupid. The intelligent people were the ones making all those inflammatory speeches which you couldn't help believing. So the balance of forces was terribly falsified; but you couldn't know that.'

There was such contempt for people connected with the military, with the army at least – not so much the navy – that they were fatally underestimated: 'Everyone thought you could dazzle an army officer's wife by inviting her to dinner, that you could charm them or talk them into doing what you wanted, that you could do all sorts of things that in fact you couldn't do: that was one of the illusions.' In 1970, when a Frenchman published a prophetic book in which he argued that, because of Chile's geographical shape and communications problems, nobody could control the nation as well as the army, which had people everywhere, it was dismissed with contempt and the author vilified as a reactionary – and anyway how could a mere foreigner hope to understand the complexities of Chilean reality?

Adriana felt that Chile in the Allende years was suffering 'a sort of collective self-delusion, a collective *voluntarismo*, wishful thinking in a noble sense: *voluntarismo* has something noble about it, but it is also stupid – the idea that because you want something very much, things must be as you want them to be. People despised their history; they didn't know a thing about their history and they weren't interested in it.'

Libertarian ideas were very attractive when opposed to

an intransigent reality; but once they became the prevailing orthodoxy, once *they* held sway, they became 'terribly oppressive'. This was the conclusion Adriana had reached, based on her own experience of the *UP* in the Catholic University: 'It was terrifying, because you found that people you were dealing with on a friendly basis, and on equal terms, had something up their sleeves; they were hiding things; they belonged to an organization you didn't belong to; they told you only what it suited them to tell you at any given moment. There was this duplicity factor, and it was profoundly shocking to me. You discovered that truth was not very important; strategy was. The whole thing went against the grain with me; in terms of human relationships I couldn't stand it, because I've always tried to be true to my own small experience. Then you find that your own small experience is being run over by a big system, and you don't know where you stand with it. For instance, you're flattered when they make you their special candidate, you're flattered to death; you're used – I was never ill-used, but I was used – I knew I was being useful to them. They would drop me the moment circumstances became more favourable; that was my personal experience, and that was what Cristián reacted against.'

She admitted to having become a cynic: 'But I know something, and that is: people who say they represent the poor don't always represent them. In fact, a very clear sign that they don't is that they say they do!'

12

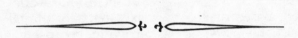

The Museo Vicuña Mackenna is situated on the corner of a
wide and busy thoroughfare near the centre of Santiago.
You relax your pace as you cross a courtyard with a fountain and climb the few steps into the cool, high-ceilinged
hall; the museum itself is upstairs and contains showcases
full of mementos of the early colonial days and battles long
ago, as well as a library stocked with leather-bound and
well cared-for books. Benjamín Vicuña Mackenna was a
nineteenth-century gentleman, who lived that nineteenth-
century life to which Cristián had aspired: like Pérez Rosales, he was a man of letters and of parts; as a young man
he was condemned to death for his revolutionary ideas,
but he survived to became a lawyer, journalist, agronomist, researcher, Chile's confidential agent in the United
States, mayor of Santiago and designer – or redesigner – of
the Santa Lucía hill, deputy, senator, and candidate for
the presidency of the Republic. But his enduring claim to
fame was that, in 'a country of poets, historians and
heroes', as Chile has been called, he was an outstanding
historian. Though he died at the age of fifty-four, he left
some 200 works behind him.

The first time I visited the museum, the curator, Carlos
Ruiz-Tagle, a novelist who also wrote a memoir of his
schooldays at St George – where he was a contemporary of
Armado Uribe and Antonio Avaria and thus a few years
older than Cristián – was away. But I left my name and he
phoned and invited me to lunch a week later. We ate in his
office, which was on one side of the courtyard and, with
its heavy wooden door beneath a Gothic arch, reminded
me of rooms in a Cambridge college; and Carlos himself,
whose white hair and shaky hands made him seem a little
older than he was, had something donnish about him. As

he was going to classes to improve his English, he welcomed the opportunity to speak the language with me.

The first time Cristián had come to the Literary Academy run by Scarpa at St George, he told me, 'he read a composition – I don't know why we didn't use the words poem or short story – about two girls living on a farm in the central part of Chile, who were in love with the same man, and I don't remember it as a very amusing composition. I found it not at all amusing, with many details and a great capacity for analysis, but I believe literature is more synthesis than analysis.'

Carlos's preferred *métier* was comedy; he liked to amuse and be amused. His conversation was anecdotal and laughter was never far from the surface. For instance, he recalled a dinner which had taken place at the house of José Miguel Ibáñez (Ignacio Valente) soon after Cristián's return from England: 'Cristián believed that we must take all our literature here in Chile and put it in the wastepaper basket. I tried to talk to him about a novelist I admire very much, but he would not consider any Chilean writer. When he went home with Paz, I stayed on with my wife, and José Miguel Ibáñez said to me, "He's very hard on our literature." ' Carlos chortled at the memory.

Carlos trained as an agricultural engineer and farmed for six years. 'I thought at first that to be on a farm is very good for writing,' he said. 'You are going to have a lot of time in the afternoon and evening to write. But I found that I had a lot of problems with the peasants and the milkmaids, and the hens and the chickens and all that. So I moved my family here to Santiago and worked in a soil laboratory in the Ministry of Agriculture. Then I worked on an aerial photography project. They took photos of the whole country from the air and we made a mosaic with those photos. That way we can determine exactly what crops are being grown where.'

A practising Catholic, Carlos was a staunch Christian Democrat and had supported agrarian reform: 'They told us that we have a kind of paternalism where the *patrón* is the father of a large family. That was a lie, absolutely. Since 1940 the *patrón* is living in Santiago and the *fundo* is an orphanage. The *patrones* started to have nice times in the Club de Union and talk about their *fundos* with other *patrones*, or by telephone to the farm-managers. So the argument that the *fundo* is a large family is absolutely false.

'For example, I had a neighbour in Curicó who had fallen out with his farm-workers and flooded their plots of land, destroying their crops. If they went to the *Inspección de trabajo*, well, the landowner was a friend of the inspector . . .

'Then you have another problem: if a *patrón*, a land-owner, is doing well, instead of giving more to the workers, he just buys another *fundo* close by, and then you have a horrible social situation. I'm talking about the days before agrarian reform. I guess that in all reforms you have injustices in some cases. That happens.'

After the aerial photography survey, Carlos set up as an independent publisher. He told me he had published about 290 books 'by people without a facility to write'. One of his projects was to produce anthologies, based on particular localities: he edited one on the *comuna*, or municipality, of Viña del Mar and its surrounding countryside. Cristián was enthusiastic about this project and proposed an anthology for La Ligua, the district where Cabildo is. 'He started a lot of conversations with the mayors there, but the mayors are not very cultivated people and don't think much of making books; they'd rather make other things, like sports. So then he wrote a whole page about one of these anthologies in the news-paper of La Ligua – to make La Ligua conscious that it needed an anthology. He was a very good friend . . .'

Another of Carlos's publishing projects was a series of autobiographical booklets, each about thirty pages long, which appeared under the generic title of *¿Quién es Quién?* ('Who's Who?'). Starting with Roque Esteban Scarpa, he published nearly fifty of these brief lives, and Cristián was one of the people he invited to contribute one: 'But he start to write and cannot stop.' That was the genesis of the *Autobiografía por encargo*, which was eventually published under another imprint. Carlos found it an interesting book, with its several beginnings: 'This was very original. You think that the book is going to continue, but no, he starts another time. It was an exercise, and I think Dr

Leavis would have been very proud of him. When Cristián came back to Chile and looked down on all the literature, it was in the name of that teacher!'

Cristián died shortly before his autobiography came out, and Carlos decided that was the time to end his series: 'I didn't want any more *¿Quién es Quién?*' He was told that Cristián had died a Catholic, that during his last days he had been reconverted to the faith. (Adriana later confirmed this, contrasting it with Enrique Lihn's steadfast refusal of such consolation even at the eleventh hour; but she reckoned that Cristián was already so severely brain-damaged that he could no longer really be held responsible for what he did.)

Before his illness, Cristián had once invited Carlos to lunch at a restaurant called the Satyricón, where the waiters were from their old school; indeed, the restaurant had been founded by a group of Old Georgians. Since then, Carlos told me, 'many times I have wanted to go to that place, but I cannot find it. I think it's a similar case to *Le Grand Meaulnes*, when they can't find the house.'

This seemed to me an oblique and delicate way of expressing his sense of loss.

At the time of the coup, Carlos Ruiz-Tagle was working for ICIRA (Chileans have a passion for acronyms; this one stands for *Instituto de Capacitación e Investigación en Reforma Agraria*, the Institute for Training and Research in Agrarian Reform), and many of his friends and colleagues there were from the *Unidad Popular*. Carlos found that the best way to help people in trouble with the military regime was to provide them with work, so he set up a printing press and gave work to some of those who needed it, such as José Campusano, an old man who was secretary of the Communist rank-and-file movement. In December 1973, three months after the coup, Campusano's wife came to tell Carlos that her husband had been arrested and taken into the detention centre called Tres Alamos.

At the entrance to the camp there were a couple of *carabineros* with a list of names, which they read out in alphabetical order, starting with – for example – Aguirre Benítez, Claudio. As soon as Aguirre's wife and daughter heard his name, they got up and were taken in to see the prisoner. Next the *carabineros* called out a name beginning with D, Danús perhaps, and *his* wife, and family went through. Meanwhile, the Cárcamo family, say, whose name had not been called out, asked where José Pedro was, only to be told that he was not there. 'But how could that be?' they insisted. 'He was here last Friday. What's happened to him?' The *carabinero* merely shrugged, told them to shut up and read out the next name. Many of the people who had been on the previous Friday's list had disappeared; for Carlos, that was the ghastly thing.

José Campusano, however, had not disappeared. When Carlos got to see him, Campusano said, 'Don't talk too loud because they're listening to everything you say.' It could be dangerous for him. In the end he was sent to Denmark, which was better than being 'disappeared'; but at the age of seventy, how could he be expected to pick up Danish and start a new life? Yet he survived, and eventually settled in France.

'I hope,' Carlos said fervently, 'that we are not going to have a division now between those who were in exile and those who were here. Armando Uribe, for example, has told me many times that he knows more about Chile than I or anyone else here because he is reading things day and night about it. Well, it is possible, it is absolutely possible that I don't know because I read *El Mercurio*, and *El Mercurio* is not giving us all the information that Uribe has – it is absolutely possible. But he doesn't know how is the ambience, the *ambiente*, he is absolutely out of the *ambiente*. I am sure that I know what is the *ambiente*, the conciliatory atmosphere, and Uribe has nothing to do with that.'

The regular articles Armando Uribe and his son were writing for the political magazine *Análisis* were highly intellectual, but they were all on the same subject – the language of tyranny – and Carlos could not help feeling that this was not what people wanted to read about at this time.

The following evening I saw another Carlos, Carlos Franz, whom I had met with Diego Maquieira. His first novel, *Santiago Cero*, had just been published to great acclaim from Ignacio Valente, no less. Indeed, Valente's review and an interview with Franz took over the first three pages of the book section of the previous Sunday's *El Mercurio*. In England, I told him, he would have been lucky if his first novel had rated half a paragraph in a multiple review. But then Franz himself had written reviews for *El Mercurio* until he had heeded Cristián's advice to desist.

It was at the book fair in Buenos Aires in 1984 that he had kept running into Cristián (who, like him, had been looking for important writers to interview), and Cristián had voiced concern about his reviewing for *El Mercurio*. At first, Franz had been inclined to put this down to envy or self-interest on Cristián's part. But he soon saw that Cristián was sincere and had his best interests at heart.

Cristián had said to him: 'You are very young, and you probably don't realize that your articles are read by people not just for their content but for their context as well. When you're writing about Pablo Neruda, for instance, in *El Mercurio* in 1984, with the rest of the press and media silenced or censored, you are exercising an incredible amount of power.' His point, according to Franz, was that 'it was very important that you became conscious of your power. After that, if you wanted to go on enjoying your power, that was up to you. But you had to be conscious of it. And it was a very good analysis, I think, because I was *un*conscious of it. I decided after that conversation, and probably two months of meditation, to stop. And the reason I gave people was exactly the words of Cristián.'

This was the time of the first big *protestas*, protest marches, organized demonstrations which started in May 1983 and continued through 1984. 'The first riots were very violent,' Carlos Franz recalled, 'and in the fourth *protesta* [in August 1983] some forty people died. Then the government enforced a state of siege and the five or six opposition newspapers and periodicals were censored or banned outright. In 1984, if you were writing articles for *El Mercurio*, you were not just writing for the establishment press, you were writing for the power – you had the power. Because what happens if someone wants to contradict you? What happens? They don't have the opportunity.'

The son of a diplomat and an actress, Carlos was born in Geneva and educated abroad up to the age of twelve. He arrived in Chile when the *Unidad Popular* was at the height of its power. He had hardly any relatives there, no uncles or cousins, since both his parents were first-generation immigrants – his father Swiss, his mother Norwegian. It took him a long time to begin to feel like a Chilean. As a child, he had believed that the Republic of Chile was a very civilized country; the parties his parents gave in embassies or consulates around the world reinforced this idea and they were always telling him how different Chile was from other Latin American countries. The coup shattered that illusion. Its effect was to divide the country into victimizers and victimized; though if you were only fourteen you did not belong in either category. 'My generation,' Carlos said, 'was essentially overlooked, through being so young, in this whole history.'

Did this mean that he, or they, did not have to make political choices?

'Living in Chile for these sixteen years for a young man, I think,' Carlos replied, 'has been an experience of making lots of political choices without knowing it, because politics was banned from public discourse. Nobody in the government, for instance, defined himself as a politician. Yet the first politician of Chile, in the second half of this century, has been Pinochet. We can return to this point of writing for *El Mercurio* as a literary critic. I thought that was just literature; I didn't realize that it was charged with political content – to an unimaginable extent.'

To grow up in Pinochet's Chile was to be condemned to an extended adolescence. 'We lived so much in dreams,' Carlos told me, 'typical adolescent dreams, both individual and collective. You have to confront your dreams with reality, but we were forced to remain adolescents in a society where the principals were engaged in a dialogue of the deaf. We had no part in that play, we could not even be porters. All we could do was dream and dream and dream.'

Apart from the limitations imposed by the state of siege, and ten years of curfew, there was the disenchantment with university, which turned out to be so different to what people of Carlos's generation had been led to expect. Through films and books they had imbibed the Anglo-Saxon notion of universities as places of culture, characterized by the interchange of ideas. But the University of Chile was based on the French model, which was more professionally orientated, and even that model had been reduced to its lowest common denominator by the military regime.

In 1974, the year before Carlos went to the school of law, for instance, the 'last democratic dean' there had been dismissed and a new dean, who was very close to the regime, appointed. This man, who rose to be Minister of Justice, quite deliberately put the clock back forty years: 'This is not a matter of interpretation, we checked it. I remember very well the programme we studied in my freshman year, and we checked it against the programme he had studied in 1936 or thereabouts and it was exactly the same. This is an extreme example, but I think it was like that for many students in our university. It was our contribution to national suffering, non-violent but still real.'

For students of a slightly older generation than Carlos's, Cristián's Departamento de Estudios Humanísticos was a refuge, the only remaining place of relative freedom in the entire university, and Cristián something of a legendary figure, about whom stories were told. Carlos himself had been taught by Cristián, not at the DEH, but when he enrolled at a literary workshop directed by Jorge Edwards. After a month or two, Jorge grew tired of instructing a group of about twenty people, very few of whom were seriously interested in writing, so he asked Cristián to stand in for him; and 'the period with Cristián', Carlos remembered, 'was much more interesting than the period with Jorge'. They did unlikely things like reading parts of Painter's biography of Proust, and Cristián and Carlos struck up a relationship that went beyond the working sessions into informal discussions over cups of coffee. Perhaps that was why Cristián felt he had a right to take Carlos to task for reviewing for El Mercurio. At any rate, Carlos found him very simpático.

For the literati of Carlos's generation, however, Cristián

was 'a sort of symbol of failure'. At the end of a joint review of Cristián's *El verano del ganadero* and a book by a right-wing novelist of the same generation, one young critic went so far as to contrast Cristián's 'empty facility' with this other man's 'realized talent'. It was a cruel judgement. 'But it expresses the general feeling, I'm afraid,' Carlos admitted. 'We felt that he was all facility and no substance, no content.'

After three months in Santiago, I was growing restless. So far all my efforts to get out of the city had been frustrated. But now Soledad invited me to lunch at Cabildo along with Adriana, who had also arranged for us to visit Nicanor Parra at Isla Negra on the Pacific coast, world famous as the home of another poet, Pablo Neruda. I had little difficulty in persuading Adriana that we should make a weekend of it, driving to Cabildo on the Saturday morning, and from there down the coast to Viña del Mar – Cristián's birthplace – where we could stay overnight, then on to Isla Negra on the Sunday.

We drove out of Santiago in the comfort of Adriana's air-conditioned Volvo. We were both happy to be leaving the city behind us. In the midst of the summer drought the landscape was dry and dusty, the hills covered with scrubby bushes and cactuses, though there were irrigated and fertile valleys between them. On one of these hills, Adriana told me, you sometimes caught sight of a hermit with a long white beard; the story was that he had been an engineer but had abandoned everything and lived in that desolate place ever since his wife had been killed there in a car crash, for which he blamed himself. Stretches of the road were lined with poplars, reminding me of the old black-and-white photos of the Chilean countryside Cristian had chosen to illustrate the issue of *Granta* he had guest-edited in Cambridge.

When we reached the village of Cabildo, Adriana pointed out the sort of house – a basic one-storey dwelling – that Cristián and Soledad had once owned, before inflation had forced them to sell it. After we left the village we missed the small turning to the *fundo* of San José and climbed the winding road into the hills beyond. We found a place to turn and stopped to enjoy the view over La Ligua before dropping down into the valley again. This time we found the turning without difficulty and bumped along the dusty unmade road till we came to the farm itself. There were one or two modest farm-buildings and a new, unpretentious and still unfinished bungalow facing the groves of avocados; the charm of the place lay in its situation near the top of a broad valley surrounded, but not enclosed, by high hills.

Jaime looked splendid in his *huaso* outfit: elegant, high-heeled boots, red cummerbund and wide-brimmed hat. Among his dogs and horses he was far more relaxed than he had been in Santiago. I met Soledad's eldest son, Ricardo, an architect, who was there with his wife and her four-year-old son. We all lounged in the shade of a tree and drank a white wine cup, fortified with cognac. Soledad was curious to know whom I had talked to and what I thought of them, but beyond that we hardly spoke of what I was doing there. After an alfresco lunch and a siesta, we went for a walk along a lane through the avocado groves; Soledad showed us the spot where she had first built a house in accordance with Cristián's wishes and it had been swept away by the flood. Then she walked on ahead with Adriana, while Jaime accompanied me and told me tales of his polo-playing past. He was reluctant to see it as his past but at the age of sixty, even a sprightly sixty, he had to face up to the fact that bones grow brittle and a fall might do him serious damage.

While we were talking, a man approached, carrying a shotgun. Jaime exchanged a few words with him before passing on. What was the man doing, I asked – shooting rabbits, perhaps? No, said Jaime, he was guarding the place, as people from Cabildo came and stole the avocados off the trees. It had been a bad year for avocados, and they could ill afford to lose any to theft. But it was a constant hazard.

Late in the afternoon, Adriana and I left Cabildo for the coast. We approached Zapallar from the north with the sun sinking into the Pacific and pelicans skimming the crests of the waves. For some reason I had expected the resort to be on an open stretch of coast, but Zapallar is in a small protected bay, surrounded by trees, with a rather enclosed, as well as exclusive, feeling about it. We parked close to the beach and walked along a promenade separating it from the houses above, their gardens bright with geraniums. At the far end of the beach there was a café under an awning, and tables with sunshades. There we had a cup of tea, which somehow seemed appropriate, though the headland was already casting a shadow over our end of the beach and families were beginning to gather up their belongings. Various people greeted Adriana when we walked back to the car; it was the kind of place where everyone knew everyone else and no one was surprised by the arrival of another acquaintance.

A short distance from Zapallar was a resort called Cachagua, which Adriana preferred; it was more open than Zapallar, both physically and socially. Marcos García de la Huerta had a house in Cachagua, which he had let for the summer; so we made a little detour to see if we could find it and Adriana pointed out other houses where she had stayed. We did not stop long, as there was still a long way to go to Viña del Mar.

The nearer we got to Viña, the more built-up the coast became. We passed the huge Con Con oil refinery, the largest in the country, blackening the sky with clouds of acrid smoke and giving the landscape of sand-dunes at twilight a hellish aspect. The dunes north of Renaca, Adriana said, had a sinister reputation as one of the places where corpses of the disappeared were found. We were glad to put these dunes behind us and come over the hills to see, spread out before us, the amphitheatre of winking lights which marked the wide bay of Valparaíso. Viña, just to the north of it, was like a Chilean Brighton or Bournemouth, a mixture of old charm and new high-rises. Our hotel was comfortable but anonymous, international and characterless.

We took the lift to the fifth floor and trekked along the corridor to our adjoining rooms, where we each had a shower before emerging to eat at a seafront restaurant Adriana knew. There I was handed – rather shamingly, I thought – a menu in English, which nevertheless provided us with some entertainment: what exactly, for heaven's sake, was 'bovine meat'? We had to consult Adriana's Spanish menu to discover. But the food (we avoided bovine meat and chose fish) and the wine were excellent, and we staggered back to the hotel, where we retired, exhausted, at two a.m.

In the morning we crossed the invisible dividing line between Viña and Valparaíso, leaving a thriving, touristic town for a depressed and dying city. (In siting the new Congress building in Valparaíso Pinochet's intention was not so much to upgrade his birthplace – his father was a customs official in Valparaíso – as to downgrade politicians by removing them from the capital.) Yet from the moment when I had first seen Tom Daskam's huge and magnificently detailed painting above the dining-room table in his and Paz's house in Santiago, I had wanted to visit Valparaíso. I was not disappointed: the spectacular site, the funicular railways and steep slopes cluttered with houses coated in corrugated iron, the faded glory of the port, its mixture of the grandiose and the ramshackle, were irresistible.

As it was Sunday, the town was quiet and we could explore it at leisure. We started at the port and climbed – by car rather than cable car – the steep and narrow cobbled streets to a museum and gallery on the famous Cerro Alegre. The paintings in the gallery were largely undistinguished, and the most delightful thing about this old *palacio* was its small garden overlooking the sea, the port and other parts of the town. Downtown Valparaíso struck me as a kind of City of London in miniature, which was hardly surprising since the English had been so influential in developing the city in the nineteenth century.

Isla Negra, despite its name, is neither an island nor black, though it is by the sea. Unlike Neruda's house, which overlooks the ocean (and was still closed to the public, as it had been since his death), Nicanor Parra's is inland, surrounded by trees, in the 'Street of the Poet' – *Calle del Poeta*, as the signpost would have informed us if it had not been broken in half. Nicanor himself was a spry and youthful seventy-five, puckish and full of fun. He had his youngest children, a teenage son and daughter, living with him; but they stayed at home while he, Adriana and I went to a seafront restaurant nearby for a late Sunday lunch.

The place was so popular that we had to wait half-an-hour before we could get in. Nicanor did not mind; he stood in the sun, his face shaded by a wide-brimmed straw hat, and spoke a beautifully clear *castellano* which even I had little difficulty in following. As he had studied at Oxford for two years during the war – physics, not literature, as he proudly told me – he could speak English, but in our conversation he chose not to; perhaps he was reluctant to concede the linguistic advantage. So we stood there reciting poetry to one another in our respective languages while we waited for a table.

After lunch, Nicanor wanted to show Adriana a plot of land he had bought further down the coast, next to the sea. I sat on a rock watching the pelicans fly south while he and Adriana discussed his plans to build a house there. Back at Isla Negra, we took a siesta and then forgathered in the courtyard of the house for tea and further recitals of poems, including one which Nicanor said he had introduced at a poetry reading in the United States by announcing that the poem he was about to read had been translated into English 400 years before he had written it – *Ser o no ser* ('To be or not to be . . .'). This was entirely characteristic of Nicanor; he was, as Adriana had told me, a very *playful* man.

It was getting late and I began to worry that we would have to leave before I had achieved the purpose of my visit. But in the end Nicanor gracefully submitted to being interviewed and the three of us went inside and I switched on the tape-recorder.

As an adolescent, Cristián used to appear, Nicanor remembered, like 'a peripheral electron' at the informal gatherings held at the house of his uncle Pancho Huneeus and Pancho's English wife Dorothy, which were the nearest thing in Santiago to a literary salon. But though he and Nicanor met on several occasions, the difference in age between them prevented them becoming intimate at that stage.

For various reasons Nicanor became *persona non grata* with the *Unidad Popular* and at the Pedagógico, where he was teaching. Immediately after the coup he was summoned by one of the 'triumvirate' of *interventores* – not Cristián – and asked in a kind of grim joke which he would prefer, to be director of the Department of Physics or go to the Stadium (the National Stadium had been turned into a prison camp in the wake of the coup). He soon discovered that he was 'director of nothing, merely a tool' required to sign a paper authorizing the dismissal of certain lecturers, which he could not bring himself to do. So, pleading illness, he made his escape from Santiago to Isla Negra and did not return until the following March, when he found all doors closed to him. At that point he remembered that Cristián had earlier offered him work at the Departamento de Estudios Humanísticos and went to see him there. Cristián welcomed him with open arms. 'You stay here, Nicanor,' he said, and immediately provided him with an office.

Naturally enough, Nicanor regarded Cristián as 'a great director, very friendly, very courteous, a director de luxe'. But it was not until he took Cristián to task for using the form of words, 'One saw that it would be as well to do such and such . . .', by saying to him, 'Tell me, *who* saw? Who is it that's hidden behind this "one", this indefinite subject?' and Cristián responded to the challenge with delight that a closer relationship developed. 'That was the beginning of the friendship,' Nicanor recalled.

Every so often the lecturers in the department held meetings, which were, in Nicanor's words, 'more amicable than academic'. At one of these, Cristián read a chapter from his thesis on D. H. Lawrence in Latin America. This gave Nicanor an idea, which he thought worth pursuing, so afterwards he announced: 'While Cristián has been reading his work, I've written a mini-text, an artefact which I'm going to read to you. Here it is: "*Argentino* [is an] anagram of *ignorante*, signed Sarmiento." ' Everyone started to laugh, but Nicanor had not finished. He explained that Sarmiento had discovered this anagram, but 'you mustn't believe Sarmiento, because Sarmiento'

– and this was his own discovery – 'is an anagram of *mentirosa* [liar]'.

This sort of playfulness, manifest in Nicanor's *El Quebrantahuesos*, the collage of newsprint and photos which Cristián and his editorial collaborators reprinted in the magazine *Manuscritos*, was (in Nicanor's opinion) largely responsible for Cristián's downfall as director of the DEH: making fun of the armed forces did not go down well with the authorities. But then Cristián always had a tendency to go beyond what was strictly prudent.

Once, for example, he invited an Australian political philosopher to come and talk on the subject of democracy and dictatorship. Nicanor did not dare go to this man's lectures, but he went to a farewell lunch for him at Cristián's *fundo*, Santo Tomás, and found the other lecturers from the DEH – Enrique Lihn, Felipe Alliende and all – there. Everything seemed to be going well when Nicanor suddenly spotted one person after another getting up from the table and holding whispered consultations. Felipe came over to him and said, 'Keep calm, Nicanor, you've got to go out, but try not to draw our visitor's attention to your departure.' Outside, Nicanor found Cristián already engaged in conversation with 'two very important individuals' under the grape arbour. One of these, who was extremely well-groomed in the manner of the DINA, said, 'You've nothing to fear, Professor Parra, just a few routine questions . . .' But behind him, Nicanor could see the second man, 'the torturer', looking over the other's shoulder as if to say, 'Wait and see what happens when you fall into my hands . . .'

In the event, they just took the keys of his car, gave it a cursory search, found nothing and told Cristián and Nicanor to follow them through a gate into the lane, where they went past a van with machine-guns mounted in the back. There the two men started questioning some of the estate workers, and Nicanor decided that he might safely leave now. So he went back to his car, started it up and drove very slowly past the van, in case they should think he was trying to run away. But as soon as he was out of the main gates he put his foot down on the accelerator and made good his escape.

In Nicanor's view, then, the two main reasons for the removal of Cristián from his post of director of the DEH were the publication of *Manuscritos* and the invitation to the Australian to lecture on so inflammatory a topic as democracy and dictatorship; there might be other ostensible reasons, but those were the real ones. (Later, when I discussed this with Marcos García de la Huerta, who had attended the Australian's lectures, he was frankly incredulous: he thought the DINA's visit to Santo Tomás had absolutely nothing to do with the presence of the Australian; in his view it was far more likely to have been occasioned by some anomaly on the estate – hence the questioning of estate workers.)

Nicanor thought that Cristián had been wrong to resign from the department after his dismissal as director, when there was nothing to prevent him staying on as a lecturer. Nicanor and Enrique Lihn, who formed (along with Nicanor's son-in-law, Ronald Kay, who subsequently left Chile for Germany) a close-knit group around Cristián, were surprised that Cristián had not consulted them before taking such precipitate action; but Cristián was a proud – even arrogant – man, and 'he believed that he had to do it to recover his lost dignity'.

After he had left the DEH, Cristián remained in close contact with Nicanor and was deeply involved when, in 1978, the government authorized the production of a theatrical work based on Nicanor's poetry, which carried the punning title *Las Hojas de Parra* (which means both 'Parra's papers' and, figuratively, 'figleaves') in a marquee in a residential district of Providencia. That it was staged at all was something of a miracle. The censors were divided among themselves: there were *los blandos*, the mild, indulgent ones, who argued in favour of the production, saying, 'Who's going to be interested in a few of old Parra's poems anyway? If we let it happen, nobody can accuse us of not allowing freedom of speech in Chile'; and there were *los duros*, the hard men, who were totally opposed to it on the grounds that it constituted an attack on the government. On this occasion, *los blandos* won, and for fifteen days Nicanor's collaborators, the actors Jaime

Vadell and José Salcedo, put on their nightly perform-
ances in front of enthusiastic audiences.

As the word got around, the houses filled to overflow-
ing and there were long queues outside. Then they
received a message: 'Close it, or one of you three is going
to disappear.' The actors came with their wives to Isla
Negra to see Nicanor and told him, 'We're being
threatened and maybe we're going to have to suspend the
production – what do you think?' Nicanor said, 'Well, let's
see what the ladies say.' Both women insisted the show
should go on, and Nicanor endorsed their view, offering
to accompany them to Santiago and show his face.

That night, after the performance, when Nicanor joined
the actors in front of the audience in that intimate theatre-
in-the-round, which was more circus than theatre, an
extraordinary thing happened: all the people got to their
feet and applauded, but they seemed to be applauding
each other as much as the show itself; it was a political act,
a heady moment when author, actors and audience were
united in a single gesture of protest. In such circumstances
it was easy to spot the secret police; they were the ones
who remained in their seats and were not clapping.

In the middle of the night there was a fire and the marquee was razed to the ground. The show was over.

Nicanor thought that Cristián had behaved in exemplary
fashion by staying in Chile and doing what he did, both in
the university and politically. True, in the first moments
after the coup, he had worked with the Junta, but so had
Nicanor himself; they had both accepted responsible positions which seemed to identify them with the dictatorship, but in reality had more to do with their opposition to
the 'mini-junta' which ran the *Sede Oriente* of the university, the Instituto Pedagógico. Their lack of sympathy with
the dictatorship soon became apparent: in Nicanor's case,
when he took off to Isla Negra rather than carry out
'unworthy acts, like burning books and dismissing lecturers'; in Cristián's, when his activities in the DEH
attracted the disapproval of the authorities and led to his
dismissal as director.

Despite occasional uncomfortable but inconsequential

visits from the secret police, Nicanor did not suffer unduly under the dictatorship. He carried on working at the university, receiving not just his monthly salary but, in addition – a point in favour of the regime – a second cheque, which he got as a result of having won the National Prize for Literature during the years of Frei's presidency. Previously, winners of this prize had had to be content with a one-off payment, but Pinochet instigated monthly payments for living holders of the prize – something never achieved by Chilean democracy.

In 1970 Nicanor had voted for Allende, but his libertarian attitudes had clashed with the regimentation required by the 'dictatorship of the proletariat'. Nicanor was a natural anarchist. (For instance, when he was interviewed for a programme on the Chilean election shown on British television, he told the interviewer that the name of his candidate for the presidency was *Nadie* [Nobody], since *Nadie* did not impose taxes, *Nadie* did not torture people, *Nadie* would do this or would not do that . . . In this way he ridiculed both the dictatorship and the parliamentary process.) Before the coup, even before the Chilean revolution, he had travelled widely, observing the phenomenon of hippyism with some sympathy and being involved in the ecological debate: he had celebrated the Day of the Earth, for example, along with Allen Ginsberg and his cronies in New York. But it was only after the coup that he turned 'from passive anarchism to active anarchism'.

He came to believe that the fundamental problem of our time was one of survival: 'So I became a citizen of the planet, regarding it as necessary to act promptly but think globally. I could hardly adopt a confrontational stance against the dictatorship when confrontation, in the last resort, was synonymous with ecological collapse and the nuclear winter. Once I began to look at things from that angle, I couldn't possibly identify with a violent opposition.'

Ecology also helped him solve a personal problem in connection with his teaching in the school of engineering, the problem of the 'two cultures' of science and literature. As he put it, 'For an engineer or a physicist, what is not expressable as an equation doesn't exist.' Students would come to the first two or three classes of a course in the humanities out of curiosity, 'then disappear over the horizon'. So Nicanor came up with the idea of offering a course on Bertrand Russell, who – in addition to being a mathematician and a writer – was a political activist. That way, he could take his students' interests as his point of departure and then broaden the discussion to cover the whole debate over ecology, for instance. His classes soon filled up, with people sitting on the floor and on the window-sills.

His libertarian sympathies and ecological outlook led him to the work of the American anarchist Murray Bookchin, who became a personal friend. When the ecological movement began to falter, and Nicanor asked Bookchin for an explanation, Bookchin replied, 'We're having to put all our efforts into fighting the eco-fascists who have infiltrated the movement.'

Even citizens of the planet, it seems, are not free of the forces of fascism.

On the journey back to Santiago, Adriana explained what Nicanor had meant when he had said to me, 'I was judged by the *Unidad Popular* and condemned to hell for the famous cup of tea.' He was referring to an occasion in Washington when he had visited the White House as a tourist. While he was being shown round, word had reached Mrs Nixon that there was a famous poet in the house and she had invited him to have tea with her. In the eyes of the intellectuals of the *Unidad Popular*, having tea with Pat Nixon was the equivalent of supping with the devil and Nicanor had been vilified for it, the facts being twisted to suggest that he had sought out the encounter. According to Nicanor, the *éminence grise* who had orchestrated this campaign against him was none other than Pablo Neruda (who had himself been vilified by the Cubans for going to New York in 1966, even though he did the politically correct thing and read poems attacking the war in Vietnam rather than taking tea with the President's wife).

In the face of such abuse, Nicanor had perhaps overreacted, welcoming the coup a little too enthusiastically, but he had soon found himself quite as opposed to the dictatorship as he had ever been to the *Unidad Popular*. As Adriana put it, people like Nicanor and Enrique Lihn would always find themselves in opposition to the dominant regime, whatever ideology it professed.

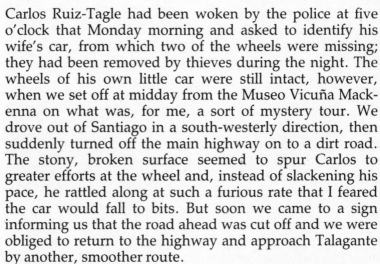

13

Carlos Ruiz-Tagle had been woken by the police at five o'clock that Monday morning and asked to identify his wife's car, from which two of the wheels were missing; they had been removed by thieves during the night. The wheels of his own little car were still intact, however, when we set off at midday from the Museo Vicuña Mackenna on what was, for me, a sort of mystery tour. We drove out of Santiago in a south-westerly direction, then suddenly turned off the main highway on to a dirt road. The stony, broken surface seemed to spur Carlos to greater efforts at the wheel and, instead of slackening his pace, he rattled along at such a furious rate that I feared the car would fall to bits. But soon we came to a sign informing us that the road ahead was cut off and we were obliged to return to the highway and approach Talagante by another, smoother route.

Carlos announced that we would be having lunch with the *alcalde* – the mayor – of Talagante, who was a friend of his, an innovative and enlightened man who had done much for the community, including building a hospital. The mayor's imposing and newish house was set in a spacious park, with manicured lawns and handsome trees. We were welcomed by his son, a tall, good-looking youth, who told us that his father would be home shortly. The mayor's wife looked in and greeted Carlos, apologizing for leaving the moment we arrived and explaining that she had to visit a sick relative in Santiago.

The son was studying 'commercial engineering', a branch of economics, and there was a translation of Paul Johnson's *History of Modern Times* on a coffee table. Its presence in a household that somehow epitomized the upside of the new monetarist Chile reminded me of a conversation I'd had a few days earlier with Armando

Uribe, when we had met by chance and had a coffee together. I had expressed surprise at the ubiquity of the works of Paul Johnson in Santiago, as incomprehensible to me as the one-time popularity of the novels of Charles Morgan in France. Armando had replied that there was no mystery about it, it was a byproduct of the ideological dominance of the New Liberalism – identical to Thatcherism in Britain – which was assiduously promoted in Santiago by the Centro de Estudios Públicos.

Ernesto, the mayor, came bustling in and apologized for keeping us waiting. He was the very model of a modern businessman and administrator, tall, with tinted glasses, jovial, self-confident and with an easy social manner. He swept us all – including his daughter, who had quietly materialized at more or less the same time as he had arrived – into the dining-room, where we were lavishly lunched. When we took our leave, Carlos's little red car, now coated with dust, looked more than ever like a poor relation beside Ernesto's dark and gleaming limousine.

Before we drove out to the Jesuit monastery that was our destination, Carlos took me to the small library in Talagante, not so much because of the books there – though he was proud of his responsibility for setting up libraries in several of the smaller towns dotted around Santiago – as to show me its permanent exhibition of terracotta figurines made by one local family, who have had a monopoly of this artisan work for generations.

I was so impressed by these examples of folk art that I persuaded Carlos to take me to the house of the family that made them. There I chose a figurine of boy and girl (*pololeo*), sitting on a bench, and also a tree, complete with flowers and birds wildly out of proportion to it, to put beside them. I was tempted to buy a figure squatting on a chamber pot, but decided that, taken out of the context of other figures engaged in everyday activities, its innocence would seem like vulgarity. The old woman and her son who manufactured these figurines did good business, selling their work all over the world. They were not interested in innovation, being content to reproduce the same set-pieces over and over again, each one hand-made but with machine-like precision.

When we got to the Jesuit monastery, we were lucky to be allowed in. There was a retreat beginning the next day and had we left it till then they would have turned us away. The *convento* had been built in the seventeenth century; it was a silent and spartan place, but its severity was softened by the flowering trees and shrubs that filled the courtyard with warmth and colour. A guide showed us round, though this was unnecessary since Carlos seemed to know the place well – which was hardly surprising as his forebears had lived there for two centuries before one of them, a Jesuit convert, had restored it to the Jesuits.

I invited Carlos and his wife to come to the apartment for drinks soon after my wife Jenny arrived in Santiago. In the few days she had been there, Jenny had already met several of my friends – Paz, of course, and Tom, who had returned from the wilds of Chilean Patagonia, Adriana, Marcos and his wife and daughter. That evening, in addition to Carlos and Magdalena – whom I too was meeting for the first time – she met Malcolm Coad (Coca was busy with rehearsals) and Ernesto Rodríguez, who looked in briefly.

Carlos and Magdalena arrived first, and Magdalena settled comfortably on the sofa beside Jenny and, as it were, took her under her wing. Malcolm came; Ernesto came and went; and the conversation remained general and amicable until a sharp altercation arose between Malcolm and Magdalena over the number of people who had 'disappeared' during the Pinochet regime. Magdalena thought the number had been exaggerated, which Malcolm was prepared to concede; what he could not concede was that the Vicaría de la Solidaridad had been a party to such exaggeration or that it had been infiltrated by Communists.

As a journalist, Malcolm dealt in facts; but as the husband of a woman who had been tortured by the regime, he was passionate too. Magdalena asserted rather than argued and, when she was cornered, took refuge in the mystique of Chilean-ness: no foreigner could possibly understand the finer points of Chilean reality; only a

Chilean could know what was really going on in the country. Mere investigative journalism was powerless against this kind of subliminal knowledge, and the more evidence Malcolm cited the more off-hand and queenly Magdalena became in her indifference towards it. Whatever he said, she knew better. Neither gave an inch and the argument was far from resolved when Carlos, who had taken no part in it, got up to go. For Jenny, this was an early introduction to the passions that divided Chilean society.

After the Ruiz-Tagles had left, Malcolm told me that the British embassy had succeeded, in the more relaxed political climate following the elections, in getting permission for somebody to visit Ledy Castro in jail, and he suggested I might try that route. The embassy was happy to oblige, and the permit that I had failed to get through my own efforts came by return of post. Before going to Santo Domingo I phoned to find out when I might visit and was told I could come whenever I liked – that afternoon if I wished. The spirit of friendly co-operation, however, did not extend to the guard at the door, who was as dour and unwelcoming as he had been the first time I had tried to visit Ledy. But when I showed another of the guards my letter of authorization, I was admitted at once; no one subjected me to a body-search, all I had to do was hand over my passport.

I was ushered into a grim little room without decoration of any sort. Two women sat at a bare table and there were two more hard chairs placed near the door; I sat on one of these while I waited for Ledy. I did not have long to wait. Ledy came in and, after expressing her pleasure that I had finally managed to come, suggested we move out into the courtyard. While she went to fetch a drink, I saw that the jacaranda tree I had noticed on my first visit, though it was no longer in flower, was clearly visible from the courtyard. Ledy returned with a Coca-Cola for me and an orange Fanta for herself; she warned me that the drink would not be very cold as they lacked refrigeration. But that simple gesture of hospitality transformed the dreary prison into a friendly haven.

There were thirty-one women detainees, Ledy told me,

living in cramped conditions, sharing dormitories and inadequate facilities. They helped each other in various ways, but the conditions tended to undermine their best efforts. She, for instance, had started to give her *compañeras* English lessons but, as always happened in that place, the initial enthusiasm waned and attendance dwindled.

Ledy herself was far from apathetic; on the contrary, she gave an impression of compact energy. She was not conventionally beautiful, but had a good, strong face and looked you straight in the eye. Her hair was short as a man's, shorter than mine; other women I saw there wore their hair longer, so Ledy's rather brutal cut must have been through choice rather than necessity; perhaps she felt it was in keeping with the brutishness of her surroundings. She spoke to me in *castellano*, though her English was certainly superior to my Spanish; she talked readily and without reserve but, though she was eager to hear about her son Julio, she was reluctant to broach such an emotionally charged subject. So first we discussed her prospects of release.

She expected to be let out very soon, as there was a law that would free her the moment it was ratified – at the very latest by the time the new government took office in March. I thought that in some respects this must be the hardest time for her: after five years inside, with freedom beckoning, she was frustrated daily by its postponement. But while she was impatient to resume her life outside, she did not seem unduly concerned for herself; it was Julio – there, the spell was broken, the name spoken – who occupied her thoughts. Where were his loyalties now? She wanted him to be happy in England, but at the same time she hoped he might want to return to Chile. On so brief an acquaintance as I had with Julio I could do little more than reassure her that he had seemed in good spirits and to be well cared for.

Ledy had a brother in Argentina and a close friend in Mexico and she wondered if she might not make a journey to England via these two countries when she was released. If that was not possible, she had heard of a scheme, fostered by – or connected with the name of – Mme Mitterrand, to pay the return fares to Chile of exiled children of women political prisoners, so that they could at least visit their mothers once these women had been freed.

When a warder came to tell me it was time to go, Ledy produced a card she had made and wrote an affectionately grateful message in it; this had to be rubber-stamped by a prison officer before I could take it out. (I have it still; it is a collage, depicting a face seen front-on with closed eyes like veined leaves and lips divided in such a way as to suggest that it could also be two faces in profile, set against a shiny purple background with different motifs on either side of the face. It is dated, 'Cárcel [prison] de Sto. Dgo., Stgo., 25 Enero 90'.)

Although, as far as I could see, the official letter I had allowed me only one visit, Ledy took up the matter with a woman prison officer, who told me I might come again. When I returned a week later the terrible Cerberus tried to prevent my entry, but fortunately the woman prison officer who had authorized a second visit was on duty and overruled him.

Ledy was already in the interview room, along with another detainee, a young girl with long hair, talking to the lawyer Camilo Marks. They were excitedly discussing the great escape from the Public Prison that had just taken place. The political prisoners who had organized it included some of those accused of the attempt on Pinochet's life, as well as those involved in the kidnapping case for which Ledy was still being held. They had spent a year tunnelling their way a hundred metres under a main road into the defunct Mapocho railway station. It was a disciplined effort, reminiscent of prisoner-of-war escapes in Germany during the Second World War. Nearly fifty prisoners had scrambled out through the tunnel before the authorities realized it existed and put a stop to this mass exodus. Only six escapees had been recaptured; the remainder had got away and two of the leaders, Mario Melo of the Chilean Communist Party and Miguel Montecinos of the Manuel Rodríguez Popular Front, gave press interviews from their hiding place.

Although this meticulously planned and executed escape boosted Ledy's morale, it made her more impatient

than ever to get out of prison and she kept pressing
Camilo for a release date. He merely smiled and told her
she would have to wait a little longer. Going back into
town ('Let's share a taxi,' Camilo suggested, then forgot to
pay his share), he told me that Chilean justice was so
Kafkaesque that the woman judge who had taken over
Ledy's case the previous September still could not get hold
of the papers from official sources and had had to ask him,
the defence lawyer, for the papers held by the Vicaría de la
Solidaridad.

Soon after I returned to England, in May or June, Sergio
Cornejo phoned to tell me that Ledy had been freed at
last, and that Julio was about to be flown out to Santiago
on a fortnight's visit. I sent Ledy a note via Julio, wishing
her well in her new-found freedom.

14

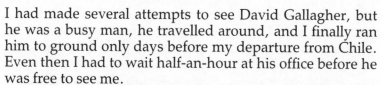

I had made several attempts to see David Gallagher, but he was a busy man, he travelled around, and I finally ran him to ground only days before my departure from Chile. Even then I had to wait half-an-hour at his office before he was free to see me.

While I was waiting, I wondered what he would be like, this unusual combination of monetarist and literary man. For David had been an academic and had written a standard text on Latin American literature before giving up university life for a career in finance; now he ran his own investment firm in Santiago. He also wrote a fortnightly column for *El Mercurio*, in which he seemed to have the freedom to sound off in any direction he chose. His ex-wife Adela, who had first suggested I see him, was Cristián's distant Ecuadorian cousin, whom I had met at the dinner Soledad had given soon after my arrival in Santiago.

Fair, bespectacled and youthful-looking, even baby-faced, David Gallagher gave the impression of not suffering fools gladly. He managed to be both brisk and slightly hesitant at the same time, but his affectionate regard for Cristián was apparent in every word he uttered. When Cristián died, he said, 'It was an enormous loss; it reduced by about thirty per cent the number of people one could talk to.'

David had been president of the Oxford Latin American Society when Cristián was his opposite number at Cambridge. They had become friends and spent weekends together, so that when David started going to Chile in 1977 or '78 (before settling there in 1980) and looked up Cristián, he felt he was calling on an old friend. He saw him in Santiago; he went to Cabildo; and he found him 'exactly the same, very much so, very much so'.

'I don't know whether he was exactly the same in what
he thought about A, B or C; he'd probably evolved in his
thoughts. But he was the same sort of terribly spon-
taneous, open person, terribly generous, honest sort of
person – a person who is really quite rare in this environment, in Chile. I can never figure out whether it has
always been like that, or whether it's the function of this
last period, that people tend to be afraid to say what they
think. There's a big gap between what people think and
what they say, I mean assuming they think more than
what they say, which one has to give them credit for. With
Cristián there wasn't that gap; he was the sort of person
who would think aloud. Whenever he wrote his column in
Hoy, for instance, or when he wrote a novel like *El rincón
de los niños*, there was a lot of thinking aloud, and thinking
aloud in Chile upset quite a lot of people and he wasn't
afraid of doing that.'

David went so far as to say that Cristián 'was the only
person in Chile practically who would speak and write his
mind; and because he had a complex mind, because he
was an intelligent person, his position was never terribly
clear-cut on any issue'. He might speak out against censorship, for instance, but his criticism would not be confined
to the current regime; David remembered him saying over
lunch, 'The worst censorship I've felt, within myself [he
meant not only censorship, but self-censorship too], was
the censorship of the left.' A favourite word of his was
'insolent', *insolente*.

Insolente or *impertinente*? Cristián himself welcomed the
return to Chile of the writer Enrique Lafourcade in *Hoy* on
December 16th, 1984 by praising impertinence; he wrote,
'Impertinence – defined in the dictionary as "tiresome and
tedious importunity" – is vital, especially in a country
where even the most enthusiastic defender of life today
would have to agree that this life is hardly typical.' Whatever the word, the point is that Cristián both felt the need
for and exemplified awkward individualism, even eccen-
tricity. In that same article, he went on: 'The eccentric is a
more characteristically English than Chilean figure, and
there are several in England. But inasmuch as it has been

said that Chile is the England of South America, we ought to find the type here too.'

David accepted that Cristián had his share of vanity, but preferred to emphasize his generosity. 'A lot of writers, especially in Chile,' he said, 'are very keen that no one else should shine, whereas Cristián, I think, obviously wanted to shine, but he wanted other people to shine too. So he was also a great listener, which a lot of people aren't. He was always very concerned about other people . . . If one felt depressed, he was a great person to go and see because he was terribly understanding, unshockable – which is quite normal in some places, but in Chile is quite unusual. People in Chile have any amount of other qualities, but that kind of enormous basic tolerance of Cristián, which makes him a libertarian to the very marrow, is very rare in this country where people – this rather Spanish syndrome – are expected to take definite positions on things.'

After Cristián came back from England the last time, he went straight to David and Adela's house, and 'from then on we were with him practically every day'. Did he know he was dying then? 'I don't know, I don't know, I don't know,' David replied. 'I mean, Cristián was such an enormously intelligent person that he probably knew and he preferred to play this game so that everybody was . . . I mean, he was always, even at that stage, cheering people up rather than the other way round. I would've thought that he probably knew.'

Earlier, when Cristián was writing the *Autobiografía por encargo*, David had stayed with him in Valparaíso, where they went for walks on which Cristián would 'rehearse his autobiography'. Whether it was just the age he had reached or some sort of premonition that made Cristián want to look back over his life, David could not say: 'But he seemed to be terribly anxious to string everything together, and very keen to talk about his past, about Paz, oh, with enormous affection, as I say, rescuing lost time, recovering it and so on. In retrospect, those conversations have an added poignancy. Literally a month afterwards he was to discover that he had a brain tumour.'

David thought that Cristián had been 'extraordinarily

selective about his life' in the autobiography, that he had
tried to turn it into 'a little literary gem'. He remembered
Cristián agonizing about whether or not to include the
letter that became the last chapter, because he realized
that it stood out; it had been written much earlier 'with
less distance, with less filter'. David advised him to
include it, not just for its intrinsic historical interest, but
'because I am not fanatical about things being terribly pol-
ished; perhaps I like hybrid forms'. He was also probably
encouraging Cristián to be *insolente*; he certainly thought it
would annoy people: 'I thought that it was more fun to
put it in.' In general, David was not inclined to see the
fragmentary nature of Cristián's autobiography as a
reflection of what was happening around him. 'It would
be nice to see Cristián as a metaphor of Chile,' he said. 'I
don't. I mean, as we talk, maybe . . . It never occurred to
me to think of it that way. I've always been rather nervous
of contextual explanations of an individual's life in that
sense.'

David never met Cristián's father, but he had read the
portrait of him in the unpublished *Una escalera contra la
pared*, which he thought was 'rather well done, a Tol-
stoyan portrait of a rather old-fashioned country gentleman'. Cristián's own assumption of that role, following
his father's death, did not mean that he was becoming – as
some people do – his father. There was far too much self-
mockery and ironical distance there: 'He would come to
Santiago and he would tell the story of some of the conversations he was having till two or three in the morning with
his neighbours in Cabildo, and they were enormously
funny and he was having a great time; he was probably
teasing them to their face without their knowing it.' But
there was also 'an element of him that was taking it dead
seriously, the farm, and trying to prove to his family that
he could make a go of it'.

His humour never deserted him. Even when he over-
extended himself and got into debt and then was hit by
the massive devaluation, David recalled, 'it didn't seem to
make him bitter, as it did some people. He was terribly
funny when he described his tour of the banks. He would
play to the hilt the role of the old-fashioned country

gentleman who was actually deigning to come and inform them that he would be rolling over his land for another year, or whatever. But one never knows with that kind of attitude how many sleepless nights are being covered up.'

David had not been particularly impressed with Cristián's venture into the erotic, *El verano del ganadero*. 'I'm not sure there is any world other than the Spanish-speaking world,' he said, 'where a writer would think it was necessary to write a "pornographic" novel. If you look around, you find that Mario Vargas Llosa has done it, and Donoso. With Vargas Llosa, and probably with Cristián as well, you feel it is done almost out of a sense of duty, a sense of revolutionary duty, taboo-breaking, part of the need to be *insolente*. You know, the moment you're not *insolente*, what are you? You're caving in, you're handing over. So maybe it's a kind of muscle-flexing.'

There was one scene in the novel, however, that David had greatly enjoyed: this was a description of a party in a house in the Lo Curro district of Santiago: 'I rather suspect I know which house it was. People got rich terribly quickly in Chile, even people from quite old families, you know, who'd never seen any money before, suddenly started behaving very, er . . . I'd been living two or three years in Venezuela before coming here and I'd been travelling to Chile, and I told people, you know, trying to be *insolente* myself, that I thought people were behaving in a more *nouveau riche* way here than in Venezuela, which had the image of being the ultimate, outside the Arab world, in petrodollar absurdity and so on . . . And the atmosphere of the party and the house in Lo Curro was terribly real; I felt I'd been there when I read it.'

I was surprised that such an enthusiastic advocate of the free market as David should be so critical of one of its effects. But he argued that there was 'a difference between observing things sociologically, as it were, and observing them economically'. Disparities of wealth and sudden riches were only the first phase of the free market system, and one did not have to approve of ostentatious gestures like having a telephone at the opera. 'But in the end a country has to make a choice whether it wants to be a charming backwater, with lots of horse-drawn carts

plodding around the countryside, lots of help – because in
the end it's true you get these new rich popping up but the
more privileged people live much better under the old
paternalist system than under the free market system,
once the free market system has really seen itself through.
The hope is that people will get a shock in a few years'
time and find they can't get all that cheap help, that wages
will start going up. I think Cristián was very much an
amused, ironical observer of these rather primitive people
– some with terribly elegant surnames – behaving like
Saudis, but at the same time thought the system was really
the right one.'

Whether or not Cristián thought that, David certainly
did. So I probed him a little about the evolution of his
political thinking.

He told me: 'When I came to Chile in 1980, and even
after a year of living here, I had the most dismal opinion of
the government and Pinochet. It took me an enormous
amount of time to see that the thing was more complex
than I had thought. I had a very stereotype image of Chile.
When the coup took place in 1973, I was in London and I
remember thinking that this was my cause – I was always
terribly involved in Chile [and] I actually did quite a lot of
work – I'm glad I did – to try and get work at Sussex
and Oxford for Alvaro Bunster, the Chilean ambassador in
London. All my thinking was of that kind, and it took me
a hell of a long time to figure out what was going on here.
It was very unusual, unique, unexpected, and it hasn't
happened anywhere else in the world that I can think of,
that you have a military regime with a lot of unfortunate
authoritarian practices actually at the same time using that
concentration of power to give up power in whole areas
where the military in other countries had been keener, if
anything, on increasing it: the economy, the social area,
pensions . . . For a time, for a lot of people, there was a
caricature about Chile where we thought the same thing
was being done as in Argentina and Uruguay, but it
wasn't. What *they* were doing was practising some kind of
open market economy – policies on the tariff, one or two
very specific things – but they weren't making any attempt
whatsoever to privatize industry; on the contrary, they

were a very statist sort of regime. If you look at Spain, its recent history is full of paradoxes on this front: I think the only really free market regime that Spain has had in the last 500 years is Felipe González's regime, and certainly not Suárez's regime, which was extremely paternalistic. So in Spain you have market socialism, and in Chile market militarism, both unexpected.'

David contrasted the position of exiles returning to Chile – who 'believed their own propaganda' and whose stereotypical view of what was going on reduced this complex reality to a battle between 'goodies and baddies', in which they were the goodies – with that of another exile, his close friend the Cuban writer Guillermo Cabrera Infante: 'When he gets back to Cuba – and it's not going to be all that long a wait; I mean, how long can Castro hold out? – he will be a real hero because he has an enormous moral capital which he has been building up for twenty-five years. There's nothing inside Cuba which is relevant to the future Cuba.'

In Chile, on the other hand, despite the 'unfortunate authoritarian practices' of the regime, there was the basis for a future, fairer society. The 'difference of vision' of returning Chilean exiles was a problem David felt he understood, 'in that I had it myself, not that I was exiled in any way'. He said, 'It took me an enormous amount of time to catch on to what was going on, to reconcile myself to it, to understand it, to face the contradictions involved.'

Paz suggested we held a farewell party in her house and invited the people I had interviewed and become friendly with over the previous four months. David Gallagher sent his apologies, but twenty other people came, which was an impressive turn-out for late February when – as in August in Europe – people tend to be away on holiday. Paz herself had only recently returned from a week's trip with Claudia Donoso (Tom had gone back to Magallanes, this time taking Tomás with him) to the tiny island of La Mocha, off the coast more or less opposite the southern city of Concepción, though this hardly sounded like a holiday. Even to get there was to risk one's life: boats overturned in choppy seas; aeroplanes fell out of the sky. But

Paz and Claudia squeezed into a two-seater plane in which there were four other people and still managed to arrive intact. The island itself, which was regarded by the Mapuche Indians on the mainland as the place where their souls migrated after death, was strange and poor, and the people inbred. It was an adventure, more than a vacation, and Paz enjoyed that, though she was relieved to have got back safely.

The party was on the Saturday night before we left. At one point we noticed that all the Chileans were sitting round the table while the English – Jenny and I, Malcolm Coad, Catherine Royle from the British embassy, and Dorothy, the widow of Cristián's uncle Pancho Huneeus – were huddled together in another part of the room. Then Adriana, who perhaps was aware of this or had tired of the male dominance of such as Armando Uribe and Jorge Edwards at the table, broke ranks and came and joined us.

A couple of days after the party, Jenny and I bumped into Armando at a small café, where he was drinking coffee and reading an article he greatly disliked by Joseph Alsop in an old number of the *New York Review of Books*. He stood up when we greeted him and insisted on buying us a coffee. Some weeks earlier I had asked him if he could arrange a meeting for me with his brother-in-law Juan de Dios Vial, who had been director of Estudios Humanísticos before Cristián and Marcos García de la Huerta, and had just resigned as rector of the University of Chile. Now at this, our final meeting, Armando could not resist telling me that the reason Juan de Dios Vial had been reluctant to talk to me was his unflattering view of Cristián whom he saw as a trimmer, someone who became a Marxist sympathizer when Allende came to power – which was how he came to be director of the DEH – then switched to being a lieutenant in the reserves after the military coup.

While this was clearly a travesty, it indicated just how narrow the dividing line was between truth and fiction, how much depended on the point of view, which in this case was a doubly unsympathetic one, since both the messenger and the message – Armando and his brother-in-law, from opposite ends of the political spectrum – were united in their hostility to Cristián. Leaving personalities aside, one might say that neither the left nor the right in Chile had any time for 'the dilemma of the liberal intellectual'. No doubt that was what David Gallagher had meant when he referred to 'this rather Spanish syndrome [of being] expected to take definite positions on things'.

15

My last days in Santiago, like my first, centred on Paz. The difference was that Cristián no longer stood between us. We had succeeded in re-establishing a relationship which was not dependent on his memory, but equally did not exclude it. I did not feel entirely comfortable talking about him with her, just as – for different reasons – I could not talk about him with Soledad. For both, perhaps, there was still too much pain involved. In Paz's case, there were also traces of anger and bitterness which would find expression at odd moments – as when she told me a story of the time she photographed a naked man (which Tom had not been too enthusiastic about, though the man was homosexual) and he found the silver-dollar wedding ring that Tom had made for her and she had lost; this reminded her of an earlier occasion when she had lost the wedding ring Cristián had bought her in the sea at Nerja: 'But that was deliberate,' she said.

The day after the party we gave for the people who had helped me in my quest for Cristián, I talked to Paz at length about her work. The exhibition of photographs of transvestites, which she had taken me to see when I arrived in Santiago, was only the last of several in-depth projects she had undertaken during the years of the dictatorship, but it epitomized both her sort of subject-matter and her preferred method of working.

In this instance, her original intention had been to photograph female prostitutes. 'I had an obsession all my life with prostitutes,' she told me. 'I always wanted to meet them, to know them, know their life. Well, it's one more subject I was forbidden to get close to. As a child in my family, you know, you were not supposed to look at children begging, or at prostitutes, or at all kinds of things in the street. Probably my work is partly to do with that: I was forbidden as a child, and the dictatorship didn't allow us to search into things.'

The project began well; Paz had no difficulty in winning the confidence of the girls and photographing them. Problems arose over exhibiting her work, since many of these prostitutes kept their profession secret from their families and – where they had them – children. By chance, Paz met a transvestite working in the brothel in the Vivaceta district of Santiago: 'Well, they like to be photographed, they have no problem, they are funny and nice and they live in this, like, triple marginality, so they have much less to lose; they don't care really.' This transvestite introduced Paz to his brother, who also worked as a prostitute, and to their mother.

'That was really the point,' she said, 'when I met the mother. I was getting involved in this triangle, photographing these *vinculos*, these links between them, and I was fascinated by that mother – to accept it the way she accepted it; the mother's was the house where they met with their friends in their free time.'

When Paz decided to switch the focus of her interest from women prostitutes to transvestites, she felt some anxiety about the world she was entering. These transvestites were not indulging in a penchant for cross-dressing, they were prostitutes pure and simple, they did it for the money; they came from the poorest of the poor and they lived in a world of violence – 'a lot of scars, of knives, a lot of drink, very dangerous'. Paz visited the brothel at night, sometimes on her own and sometimes with friends, and occasionally, on Sundays, she would go to the mother's house and spend what was, especially for the mother, a family day – though she had to be wary because the sons drank so much in the course of their work that they could be very morose.

As a woman working with transvestites, Paz found them eager to transform her appearance; they wanted to know why she did not make up her face, wear ear-rings, or high heels, do her hair this way or that. She had experienced this before, when she had worked with gypsies: 'They wanted to dress me up; they gave me all their clothes and I said, "Look, I can't work if I become a gypsy.

I would love to, it's my life's ambition, but if I dress like a gypsy I can't work." ' Maintaining a distance, a difference, while at the same time empathizing with her subjects, was essential to Paz's quasi-anthropological working method. 'It's very strange,' she said, 'what happens in two worlds. You belong; every time I've done similar things I feel I belong – the circus, whatever. Or I want to belong so much I feel I do: it doesn't matter which.'

Once she gained the transvestites' trust, they told her amazing stories. She had always wanted to write and had felt that she could never be satisfied with photography, until she hit upon a way of working which engaged her imagination. She envied the American photographer Susan Meiselas her freedom to embark upon long-term projects, such as her work with topless waitresses in the United States, in which she both recorded their stories and photographed them. Family and financial pressures made it impossible for Paz to work in this way; so, for the first time, she looked for and found, in Claudia Donoso, an ideal collaborator – as adaptable as herself and with a necessary streak of craziness, as well as some journalistic experience.

There was a further reason why she needed a collaborator, which had to do with political developments. In 1983, or '84, when Paz started working with the transvestites, Pinochet's wife was agitating for legislation to outlaw prostitution; and the police, taking the wish for the deed, set about making life as difficult as possible especially for transvestites, whom they beat up and harassed to such an extent that many were forced to leave Santiago. One group, which included the brothers 'Evelyn' and 'Pilar', went to Talca in the south, to an all-male brothel called La Jaula (The Cage) – 'Nobody knows why Talca; it's a corrupt province. They had friends in the police there and paid them off with wine so they wouldn't harass the place; I think that was how it worked.' In the nineteenth century several of the ruling oligarchy had farms in Talca, which became a byword for elegance, giving rise to the ironic saying, '*Talca, París y Londres*'.

When one of the brothers wrote to Paz, 'You must visit us because we're going to have a Beauty Queen competition', she very much wanted to go, but was frightened to go alone – how would she explain her presence in a male brothel if she were caught in a police raid? For various reasons she could not invite a man to accompany her: apart from anything Tom might have to say on the subject, the presence of a man would jeopardize the relationship she had built up with the transvestites. At that time Paz had only just met Claudia, but she sensed she would be just the person to go with her, so she invited her along.

In Talca they stayed at the brothel under the watchful eye of Maribel, the male madam. The *travestis* demonstrated pickpocketing skills worthy of the Artful Dodger on unsuspecting clients; but at the same time they looked after Paz's expensive photographic equipment with fanatical devotion. Claudia was quickly accepted by them, her blue eyes making them envious, since 'in Chile to have blue eyes is like something out of this world'. The transvestites lived entirely by night, never emerging into the light of day except when Paz and Claudia invited them all to take a boat trip on the river one Sunday afternoon; then they put on jeans and woolly hats – to hide their long hair – but still managed to seem exotically out of place, with their long, painted fingernails and outrageous behaviour. They could be very aggressive, and a boat-load of them was a fearsome sight.

The *travestis* from Santiago made out that they were bored with Talca; the clients were all *huasos*, crude country bumpkins. Yet these clients seemed to Paz like normal, lower-class men, a surprisingly large number of whom were married. 'Oh, March is a very bad month for us,' the *travestis* would say, 'because all these men have to buy books and things for the children, uniforms for school.' The attraction of the *travestis* for their clients was that they had more imagination and fantasy, were more sexually inventive, than women; they were always beautifully dressed and, playing the role of wife, were ready for anything. Even so, Paz and Claudia had to be careful not to get too involved. The atmosphere was very relaxed, there was music and dancing and drink, and more drink; and as they were the only two women in the place the clients sometimes wanted to dance with them. This was fine so

long as there were enough clients to go round, but sometimes, at about two in the morning, Maribel would come
up to them and say, very politely, 'Look Paz, from now on
the atmosphere gets very thick and dangerous, so I think
it might be better if you went to bed.' Paz would take the
hint and say, 'Yes, we understand – goodnight, everybody.'

Paz and Claudia went to Talca in 1984. The project went
on for four years. It ended with the Pope's visit to Chile,
which made such an impression on one of the *travestis* that
he cut off his hair and sent it to his mother, gave up
prostitution and started selling sandwiches in the market
in Santiago. Then Mercedes, the mother of Pilar and
Evelyn, died. Pilar had been in Europe for a year, which
he had spent entirely in jail since he had been apprehen-
ded for smuggling cocaine the moment he stepped off the
aeroplane at Frankfurt. When Mercedes was dying, Paz
and Claudia would read her Pilar's letters and write
replies for her since she herself could neither read nor
write. Evelyn, too, was spending so much time in jail in
Chile that he had finally abandoned the *ambiente*, the
milieu, and grown a moustache – 'I couldn't believe it,'
said Paz, 'because he had a most feminine face.'

Paz met him by chance in Valparaíso and he told her he
was waiting for Pilar to arrive from Sweden. 'Pilar came
with a Swedish boyfriend,' she recalled, 'and I met them
in the street again by chance and we had this long evening
together with the Swedish guy, who was an expert on
French cooking. And then – this fabulous *culturisación* –
Pilar confessed to me that he wanted to be a gay, not a
transvestite any more. He had acquired this terminology,
"gay". In these very low groups you are called *maricón*:
gay is much classier; so he was very proud he had become
a gay. He said he had to stop himself running away and
dressing up as a woman, but it was more cultured, more
modern, had more status, to be gay. It was absolutely out
of fashion to be a transvestite.' Evelyn stayed in Chile long
enough to attend Paz's exhibition along with the rest of
the group, but afterwards he went to join his brother in
Sweden. 'The others separated,' Paz said. 'Some stayed in

Talca; one of them was killed in Talca; and others are here in Santiago, and Talcahuano, or San Antonio.'

Paz had begun by photographing children. To supplement her income as a infant school teacher, she accepted commissions to do portraits of children; and with the encouragement of Isabel Allende, who was then editing a series of books for children, she published a story with photos about the exploits of a silky hen called Amalia. Then she started photographing drunks and down-and-outs in the streets of Santiago, collecting a sequence of images which she called 'the sleeping people'; and she followed that up with two long-term projects, one with old people in retirement homes, the other with patients in a psychiatric hospital – which she had to wait a year and a half to get official permission to visit.

Although her interest was not primarily political – 'I always photograph *behind* that' – it took on an immediate political dimension when friends asked her to take advantage of her access to the mental home to check on whether such-and-such a disappeared person was being held there, a common suspicion in the immediate aftermath of the coup. The real focus of her interest was the condition of marginality itself. 'I feel terribly identified with all these worlds,' she said. 'It's something very difficult for me to explain because it's so personal. I had to work it out with a psychiatrist and suddenly I understand why. I told you I was brought up by this nanny, that actually she was my mother, you know, and this nanny was a very poor maid originally; so probably I'm confused in that respect. I have a strong, strong need to find out things, though people who know me only superficially will say, "Oh look, I mean, Paz Errázuriz, what does she have to do with this world?" That's why I can't talk about it.'

Tom helped her both critically and in practical ways, setting up a darkroom for her; but even when she earned some money for her work, she still thought of it as a hobby, or private obsession, rather than a career. Paz was accustomed to subordinate her artistic ambitions to those of her husband: Cristián had been very much the Writer, with a capital W; and now there was Tom, who lived for his painting in a way that left no room for doubt as to who was the artist in the family. And she had children, of course: in addition to Daniela, there was Tomás to look after.

She was handicapped, too, by the fact that she had lived outside Chile for an important part of her life. She had felt very lonely on her return from England, and no sooner had she begun to make friends than her separation from Cristián and involvement with Tom, himself a foreigner, plunged her back into isolation; then came the coup and, once again, she was deprived of such friends as she had, a number of whom either left the country or disappeared. For that reason, her friendship with the artist Roser Bru, an older woman born in Barcelona and exiled from Spain since the Civil War, was important to her, as Bru was the first person to suggest that her work merited an exhibition; not only that, but she helped her arrange one. It was held in 1980 in the Instituto Chileno-Norteamericano de Cultura, though it almost did not take place when the organizers saw the kind of pictures Paz intended to exhibit.

'And then I realized that in Chile,' Paz said, 'we didn't have any photographic culture at all. I think something might be starting now, but at that time we only knew conservative photography, like portraits of Pepe Donoso, factories, social realism, that type of photography – big things, important people, or a beautiful volcano. Then for the first time there were hung on a wall photographs that were not supposed to be hung in a gallery – drunkards in the street, crazy people in a hospital, dying ladies in an old people's home.'

When the exhibition opened, Paz was very nervous. Enrique Lihn came with Adriana, she remembered, and talked about Diane Arbus, whom Paz had never heard of: 'Then I asked for a book of Diane Arbus, and I was fascinated to discover that we had a similar background: she was a rich Jewish woman from New York and she had the same prohibitions as a child, and an interest in more or less the same people. When people tell me, "You're the Chilean Diane Arbus", I can't stand it. But I love her. I was obsessed with Diane Arbus the minute I saw her work and read about her.'

Enrique Lihn agreed to sponsor Paz when she applied for a Guggenheim fellowship. Her project, as she summarized it, was 'to make the invisibles visible', and that really was the aim of all her work. When the award came through, she was overwhelmed: 'It was the first time they'd given a Guggenheim to a photographer in Chile, and only the second time in the whole of Latin America – the first was given to the famous Mexican photographer, Manuel Alvárez Bravo.' Then, just as she was about to leave for New York, where she planned to buy up-to-date equipment, Tom fell ill. That was when he was so ill he nearly died. She could not leave him and at first she thought she would have to renounce the Guggenheim. But Tom began to get better and she resumed her work, slipping out in the evenings while he slept to photograph boxing matches. Some of these bouts were televised and friends were amazed to catch glimpses of her at the ringside, and wondered what she could be doing in such a raffish milieu. Indeed, the boxing authorities themselves had been reluctant to co-operate at first: 'They said I was going to get robbed, get hit, and this and that – and how did my husband allow me to go. Then they invite you out!' She persisted and succeeded in the end by 'being charming – as a woman in Chile it still works'. Taking photos at the ringside was part of soaking up the atmosphere; she never used those pictures: 'My obsession again was to be face to face and look at a boxer's *eyes*. And that's what I did: I did portraits, very painful portraits.'

Wrestlers were another group, like the transvestites, to which she came in a roundabout way. She had wanted to photograph topless waitresses (this was before she heard that Susan Meiselas was doing precisely that in the United States); she went to the Plaza de Armas, the place in Santiago where all the jobless popular artistes gathered, and started talking to people there. She already knew some of them from the days when she had photographed circus performers. Now she discovered that these artistes had a manager, who was a wrestler, tough and tall, but also very pleasant and approachable. This was La Momia, whose death soon after my arrival in Santiago had been such a shock to Paz. She went to his funeral and the newspapers published her pictures of him; normally he was never seen other than swathed in bandages like the mummy he personified in his professional contests.

La Momia introduced Paz to his wrestler friends and she was so struck by their appearance that she invited Claudia Donoso to go with her on a tour the wrestlers were making to Illapel, 'a lost town in the north'. But then she discovered that this subculture had a sinister side, that wrestlers were not only being used by the regime as bodyguards, because of their toughness, but some of them were also involved in drugs traffic: 'I mean, the poetical thing changed into something very dark and I got mixed up and then I stopped it.'

At the other extreme from the cynicism of the wrestling world was the sentimentality of the circus, and Paz eschewed that too. There were no pictures of clowns, for instance, among her circus photographs. 'I avoid clowns,' she told me. 'I dislike clowns, the same as Father Christmas, I can't stand them.' She also disliked the picturesque, and one of the reasons why she had never exhibited her photos of gypsies was that they were 'too beautiful and too colourful'. Another reason was that they were not Chilean in the way that her other subjects were; the gypsies lived in ghettos and did not mix with other people.

Paz was not easily distracted from the main thrust of her work. Once, when she suggested doing a portrait of Santiago, the commissioning editor said, 'Why don't you photograph upper-class people for a change?' She said she was not interested and anyway she was no longer in touch with them. The editor persisted, saying his sister was a member of the Golf Club and would provide introductions. So, against her better judgement, Paz started taking photographs; but she was filled with a passionate hatred and the pictures were ugly – the society women she photographed all came out looking like transvestites. Her lack of sympathy, or empathy, made it impossible for her to continue. Photography for her was 'an act of love, a possession of somebody or something'; she believed in 'what the Indians here say, that you rob their souls – but with a lot of love'.

Portraiture, she agreed, was central to her work, but she thought she might be getting a little tired of that; perhaps it was time for a change. 'I think I've already acquired what I needed,' she said. 'I've robbed enough souls.' She had just been reading Italo Calvino's essay on lightness (one of the last things he wrote) and this had encouraged her to explore a side of her work and personality largely suppressed during the years of military dictatorship, the part of her that responded to the lightness of Lartigue rather than the freakishness of Diane Arbus.

'Look,' she said finally, 'I've worked as a photographer up to now only under the dictatorship, and it's stained with pain, a lot of pain; it's very hard, people have been beaten up on all sides. It's such a terrible identification. It's strange, but this air that one starts breathing now makes me feel a bit different.'

My two Cambridge friends, Paz and Cristián, had both, in their different ways, borne artistic witness to their turbulent times, Paz by 'making invisible visible', Cristián by assuming the fictional identity of 'Gaspar Ruiz' and – in his own words in praise of the poet Diego Maquieira – inventing 'a grotesque character to speak through and say those things which there would be no way of saying – or even perceiving – directly'. I was proud of them both for their courage and for what they had achieved – even if, in Cristián's case at least, it fell short of his high ambitions. *El rincón de los niños* may have struck many of its original readers as ' "hermetic", "pretentious", "unreadable", "obscene" ', as he had informed me in the letter he wrote me in 1984, but a generation or two on it could be rediscovered and revalued. Indeed, this was already happening; shortly before I left Chile I met someone who had written a thesis on it.

Coral Pey had spent the majority of the last sixteen years in exile, in Bolivia and Peru, just as her father, a Catalan (like Roser Bru, he had come to Chile on the *Winnipeg*, a ship chartered by Pablo Neruda to bring over Spanish refugees), had spent long years in exile from

Spain – to which he had been obliged to return, against his wishes (he had sworn he would not go back while Franco remained in power), after the coup, because he had been one of Allende's advisers. Coral herself was a radical feminist, and it would have amused – if not amazed – Cristián to think that his novel had been appreciated and made the subject of a Barthesian thesis by a *mirista*, a member of the revolutionary left.

In her thesis, Pey examines the form and content of the novel in the light of what she sees as the crux of it, the battle between Tradition and Rupture. From this point of view the apparently trivial lives and loves of a group of idle rich young men and women take on a new significance: they are treated, not as in Cristián's own earlier writing (though Pey does not say this) simply as stories of personal success and failure, but more as case studies, caricatures even, revealing the behaviour of ruling class youth at a particular historical moment.

The distancing effect Cristián achieves through, as it were, splitting himself into two fictional halves and looking ironically at his own intimate behaviour and that of his peers enables him to criticize – in Pey's words (which are not entirely free of literary jargon) – 'the values of "tradition" as much as the discourse of "rupture" '. Above all, in this reading, he is critical of all 'discourses' that emanate from, or reinforce, a position of power: 'The narrator, in this sense, is not identified with any discourse – or, therefore, any ideology – that appears in the story, which represents a wide spectrum of the country's political life.'

In other words – and this is my interpretation – in *El rincón de los niños* (and its still-to-be-published sequel, *Una escalera contra la pared*), Cristián found the form in which he could transcend his personal history and prejudices, and turn them to account in documenting the wider history of his class and generation. And it is here, as in the two halves of 'narrator' and 'Gaspar Ruiz', that the moralist and the hedonist are engaged in fruitful conflict. The moralist wins; he presents a portrait of a decadent group, whose pursuit of pleasure – 'a self-regarding and narcissistic pleasure', according to Pey, 'at the expense of others, in an eminently bourgeois world, where human values are subordinated to the power-pleasure axis' – opens the way to 'rupture' and beyond, to what Pey calls 'the end of the party' and the forcible reinstatement of 'tradition' in the form of the military dictatorship.

In life, of course, things do not happen in quite so schematic a way; and in Cristián's life, in particular, the conflict between the hedonist and the moralist was never entirely resolved, as his obsessive and nostalgic returns to the days of his youth testify. Chilean childhoods, when they are not blighted by oppression, poverty or disease, tend to be idyllic, as Adriana had remarked to me when we were driving along the Pacific coast, and Cristián's was no exception. How could it be otherwise in a country blessed, in its most populous region, with a Mediterranean climate, vineyards, high mountains, wide beaches, sea and, above all, space to dream in? To grow up in such natural surroundings, and to be the heir to an estate, secure in the love of family and friends and the deference of servants and labourers, was to be a prince indeed: why not enjoy what nature and nurture alike had so bountifully provided?

Of all Cristián's works, the one I find myself returning to is a story, or meditation – since it has no plot or characters, only an autobiographical 'I' and a 'you' readily identifiable as his loved one. *Al otro lado del mar* ('On the Other Side of the Sea') is thirty pages long and acts as a makeweight to his early novella *Las dos caras de Jano* ('The Two Faces of Janus'). It was written in London in 1962, the year before I met him and Paz, and it charts their disillusionment with England (before they went to Cambridge) and suggests beyond that another, deeper disillusionment, not so much with each other (the writing is imbued with an aching tenderness and a profound sense of guilt) as with love or life itself – or their impossibly high expectations of both.

The London Cristián evokes is a predictably drab, cold and grey metropolis, in which this lonely Chilean couple find themselves identifying not with the Europeans they feel themselves to be at heart, but with outcasts like the Blacks who were being shunned by fastidious landladies advertising for lodgers with the proviso, 'No coloureds need apply'. Instead of making them feel more European, London has the opposite effect: it makes them feel, perhaps for the first time in their lives, *South American*.

Lost in the huge impersonality of London, confined to a dreary Earl's Court hotel room in which the miserably inadequate gas fire dies for want of a sixpence in the meter, the couple try to warm themselves by reliving the early days of their love – *el comienzo de nuestro amor* – in 'the parks and gardens of our families, the presence of our little brothers and sisters, the white beaches, the beautiful lonely white beaches where we spent our adolescence'. Everything they see or do in London triggers off unbearably poignant memories of the Chilean paradise from which they have been ejected, or have ejected themselves.

What ails Cristián, and Paz too – to the extent that she shares his psychological discomfort – is the feeling of being powerless and anonymous in an alien land in which he/they have invested such hopes. The higher the hopes, the more disillusioning the reality. That is what fills each day with horror for the stranded couple as they go out sightseeing or shopping or looking for a flat.

'What happened when we were living in Earl's Court?' he asks. 'What happened? . . . Although we were always together, there were moments when I couldn't reach you, and I felt horribly alone. I looked at you sleeping, I came close, I touched you, listening to your breathing and kissing you, and still I couldn't melt the circle of ice shutting me off. I spent hours lying awake, staring into the gloom of the ceiling, as if neither you nor anyone else existed or had ever existed. So a new chain of regrets was added to the one that had reduced me to that state.' He felt as though he were in a straitjacket which prevented him establishing normal relationships with other people; he tried to breathe deeply, flex his muscles and break out of it, but he couldn't. He grew tired of blaming God, or the wickedness of the world, or even himself: 'But don't imagine, because of that, that I feel free of guilt; only that I shall go on searching for whoever or whatever has got me into this mess.'

The search takes him back to his childhood on his father's estate, where his favourite day of the week was

Saturday, when all the staff came to be paid. They gathered outside the office window and waited to be called in by the foreman. When Cristián approached a group, conversation would cease – probably, he thought, because they had been talking about women. Now they ruffled his hair and asked when the young master would be coming out for a ride. He moved on to another group, of young men talking about football; these he liked least because they answered his questions ironically, and he found that disconcerting. It was a relief to meet up with the children of his own age, who came along with their fathers or elder brothers, or stood in for them to collect their pay.

With these younger children he played games, including a primitive kind of golf he initiated when he discovered an old bag of clubs in the cellar. One of Cristián's wilder swings ended with the tinkle of breaking glass; fortunately, his father was out that day. On another occasion, some visiting cousins joined in a game that sounds more like hockey than golf, and in the mêlée one of them was hit on the shins. As he limped back to the house, covered in sweat and grime, he said, 'Of course, if you play with scum, they hit you on purpose; the shitty scum.' Cristián was outraged and – 'like the innocent I was' – shut him up: 'Who do you think you are? You think you're different because you've got money? Aren't we all children of Adam and Eve?'

The point of dredging up such memories, he says, is not to wallow in nostalgia, but to see how the past connects with the present: 'Don't you think the past changes just as the present changes, that different lights illuminate and transform it?' Cristián cannot say exactly when he began to understand the sham concealed in the idea of everyone being a child of Adam and Eve. Perhaps it was after another such game, in which he himself was hit on the shins: 'That made me see that the motive was bitterness since, though we were indeed all children of Adam and Eve, there were certain differences it was as well not to forget.'

Later, he goes on:

I was told that there was a profound reason why things were as they were: God had made them so. No doubt that was terrible; and our privileged position imposed on us the duty to amend God's work and help the poor. I found this very strange. Nevertheless, I had to get used to the idea that poor people were not people: that's to say that, although they had the right to receive our help, they did not have the right to help themselves. That would be presumptuous, impudent and arrogant. That had to be stopped. At all costs. But something very annoying, something inexplicable, had happened in the world: with every day that passed these people seemed more and more resolved to turn up their noses at our help, regardless of the fact that – thanks, no doubt, to a change in the divine plan – this help increased daily. We went so far as to make the noble gesture of allowing them a reasonable education. But that wasn't enough for them. Evil was taking possession of the planet. We went even further, offering to share our lands. Just like that. They didn't rise to the bait.

The story ends with the couple finding a flat in Hampstead (though he does not name the district) and putting the anguish of Earl's Court behind them. They unpack their books on to the shelves, their clothes into the wardrobe; they make the bed and then go out, hand in hand, into the street. The sky is blue, there is a light breeze, and the clamour of the city seems far away. They can hear birds singing in the tops of trees and someone trying unsuccessfully to start up a car. On one side of the hill there is a cemetery, a forest of standing stones surrounded by pine-trees and enclosed behind a long black fence. Still holding hands, they tell each other they should be happy to have found somewhere to live: 'The truth however, is there, where we still have to do it, on the other side of the sea.'

How the past connects with the present . . . As Paz drove Jenny and me out of Santiago to the airport at Pudahuel, and then stayed and had a coffee with us while we waited nervously to board the plane, I understood that my friendship with her and with Cristián had been such an important one for me not just because of the way they had complemented one another when I first knew them, but because they had each complemented me as well. At Cambridge we had all had leftist political sympathies;

Cristián's, it had sometimes seemed to me, were over-intellectual, Paz's too instinctual, and my own, of course, a perfect blend of the two . . .

In Cristián's 1962 story, the couple discuss the possibility of revolution in their country:

> You said a revolution would bring too much cruelty, and I replied that in peace there could be much greater cruelty; that in the last analysis it was a matter of whose side one was on, since there were forms of living which, during a revolution, were nothing but forms of dying.
>
> One could meet death miserably, without knowing how or why, trapped between two fires like a hopeless idiot who does not understand what is going on. One could die heroically, fighting for what one believed to be the truth – and such a death exalted a life, making it even more alive than it had been when blood flowed through that person's veins. One could die like a hunted hare – or even a hunted lion – defending one's own burrow and be condemned, as a result, to the scorn of all future history. The problem lay in freedom of choice. It was limited. One died as one had lived.
>
> You answered that that was to look at life from the point of view of the importance it held for others rather than oneself. Be that as it might be, you thought that all life was beautiful, and noble, and ought to be respected . . .
>
> It did not take us long to recognize that essentially we were in agreement, but were speaking on different planes . . .

If indeed 'one died as one had lived', then Cristián's brain tumour might be ascribed to too cerebral an approach to life; but such an attribution of cause and effect would be simple-minded, if not entirely specious. The sense in which it is true to say of Cristián that he died as he had lived is in his dignified refusal to court sympathy or pity in his last months, weeks, days and his determination to live fully to the bitter end. This was of a piece with his courage in speaking his mind regardless of dangers and potential unpopularity, whether it was in the years of the *Unidad Popular* or during the dictatorship.

There had always been something *voulu*, something forced, about his revolutionary fervour, and he was not destined for an heroic death at the barricades; 'in the last analysis', as he puts it, he was on the other side – though he preferred to fudge the issue by describing himself as a liberal or, as he was wont to tell his students at the DEH, an *English* socialist, as if that exonerated him from any serious commitment to the left.

I am not saying his liberalism was a sham – far from it. Twenty years after he wrote the story from which I have been quoting, he spoke out against abuses of language in a New Year's article entitled 'Liberal Sermon': 'It is enough to note that in today's world people go to war in the name of peace, impose dictatorships in the name of freedom, discriminate and persecute in the name of justice, practise profiteering in the name of the common good, kill in the name of the love of humanity.' He went on to suggest that it might be better to rest the grand words in favour of lesser words like 'tolerance, sympathy, discretion, straightforwardness, sense of humour, calmness', and so forth. Though the article is couched in generalities, no Chilean reader in 1982 could have missed its particular application.

Paz, fortunately, is still alive and working. She has never seen herself as an intellectual, though several of her friends are intellectuals, and she is not given to making political statements. But even a cursory examination of her work reveals the depth of her opposition to the dictatorship: her photographs are a standing reproach to its inhuman policies; her focus on outcasts emphasizes the narrow limits of acceptable citizenship under so rigid a regime. The appeal of photography in times of catastrophe, as Adriana Valdés has written in an essay, is that it provides 'a material trace of people who have left no trace in official history'.

Of course, there would be drunks in the street, prostitutes and transvestites in brothels, people suffering in psychiatric hospitals or old people's homes under any but the most Utopian system, and Paz's involvement with them is as romantic as it is political. But the contrast between her particular talent for exploring marginal social worlds and the dictatorship's determination to suppress such undesirable excrescences is what gives her images additional force and poignancy.

*

And what of the third party in this triangular relationship? Did my brief sojourn in Chile influence my political thinking? Did it restore the radicalism of my youth or confirm the conservatism of my middle age?

I had gone to Chile by and large accepting the exiles' version of events which had dominated the world's media. I had read (and even been instrumental in publishing in *New Society*) passionate articles by Ariel Dorfman – an exile who seems to have cornered the market in Chilean comment in American and British newspapers – without taking into account that his was the point of view of an unreconstructed *allendista*. I had been excited by the Nobel prizewinning Colombian novelist Gabriel García Márquez's rip-roaring, real-life thriller, *Clandestine in Chile* – in which the Chilean film-maker Miguel Littín returns to Chile disguised as a Uruguayan, outwits the authorities to film there secretly and escapes to tell the tale and show the film – without questioning precisely how much of this cloak-and-dagger stuff was actually necessary, and whether Littín might not just as easily have masterminded the whole thing from Europe and thus spared himself dangers, real or imagined – including that of flying, of which I share his dread.

The only other country I can think of where the exiles' view has prevailed to a comparable extent is South Africa, from which there has also been a massive exodus of articulate middle-class professionals. But there, perhaps due to the size of the English-speaking population, some powerful voices from within, from Alan Paton to J. M. Coetzee, from Nadine Gordimer to Rian Malan, who speak complex and often uncomfortable truths, have also been heard. From inside Chile, during the dictatorship, so little was heard that I had expected to find widespread evidence of censorship when I got there – instead of which I was surprised to see books highly critical of the regime on sale openly in the bookshops of Santiago. Of course there had been censorship and, more damagingly, self-censorship in the earlier days of the dictatorship. But in this respect, if not in some others, a dictatorship differs from a totalitarian regime. Vaclav Havel, whose swift promotion from prison to the presidency of Czechoslovakia entitles him to a hearing on such matters, made the point succinctly in an interview published in the *Washington Post* in February 1990:

> The substance of the totalitarian system was that all of us were drawn into it, and all of us became guilty. This is the way in which a totalitarian system differs from a dictatorship. In a dictatorship, there is a strict dividing line between those who grab the government by force and those who are powerless and have to submit. But the substance of the totalitarian system is that there are special rays which get into everyone's soul.

This is a useful, though perhaps not an absolute, distinction. The people I spoke to in Chile, whether they had spent years in exile or remained in the country, often used the word 'guilty', as in 'We were the guilty ones' or 'They were the guilty ones', but they used it ironically to demonstrate how others regarded them or they regarded others, rather than how they regarded themselves. Nobody I met gave me the impression of having colluded with the regime in the sense that Havel means when he talks of 'being drawn into it', and of 'special rays which get into everyone's soul'. People might be forced, or frightened, into silence; but they were not duped, or cowed, into spiritual submission.*

---

*Malcom Coad, with the benefit of vastly more experience than I have in this area, comments: 'On totalitarianism and dictatorship. It may be that I'm oversensitive to this after years working at *Index on Censorship* as Latin American editor and constantly having to deal with it from the Eastern Europeans, but I always find myself wondering just what is the point of this comparison. Perhaps there are quantitative and qualitative distinctions to be made between different forms of tyranny – more freedom to read books and more death squads in one; less fear of hunger and more psychiatric hospitals in another – but I seriously wonder where they get us, particularly since 1989 removed the argument about dictatorships being easier to overthrow . . . Certainly there were greater pockets of freedom in Chile after 1983 than in most of the states generally called totalitarian. But I can't agree that "people might be forced, or frightened, into silence; but they were not duped, or cowed, into spiritual submission", or that Havel's "special rays" haven't got into people's souls and that guilt is merely referred to ironically. This is not my impression, either from living these things, or speaking to many ordinary people, or talking at length with psychologists and psychiatrists who have treated the syndromes of mutism and deep trauma directly traceable to the dictatorship – not just in the individual cases of those who have suffered repression, or their families or children, but more generally, as social phenomena.'

In saying that the totalitarian regimes of Eastern Europe were in some respects even worse than the Chilean dictatorship, I am not trying to exonerate the latter. I was delighted with the collapse of both systems in those extraordinary last months of 1989. But, as soldiers say, in dealing with an enemy one should try to understand the nature of the beast, and Pinochet's dictatorship was more Francoist than Stalinist – or Castroist (though it is not entirely surprising that Pinochet, in a book of interviews with two women journalists published while I was in Chile, *Ego Sum Pinochet*, should express some respect for Castro in person and praise him for his 'bravery' and 'charisma' even while deploring his Communism).

My impression of Chile is inevitably coloured by the kind of people I met, mostly middle- and upper-class intellectuals with liberal or left-wing leanings. Almost everyone I interviewed would have voted for the *Concertación* in the election. Yet, just as that alliance of convenience covered a wide spectrum of political attitudes, so there were considerable disparities of outlook between, say, Nicanor Parra and Armando Uribe. Political or ideological differences, it seems to me, were often less significant than differences of experience, particularly that of being within or outside the country. In the case of the returned exiles, their attitude often seemed to be determined by how long they had been back in Chile, with those who had returned a few years back becoming almost indistinguishable from the people who had remained in the country throughout the period of the dictatorship. Such recent returnees as Uribe and Mario Valenzuela might have ideological differences, but they were united in their uncompromising attitude to the crimes of the dictatorship, the edge of their outrage having yet to be blunted by sheer habituation.

The view from a university is, of course, different to the view from a prison cell, and the liberalism which seems appropriate to the one may be entirely inadequate to the other. The most remarkable event which took place during my stay in Chile was not the election, however much television coverage it got, but the mass escape from the Public Prison in Santiago, masterminded by political prisoners of the revolutionary left. The discipline of these men matched that of the military, and in this manoeuvre they easily outwitted their captors. They were indeed prisoners of war; it was impossible to think of them as common criminals. The press photos of two of the leaders were as revealing as their comments: these were young men with a mission, with the clear, proud gaze of untroubled conscience. Whether wrongfully imprisoned, like Ledy Castro, or – in terms of the military regime – rightfully detained, these were not evil men; you could see that at a glance. But will they, as the bishop had said after the *atentado*, come to be considered as 'heroes in the history of Chile'? Perhaps only history can answer such a question.

Almost exactly a year after Pinochet officially handed over the presidency to Patricio Aylwin, Malcolm Coad wrote to me from Santiago: 'Here the transition continues its extremely Chilean course. I never know whether to admire how civilized it all is (or most of it) or shriek in exasperation at the concessions and *mea culpas*. Is there anywhere else where it is so hard to know where principled compromise ends and pusillanimity begins?' (The Rettig report on human rights abuses under the dictatorship had just been published and 'was hard hitting and as blood-chilling as you might expect'. Writing before the assassination of the high-profile and clever right-wing political leader and lawyer, Jaime Guzmán, Malcolm added: 'So far, the only violent reactions have been from some retired generals and a couple of highly suspicious murders of a medical army officer and a police chief, which have the hallmarks of the extreme right stirring it – though again, you can't be sure.')

Principled compromise or pusillanimity – not a bad definition of opposite views of liberalism. Liberalism flourishes in times of economic well-being; in hard times it gets a bad name. In Britain in the Eighties, the more liberal government ministers were nicknamed 'wets' – i.e., pusillanimous. Mrs Thatcher, by contrast, was the 'Iron Lady' (Pinochet, in *Ego Sum Pinochet*, talks admiringly of Castro's 'hand of iron'). Under Mrs Thatcher, as under Pinochet, compromise was a dirty word; the liberal, or welfare, consensus was blamed for a host of ills from inflation to stagnation. In both countries economic liberalism, or monetarism, went hand-in-hand with social authoritarianism, the rule of law, a powerful police force and 'the enemy within'. Without wishing to push the parallel too far, one might also see some resemblance in the social constitution of the two regimes: the lower-middle-class Toryism of Thatcher and Tebbit finding an echo in the comparatively lowly social status of army officers in Chile – who might well wish to revenge themselves on upper-class socialists such as Carlos Altamirano for more than political reasons.

So what were the political lessons of my Chilean experience for me? In sum, it both confirmed my liberalism and at the same time made me more than ever aware of its limitations. If the great goals of liberty and equality are indeed irreconcilable, then liberalism will never go unchallenged; the end of ideology is as much a mirage as ever. For me, liberalism – like peace – represents a desirable social condition. But it is a precarious and privileged one. Just as wars still break out all over the world, so the liberal world view will continue to be challenged by other ideologies better suited to the social conditions out of which they arise, social conditions not amenable to liberal solutions.

Whether or not Chile comes into this category remains uncertain; it has had a revolution of sorts, and a bitter reaction, and in the process some things have been lost and some gained: the feudalism of the land is largely a thing of the past and economically the country may be better off than many of its neighbours, but the cost in human suffering has been huge and Aylwin's incipient democracy is still a very fragile plant, exposed to rough winds from left and right. For the sake of my Chilean friends I hope the Chinese curse, 'May you live in interesting times', has finally worked itself out. But I would not bet on it.